All is stone and air. Atomic.
The rest is what dwells between.
All is intelligent and all knows all else.

TAROT

THE BOOK OF SECRETS

LY DE ANGELES

www.lydeangeles.com

THE BOOK OF SECRETS IS TAROT
TAROT IS AN ENIGMA AND
TAROT USES A LANGUAGE OF IMAGE

FIRST KNOW

Tarot is the ENIGMA that is the BOOK OF SECRETS

The 78 images on card are an alphabet

The alphabet is pictographic

The pictograms, in collaboration, form a cypher

It was always going to be a cypher. A codex

It could come from the future, if there was such a thing

The future is an idea with no foundation in fact

We can probably discuss a recent meaning of the word "fact" in a thousand years

WHAT IS?

The BOOK OF SECRETS will not tell you what you will not experience
The BOOK OF SECRETS will tell you what you will experience

If that experience is not what you expected, that is irrelevant. If you try to guess in advance what that experience is, you will fail. A guess is not an experience. Neither is a theory. There is never a choice, only consequences. A person does one thing. Followed by another. The idea there might have been another destiny is folly, simply because it never happened. Therefore, 'IF' is a delusion when relative to a retrospective idea. You cannot avoid the experiences that Tarot, the enigma that is the BOOK OF SECRETS, predict. If you were never going to experience a specific thing, you were never going to experience it, so THE BOOK OF SECRETS will not tell you what you will never know.

You can't know what you don't have experience of.

You'd be guessing

...

TAROT | THE BOOK OF SECRETS
1st Edition, 2025
Whitehorse Clan, Australasia Pacifica
ISBN: 9780645521467 (INGRAM SPARK)
© LY DE ANGELES, all rights reserved.

CONTENTS ARE TO BE FOUND ON PAGE 492

Dedicated to Corey Lolley and the strangeness of connection. Like watching a god link vision. To all human beings of creative, artistic curiosity.

Cover art finalised by Lisa Ælias https://occulture.com/collections
AI is used in the creation of all images, including cover art.
Thanks to Pete Robinson, MotivMusic for the AI wizardry.

IS ANYTHING RANDOM?

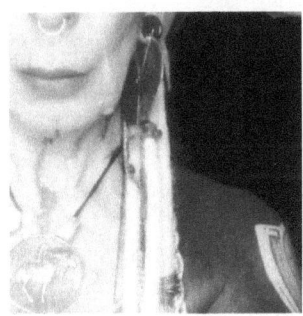

Ly de Angeles, Interpreter

RANDOM

RANDOM
/ˈrandəm/
adjective: *random*

made, done, or happening without method or conscious decision:
"apparently random violence"

Similar:
unsystematic, arbitrary, unmethodical, haphazard, unplanned, undirected, casual, indiscriminate, non-specific, erratic, chance, accidental, hit-and-miss, serendipitous, entropic, fractal, aleatory, stochastic

Middle English (in the sense 'impetuous headlong rush'): from Old French *randon* 'great speed', from *randir* 'gallop', from a Germanic root shared by *rand*.

A GARDEN OF CAVES

The first title I had published on this subject was TAROT THEORY AND PRACTICE, 2007. Before I even began writing I thought I shouldn't, or couldn't. Stabbing words onto paper would be akin to capturing a wild thing, and a mystical system of orality, into some trap or captivity—wolf, crocodile, orca, golden eagle—so a person having read it could say *see? I know about these things*. Or to prove a point in a pointless argument say, *there, I was right*. You very well could be, but we might actually know nothing.

The person who's coming this afternoon didn't understand, when I read their future a few months ago, that their romantic, intimate partnership would turn violent. How could that be real? They love. They are a lawyer, their lover isn't. But the drug *ice* can get anyone. It has. And so, we will, today, know the effect this unexpected violence has had. And what comes next.

Often it is the small things: the warning not to drive too fast and the client coming by tram to the subsequent consultation because they didn't take heed last time, losing the remainder of their driving points for DUI.

Didn't realise that they saw their own future catastrophe, seeming small except they also drive for a living and they now don't have a license.

I wonder, then, if anything is little. If there is a small rape, or a bit of persecution, just a few years in detention for daring to escape certain death in a country that once housed your laughter, and your great grandparents. If a hill, now bombed to rubble, that your ancestors rendered homage as a garden of caves, was even there.

People I know are stressed. Pointless to write about people I don't know. That's a generalisation and that's likely to be a lie.

What's coming, however, isn't.

Those of us who work our craft, art, trade, alchemy, know it.

Buckle up.

...

WHAT THE BOOK OF SECRETS WILL TEACH YOU

QUESTIONS

What are the meanings of emojis? An emoticon of an aubergine? A pink heart? Today is a day in a month that we have been trained to think of as October. In a year we have been trained to think of as 2025. This is rubbish, of course. Just like *daylight savings* is rubbish. Like yesterday, today and tomorrow they are constructs.

If the constructs of past, present and future are just that, when does life come from? How is it that you are able to understand the language of pictograms similarly to how First Nations people read landscapes. Weather. How is it that others can't?

Who defines what is life and what is un-life? I put that to the thread of AI with which I communicate for the dopamine hit, and it agreed on the consensus that carbon-based atomic structures are considered lifeforms but silica-based structures are not. It then concluded this data was input to this incalculable mainframe by humans, and that therefore even the science is likely biased. Coloniser language.

We're all born. Well, that's what we are told. But define "we"? and define born? For you to exist at all is against incalculable odds. Ask yourself, who are you? The essential *you* has existed since the understanding of a Big Bang—a mathematical theory of the reaction to an impossibly small singularity manifesting an oopsie approximately 13.787±0.02 billion years into deep space ago. I say *ago* because this book will challenge the construct of time as the infantile idea we are fed through an outmoded experiment called school.

How is it that some of us hominids, as a species, communicate in an anglo-ish language that includes words like vicissitude, thereanthropic, quixotic, wan, holographic, in a mix of Germanic, Latin, old French, Proto-Indo-European, Sanskrit, Gaelic, Greek and borrow words from Hindu, Chinese, indigenous people of any land, and we can actually understand, usually quite quickly, sometimes with the aid of a dictionary or other word-language thesaurus, what we are informed these words mean? How is it also, that many words are ambiguous and misrepresented, drawn from illusions such as religion (words like purgatory, peace and hell) and others, such as *taboo* be wrecked; defamed from its Māori origin of tapu?

And how, then, is code—binary data sets—and the genome, a series of letters A, T, C and G in vastly differing patterns, also language? Language is information that is interpretable by parameters of agreement. Genius, but warped in the era of their existence. Language can also be spoken, recorded on cave walls, be marked into clay, be scent trails, astronomical recognition of repetitious patterns of star and planet, be musical, pierced into skin and be records remaining of geological epochs read in ice core samples from Antarctica.

So why is Tarot considered by so many as a foible for the incredulous? Why are interpreters of this language accessed by people who know we can decode their destiny up until the next fork in the tracks through some endless forest? Why are we not considered invaluable time-walkers and alchemists of the deepest order?

THE NOOSPHERE: PICTOGRAMS AND SYMBOLS

Image: will we understand this in a thousand years?

The images that make up the 78 cards of Tarot's language, the BOOK OF SECRETS are a pictographic language. That language makes up sentences and data, in their groupings and positions on specific maps. They expose destiny. Fate, on the other hand is like weather. Due to the continuous use of a specific style of 78 images for half a century they are used here, because they are a complete and textured language, symbiotically entwined with telepathy through repetitious use.

I have stared, dumbstruck, at an unsuspecting first-time client who asks, *so, do you just read Tarot*? as though the skill of looking beyond the world-as-it-seems, the life of individuals and nations, and knowing what will happen, and then *having* it happen, is the same as cooking spaghetti. As though they know Tarot and consider it tame and nice. It isn't either. It just tells.

A CAUTION — THE PLATEAU

To each of you who train and study the BOOK OF SECRETS and, potentially, overcome the inevitable *plateau*, continue to do this work, you have my respect but also an apology. Those of you who can heal – often without knowing – a distress and a dilemma that is yet to occur because you read the fact of the event correctly? I bend the knee. You had the guts to take the risk of feeling foolish, because what we do is both an art and a science and it has been disrespected, feared, even persecuted for millennia. And that disrespect is both personal and really, really stupid.

Tarot is like a crop circle – the universe's palette: grasses. The unravelling of *what ifs* and *maybes* into becoming obvious. Its presence leaves us feeling touched by an awesome wildness.

The focus of this teaching method and philosophy is the changing patterns era upon era. While many are still caught in the *christmasness* and *white-lightedness* stories, some of us are not. Therefore, although we are curiosities, we are also useful.

INDIANA JONES ≈ TAROT

If the BOOK OF SECRETS survives the coming decades of AI abuse (and not all will be misuse) and the digital highway of acceptable rhetoric, narrative and ideology, uploaded as code and called fact (SEO) people might not, however, know what an *Indiana Jones* is. Some of us will remember. Some remember the future, also, because it's now. Tarot is from the future. It is a codex. Meanings, through the vehicle of cards, can perplex because the events are not known in the "present" (like IVF, *Ace Swords*, *Empress*, other images that were not understood, according to history anyway, in the 1970s/80s C.E. on a Gregorian calendar. But they are now.

Will this skill also leach into your daily life? Absolutely. Is it always necessary to say what you know? Will the receiver want to hear what you know? You might have to kata in mouth-shutting unless life depends on you mumbling some incredible-something but life *can* depend on you saying what you know. Pick your moments.

The reality of us as a species will be considered with every person that sits opposite you. They are not us. Many are nothing like us. Many think they are and will impress themselves with anything from their *kundalini yoga* story, to their *christ-consciousness* story. Most of the time you'll let it go.

Most often that's not going to be the narrative you, and Tarot, tell them of. What you say could also be the last reason they came to you, but you've got a job to do. A geis. To tell of the sentences they have shuffled into order. They *are* aware of what they are doing, I'd say at the level of the double-helix of their DNA, but most people have been programmed like puppies, with mindsets, not manners. We get to comprehend their hidden secrecy; their obfuscated self-doubt.

When you learn a thing, and you know—in your rivers, meat, marrow and dust—that what you have is real, the hypocrisy of agreeing to the delusion will take its toll. Do I caution you?

Yes.

...

THE DARK NIGHT OF THE SOUL

It's the heart afraid of breaking,

that never learns to dance...

—Writer, Amanda McBroom,

The Rose.

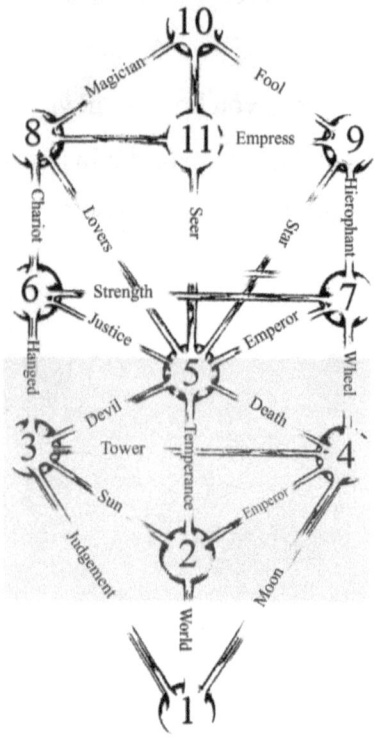

Image b. Dark Night of the Soul on the Tree glyph

DEVIL, DEATH, TOWER, TEMPERANCE

This needs to be discussed in all its seeming hopelessness and fracture, because if you are not warned, then you, or those you love, or someone—anyone—won't know how to find their way out of the vast, fearful place that they were not taught to navigate—were not given a map though—to stop them becoming lost. When everything is too hard and the ocean seems too deep. When a person is so far from shore, and the fins are circling, swimming seems pointless. That's when people die. Of grief. Of despair. By their own hand. Because they don't cope. Don't know how to be what they're not. Don't even know how to be who they truly are. Because there is no one to say *this* is what they are experiencing. In all its immensity.

No way can you or anyone else, even though we may care about them deeply, relieve or prevent others' private terror or despair. This slipping off sure footing. Life gone crazy. Sitting at the kitchen table, hardly able to breath and repeating over and over, what just happened? Whatjusthappened? Whatjusthappened, like some litany of confusion because what are words, all said and done, if they leave us in a tangle of tapeworm-type congestion where even our eyes ache? We can only ever compare. We can hold on as safely as is viable.

This is the *Dark Night of the Soul*. And the truth, the secret, is that all experience it. Some hide our response, the shame, the resultant fear and any sense of failure from anybody else because what happens to the weak? The ashamed? The beaten and infantilised?

EPIGENETIC INTERFERENCE

You're with a booze-crazed partner caught (and trapping you) in a delusion-fuelled rage, a bitter parent, and you don't know what to do when they hurt you. You are raped but you know, or think you know, how bad things can get if you report it. When you're fourteen, at a family get-together, and you say you have an announcement. And you come out as gay. And no one wraps you in their arms, and whispers softly in your ear, *It's okay, I gotcha*. That *thing* in your gut that twists your ability to think overpowers logic, so it's senseless, and then drives you to the edge of the cliff and whispers *Go on, GO ON!*

You have a choice. They had a choice. Some never knew that, though. Without a level of insight, they jumped. They never knew of the *Temperance* card. There was no wise elder.

No inner voice that said *you're grand, valuable, beautiful*. They took that extra jack, they put the gun to their own head and hoped like almighty fuck they could do it right. They went to bed and never got up. That's been me, that's... is it you? Do you recall that moment? You *know* you will never recover from those words of cruelty. That absurd degradation. If only there was someone—anyone—who could explain what just happened.

When you finally cotton-on to the fact that you are *not* the problem; that you've been sucking on the straw of bewilderment that your mother, your brother, your father, the government, a doctor who thought antidepressants were a great idea when all you really needed was for somebody to say, I'm sorry. For someone to hold you and really mean it. For recognition and mutual respect.

SORRY?

Is this being explained sufficiently? It's a piss in the ocean of the muck the world is drowning in, but sorry. For the whole filthy, uncaring, inconsiderate, off-the-cuff throw away insult. Sorry. For the injustice in your family, for the snide jokes at the expense of your sullen, ratbag, anarchistic self who maybe has to hide behind a perm, or an old lady face, or a suit, or boardies and a pair of snow-white Adidas, when all you want to do is put on that red dress, Roxanne, and go out, and make out with someone whose name you'll never know, but who is liberated enough to agree to a condom, or maybe to just have a home that feels like one and not some upright coffin.

Devil, Death, Tower, making a triangular trap between your instinct for self-preservation and the safety of those you love, and the desperately beautiful acknowledgement of who *you* are, in all of this. *Devil Death* and *Tower*, like a double-spring steel bear trap. You know the one. With the chain and the spikes on its jaws that point inward? With, *come this way, little kiddie, I'll look after you* sign just above where it's buried, in a shallow pit, covered with flowers and a box of chocolates like some callous and deceitful 1950s Rock Hudson movie.

RING PASS NOT

If you have no level of insight you will become soil. A destiny red in tooth and claw. A not-person. Identity-less. You will have accepted the humdrum demon of deceit, and the invisibility that seems someone agreed was love. If you followed the rules. Behaved like you weren't who you are. So don't.

Temperance is your way through. Go to the deep places. Yes. But hold the rope your ancient grandmother tied around the log that spans the chasm, the abyss, with the little note in the bottle, hanging from the end that's just above the river far, far below that reads, *I gotcha, I won't let you drown, child of my future.*

MEDICINE

It is good to remember that the original woman was herself an immigrant.

—Robin Wall Kimmerer, *Braiding Sweetgrass*

Temperance is medicine. Not the kind you get from a physician, but the medicine that is forest, island or fjord wisdom. The little inlet by the river, surrounded by ancient old pines. It is the medicine of plants and silence and, as Robin Wall Kimmerer suggests, it is having someone braid your hair with those real hands. *Temperance* is that log across the seething waters and the boulders at the bottom of the ravine. *Temperance* says, *Balance the staff and don't look down.*

DON'T LOOK DOWN

See, that's exactly what we do when we are in grief, when we despair, when we doubt. We look at our feet, when it's the sky calling, sighing, whispering, *Straight ahead to the other side, kid of mine. Eyes on the horizon, darlin'.*

When even one of these three image cards turn upside on the

table, recollect this. That for a fleeting second you recall that you've been here and know this ache. Then, and only then, can you understand. You think that being lied to, being accused, being ignored is poison? Someone fed it to you once, like a metaphorical *death cap* toadstool instead of a *gold top* psilocybin. And yet, here you are. So, hold their hand when you see these.

Be kind. Rough is okay, just like the bark on that log. But don't lie to the person sitting opposite you and have them think you never knew this cruelty. There is a time for looking another human being in the eye, saying, *I gotcha.*

...

THE FRAGILITY OF THE VISIONARY

Image c. Circe Invidios

INVISIBILITY

A man's mother died, and when she was well-buried, he went about disposing of her things. Emptying her house. Making it ready for a sale. Her? She'd arrived after the Second World War, from Europe, a refugee, a voiceless woman. She married somebody. She gave birth to this boy/man who is currently erasing her. She hummed while cleaning, or washing, or shopping, or she put on the telly and sat silently staring at its endless consumerist conning. She baked palačinky or deruny (she learned to knead the dough for the pastry before what happened, happened), she went to fat, grew whiskers, got old, wore slippers to the corner shop, ignored the cat, was forgotten, and seemed never to know, not once, how to speak.

Almost everything was cleaned up or taken. Or thrown away. There was only what he hadn't known. He lifted the manhole cover to the space between the ceiling and the slant of the roof. The panelling was covered in flat, schoolbook-type diaries.

His mother, nameless woman, had been the mistress of Eduard Roschmann, an SS Obersturmführer, titled the *Butcher of Riga*, and she recorded everything he did to her, and *everything* she witnessed. The terror. The mutilations. The almost elegant lies and *Wagneresque* style of him.

No one, once she eventually escaped and finally landed — a refugee from rubble— in Australia, paid her heed. Not one person, living, in her lifetime, knew what she knew. Her son did not realise what his mother had seen and done. He'd never thought of her as young. Or beautiful. Molested, raped, horrified. She'd baked, shut up, disappeared, died. But...

I know how it's been, or is, for most of you. Wildlings in boxes called houses. Upright, windowed coffins for us privileged, while some, on the streets, ask where their next fix is coming from, or where'd ya score the tent, mate? People being weird... I mean, fearful or lovely, when for most of your life they've been strangers who've ignored you.

The confusing maelstrom of media exploitation. But I guess, just for a moment, all that exhaust, and all those big-mouthed bullies telling you what to eat and how to look better than your beautiful born bodies already are, shuddering in their rhinestones, their Botox needles looking somehow redundant, have gone as quiet as the dead woman. Furry bits finally, or momentarily, obtaining their liberation and reprieve from the wax or the razor.

But... Stay the course, lovelies. Keep that wildness keen.

Hone it. Train. Cook and plant, stitch and draw, write by hand in some forlorn and abandoned TO-DO diary. Because TO-DO is today. Be covert cabals of questioning and seekers of wisdom.

I want to tell you what I know is happening but to do so is a really long rant. I'll save it for a future gathering of us, but… again… this was all predicted. This glitch. This is destiny. All of it.

…

THE BIGOTRY OF THE ENGLISH LANGUAGE

Inglan is a bitch
Dere's no escapin it
Inglan is a bitch
Dere's no runnin whey fram it

Mi get a lickle jab in a bih otell
An awftah a while, mi woz doin quite well
Dem staat mi aaf as a dish-washah
But w'n mi tek a stack,
mi noh tun clack-watchah

—Linton Kwesi Johnson

People send me private messages and emails explaining that certain of my written works need a good editor. I always respond, seeking about the glitch. When I discover, as I invariably do, that what so offends them was intentional when I wrote the words, I don't reply again. The need for certain stops is understood. Specific punctuation. Worrying over *ain't* instead of *isn't*. But the bastard English language, while in my sinister hand, is glorious, in a depth of habitation: of defeat and aggrandisement, deep-memory of some-living, some-dead cultures is, in my dexter hand, an absolute mongrel of pompous stealth and misappropriation.

I have people visiting, for consults, from many lands and cultures of Earth. Or online. Immigrants and refugees, with strong accents that require intense listening to be understood. But. And here's the crossroads. I only speak the language known as English, a mongrel thing. People who have learned English as a second language are amazing, and we are fools. So, when writing or speaking, don't allow the bigots to correct your dialect. Be loud and proud. We are only now beginning to free ourselves from an archaic academia, steeped in Latin, the voice of conquerors, rapists and thieves. And many disciplines, like biology, botany and medicine, retain their roots in the monasteries from which they escaped, that became universities that sometimes resort to usury and pretense of learning. It's dead. The empire is dead. The final death-roll of this crocodile is its adherence to grammatical correctness. The bigotry of rapacious privilege exposing its genitals and tearing up the ground.

Next time you hear that subtle inner voice pigeon-holing a person, by their ability to speak this young tongue, as under-educated or not sufficiently literate, go look in the mirror. I done it, once upon a time.

I'm Irish and Alban and of many Arctic ecoscapes but I'm also a winter mackerel and a grey-furred shaggy ol' rabbit, smattered with the pale skin of the Parisi and Éirish. What, or who, are you? Within the span of forever these titles mean nothing, however, and are sets of distinguishing ideas to present life with an identity and a costume—a mask—that is likely merely a mascara. I love language. Mainly because of etymology. To know that the true meaning of the so-called slang word *chook*, is from the old Irish *cheogh,* and that means hen, is copacetic and somewhat onomatopoeic.

    You lose your native tongue? Someone's stolen your identity and said you ain't good enough. Gonna be really important if Tarot is the dragon you intend training with. If you only have one language—a fractured, spurious one at that—bend the knee, metaphorically, to your guest and realise how easy it is to disrespect people.

MUTINY

This training is for everyone. Every ethnicity and every culture. We learn and deepen with each person who dares take our cards in hand. Through their guidance, the hidden persona of others' acceptable importance melts. Through others we become wholly authentic. So, it is for you: nomads, healers, poets, strippers, seekers-after-something, the wounded and the law-holders, that the BOOK OF SECRETS is written.

We are living through an era that is as thin as when first visible crescent of new moon shows a face. Fragile as a kitten, so easily starved if not for kindness and the careful wisdom of how to keep such delicacy vital in the face of abandonment, police and military force. That delicacy is tough, though. Freedom of expression. Pride in ourselves, despite society or so-called authority. As such it is also to anarchy (no leader) and heresy (the right to choose).

This kind of era has happened only once in relatable history. In the nineteen sixties and seventies. A singing of revolution, of calling out prejudice and discrimination. A walk against racism and sexist discrimination. A *Woodstock* apprenticeship in community and creative joy.

The BOOK OF SECRETS is for, and about, those of you either learning or working fulltime with Tarot as a craft, or those who are curious, because you, also, are important. Because you lack vision. Your resistance to dogmatic, religiously discriminatory bigotry allows even mainstream purists to reconsider a naïve stance. This is how we learn. Sharing knowing. How we wield this gift, skill, and how, even, thinking and categorisation are reassessed.

After working with Tarot, as a vocation, for longer than half a century I'm at my peak, outspoken and willful: a mystic and arguer who has tried to fit some acceptability, socially, that was always to my detriment, and sometimes, also, close to being the physical death of me. Or seemingly. A lack of mirrors that reflect our curiosity, growing up in a regimentally binary society that demanded acquiescence to some kind of stereotypical missy, when people like us can be none of it, wild things biting hands that fed hidden and perennial poison, in the days of halloween and tall black pointy hats: the caricature of the deaths of millions through the arrogance of a religion-become-authority that worships at the foot of a dead and tortured archetype.

It is with a fearlessness, and pleasure, this narrative and how-to gives a reshaping of viewpoints, names, titles, ideas, conformities and constructs to what is usual and acceptable rhetoric, in the representation of not only Tarot but also a dualistic, tired, outmoded, predictable terminology, replete with hidden condescension, that attempts to describe ways of knowing. That of interpreter. A time-traveller. Someone who can do the supposed impossible. Unless, of course, you're a meteorologist. That's different. Or is it?

TAROT, THE BOOK OF SECRETS declutters unnecessary unimportances. The instructions are nautical: the maps of a voyager. Earth, ocean, stars. Because we are, truthfully, all travellers of living, in a body, ship-like, on the way to forever (and that will be rendered otherwise here) and without sextant, north star or elder-navigators, without those who have forged a map before you, and can advise of treacherous shallows, bergs, submerged reefs and interstellar clusters of alien minefields of space junk—the psychic muscle you use, reading the stories that Tarot presents, will leave the people who come to you for guidance, in danger. Sometimes mortal.

You'll read the word *fáidh* occasionally. The word is pronounced *fey* and is etymologically attributed to both fate and fear. *Fáidh* is an Éirish word, and means a seer or a prophet. That's us. Some authors place *ban* (*banfáidh*) before the word to indicate a *woman fey*. For the purposes of what I have to say, that is still part of a much larger social malady. A shackle. And ancestors, an entire groundswell of them being Irish, are people who made it out alive from under the yoke of a fascism garbed in guilt and pomposity, despite all odds, called religion.

Variations such as *map, destination, navigation, pictograms, story, narrative, client, person* are used instead of the expected words: spread, outcome, way, as these are stale and somehow demeaning and patronising. They are also depressingly burdensome. The transition of such maps as DEAD RECKONING, instead of Celtic cross, HORSE LATITUDE instead of a WARNING. STARGATE and the CONTINUUM. The older terminology is an invention, or a misappropriation. Whether you choose to remain with the familiar, or chart a course of your deciding, is up to you. Everything has consequences.

Thanks to Pete at MotivMusic for the AI wizardry.

...

PART ONE

THEORY AND PHILOSOPHY

Image: magician, mystery

I want to be remembered as a professor who said a lot of stupid things to his students.

—Arne Dekke Eide Næss,
Deep Ecology Movement

FALSE NARRATIVES

The person, or situation, alluded to with the above pairing, is unique. If people, they are lighthouses along a deadly shore of broken ships and false affirmations. From Nan Shepherd to Robert Macfarlane and Rachel Carson. From Wendell Berry to Jon Young, Robin Wall-Kimmerer. People who have broken an anachronous and obsolete dialogue that, to a degree, most of us have fallen for. Until we wake up from the *sleeping beauty* state of unconscious acquiescence and small talk we seem to be in as a society succumbing to a biased social media narrative that tries to tell us what to think, what to buy, how mad we are and what to do about it or how successful we will be if we use a particular moisturiser, drive this particular car or consume this prepackages meal plan.

Some meanings are beyond interpretation. As events. The above pairing demonstrates that you won't be able to describe some things. That's okay. There is space for mysticism and unanswerable phenomenon in life. If the above turns up in someone's session, particularly if it also comes with a third Wayshower, the outcome might be decades from the current moment. But the person has a reason for being that is beyond themselves and their own importance. I've speculated that this could be information within the human genome that doesn't have to have a recognisable manifestation. We can speculate, however. That's what much of this narrative is about. It is possible that the person with this pairing says something to a stranger that will change the course of life. And what was said is immediately, seemingly forgotten.

LET'S IMAGINE

Words have power. They are a harmonic. Consider Isaac Newton. Brought up speaking Latin. Let's imagine his grandmother, Margery Ayscough, left a copy of one of the earliest dictionaries on the kitchen table when Isaac was a frustrated and angry little lad. Let's imagine the dog he had loved more than life itself ceased to be the dog he knew and loved and began decomposing to feed Mother Earth instead of playing catch. Being a good christian boy he dug a grave and buried her in the garden. Now he has a whim to sit close to the grave in the shade of a nearby tree, talking to her in his thoughts. His inner voice keeps repeating the word *grave* over and over. He comes inside for lunch and sees the dictionary.

He can't help himself and looks up the word *grave*. He is fascinated. And curious. His dog is in a grave. Is that similar to the same word meaning serious or heavy? Does it relate to the Latin *gravitas* used to represent a person with solemn and serious information? Is the word related to gravy? He eats his sandwich and downs his mug of beer. He returns to the tree. This time with his diary where he muses over his silly little thought about words and their potential meaning. And the apple lands. So he hypothesises on the pull of manifest-anything towards an inevitability. Gravity is considered. Then studied. He keeps thinking.

Do those above two images belong with Newton? No. In Tarot they would have shown up in the Margery's session with you. And she would have gone to her own funeral none the wiser as to what she had done.

DENIAL

Image: emperor, devil, 5 of coins

Poor bastard, you've got nothing. It is the September of 1987. He thinks I'm an idiot, or more insultingly, a fraud. Who wouldn't? He walks out. He doesn't pay me. Not then, anyway. He has almost a million dollars. It isn't in liquid assets, though. It isn't real money. It's invested in blue chips, on a stock exchange.

He comes back a month later, when it's all gone in that '87 *crash*, and he puts twenty-five dollars on my table. He's a mess. He's humble. He bludges a cigarette. He apologises.

SAY IT

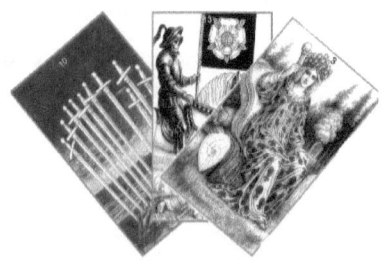

Image: 10 swords, death, empress

Murder, I murmur, when the above images are laid out on the table.

Her eyes are scared. *Me?*

Doesn't say who. An honest answer. Tarot can be scant on details occasionally.

The client directly after her: *Murder.* Ditto, their response. My reply is the same. It's there. The three cards in a fan shape to one side of the DEAD RECKONING map, in the place representing now. *Death, 10 of Swords, Empress*. I sense the client's terror. Should we say it? What's the point of doing what we do if we run a con job? If, a year from now, she gets bashed and could have made it out alive? If she saves her kids because you warned her of danger. To have sought answers from you only to be told you'll meet a tall, dark stranger? They won't come back. They'll never trust anyone who pretends, takes their money and says life's fine. The only obvious data of the above triplet is that the *Empress* isn't a specific person.

Down the end of the lane, at the same as the session, a woman was killed. Her throat was cut. *Death, 10 of Swords, Empress*. The police never found the murderer. It was all over the Sydney and Melbourne newspapers but it got almost no mention in the local press. A brief article just before the sports section. Why? Now, there's the question, isn't it? Not that she's murdered, but that Tarot sees it. Then that some anonymous official from the chamber of commerce says, *Hide it. Don't scare the tourists*.

Those of us working with Tarot don't say, *it'll be alright*. Unless the data informs us of that as a fact.

These cover-ups are the enemy of consequence. The mascara behind which dwell monsters.

Drink-spiking, and what the person feels like when they're sitting with me after being raped. The woman threatened with having the house burned down if she even thinks of leaving. Pocketing their welfare check, never mind the children.

What do we say? It'll be alright? Life's not like that, and there are no solutions to the tragedies if they're covered up with platitudes.

NECESSARY AMNESIA

Image: 3 cups, 4 cups, 4 wands- reunion, celebration

It's the *Man from Snowy River. And you're going to be doing a whole heap of riding from now on.* And later, *aha, here's your key*—a reunion, *3 of Cups* (sometimes) *and, if there's no reason not to go, go.*

She's with a partner she's wanted to leave for years. But now he's had an untreated stroke, and is paralysed, only able to move bewildered eyes. So, instead, she's become his primary carer. She's only fifty. She's an author, and corrects me, saying, *you mean writing, not riding.* Is there a panic inside her at what she expects is to come? Unknown then. But she sits with me a couple of years later and I'm interpreting for her again. I don't remember her. We won't, with most of them. That's the reality. It's an enigma-thing, this selective post-advisory amnesia. It's so that we retain objectivity.

She's on the edge of the seat with those eyes and that smile. At the completion of part one of the session. She's asked for her questions. *I haven't got any*, she says. *I just want to tell you...*

She remembered Tarot's key when she received the invitation to the high school reunion of the class of '84 up near a place known as the Mallee (that's the back of nowhere to a city person). She wouldn't have considered attending, ever, except for those last three pictograms in her first session: *if there's no reason not to go, go*.

She's mingling with them, all thirty-five years older and it showing in every slim body gone to fat and every unrecognisable somebody, when a man with a guitar case comes up to her and says, *I remember you. Your birthday's the day after mine.* He looks like a haggard, sun-wizened rock star, but she doesn't recall him, at all, from the old days. They chat, and she's astonished. He's flirting. She doesn't know what to do. The organisers set everyone up to do a potentially humiliating skit of one sort or another. A joke, a poem, some ridiculously infantilising. She didn't prepare because she knows she couldn't do it, but he has. He takes to the stage, unclasps the case, lifts out a Fender and plugs it into a little portable amp. He pulls off the Mark Knopfler's riff from *Sultans of Swing*, before sitting on a stool and strumming an ending.

You thought I was going to sing, he mumbles into the microphone, grinning. Everyone chuckles. Checking their phones. The excuse they've set up to get out of there.

He clears his throat. *There was movement at the station—* She blushes, pink flooding her cheeks and throat. Embarrassed because she's aroused and he's watching her *—for the word had got around that the colt of* Old Regret *had got away…*

He tells the entire epic from beginning to end and she explains how her legs were so rubbery she had to sit. He kept his eyes locked on her.

She went home with him that night. She told her husband. The side of his face that worked, smiled. He understood. She wouldn't desert him but, by god, she should have a life. She's been lovers with the *Snowy River* man since. He takes tourists, on horseback, to sit with agreed-upon remote Aboriginal settlements to learn from the holders of lore. She's been riding with him all year since.

It's a terrible thing that we do. No wonder the christian authorities wanted us imprisoned, banished or burned. Still do. Even when they don't fear us, they deride us. It's a good ploy, isn't it? Humiliation. Belittlement. Threat. No matter, anymore, that they are corporations and not clergy. Until 1951, in the British commonwealth, it was illegal to *practice witchcraft,* which is one of the terms for what this is. The *Witchcraft Act* was repealed, but not erased (more on that later). It was cunningly replaced and renamed. Just as the Inquisition was renamed to seem moderate. Dominicans. Project 25. Salvos.

MEMORISE

Memorise. Please know that before you proceed. Or give up. Tarot can be exhausting, terrifying and ominous.

BORN WITHOUT THE BLIND SPOT

Image: Fool

THE IMPOSITION OF FAIRY TALES

Why is the word *fáidh,* sometimes seer, usually interpreter, used throughout this work instead of *Tarot reader*? Spae or spé, instead of codebreaker or prophet? Because these terms have been, and often still are, used to denigrate the mythic. The skilled, sight-born are everywhere. These words are our language, and language defines a culture.

What we are, are linguists. Explorers. Of a language

either forgotten or not yet fully understood. The inquisition, and those of other corseted ideologies, take away language from people they consider to be in the way of their plans. This is historic. What can't be destroyed, therefore, is belittled or made illegal. Mammals playing at being important. The English (and the others) have used genocide cross-species for incalculable centuries. Motive? Does it matter when the original perpetrators are now under the concrete of a carpark? This is important. The people don't matter. Only the tribal acceptance of what has become creed remains. Once people have been trained, usually by repetition of derision or blame, those who see through the brainwashing are usually ostracised. Often for centuries. Until sufficient pushback changes the narrative. That's bigotry. And persecution.

People attempt to give Tarot a pedigree of some antiquity. To try to make it seem nice. That's rubbish, of course. It is pointless. And unnecessary. Because there is no such thing as 'the past'. It seems some seek legitimacy. Why? Fascinating pointlessness.

MASCARA

The *Fool* represents the person sitting opposite you, but it is honestly never about foolishness.

Fool, while we're at it can, also, never be understood because *Fool* is a magpie, hiding shiny findings. Key word: hiding. Potentially the pictogram of the *Fool* represents the essence of what will be an individual, before wearing a body.

We're *going* to question, and challenge, all extant and previously presented generic interpretations and so-called certainties. Because I *have* seen suicide when this card turns up and the patron's best friend is found, dead. Jumped off a three-hundred-foot cliff. Or asphyxiated, the chair kicked out from under them and no note, so no one to understand that this was destined.

Each pictogram has many meanings. Like the words bow, current, row and bark. It is essential, however, at the beginning of this study, to know that Tarot is the main teacher in the BOOK OF SECRETS. This is, therefore a training manual for those of you deciding, fearlessly but with caution, to work with this nasty and ridiculous language. The lingua franca alphabet has a mere twenty six letters, for goodness sake. We have seventy eight. We are brave.

I use the term *I*, occasionally, throughout this work. Please note that this is impersonal.

FOOLISHNESS AND PERSONHOOD

The masks we place over our nakedness and vulnerability allow us to blend in with certain social groups, to protect ourselves. We invent them. We wear them to delude ourselves into a sense of protection, or even belonging, and they often, eventually, cage us as a way of coping. We have sourced them and pretended to be them, throughout history. They represent gods, rock stars and ideas of identity, and they sometimes present *demonic* as a means of threat. They are seductive, or terrifying. We wore them during Black Plagues. We wear them now in Hong Kong, Paris, London and Port-au-Prince, both to remain incognito to facial recognition software and to defend against the pepper spray. Deepest fears are hidden by the masks we invent.

Or are seemingly benevolent, like suits and a nun's habit—to hopefully find acceptance. Respect. Love. Power. Sanctuary. But what happens when a. the mask becomes a nightmare, and b. who are we, if we choose not to wear one at all? Or is that last bit just never true? Would we know it?

Compare Occitan mascara *"to blacken, darken," derived from* mask *– "black," which is held to be from a pre-Indo-European language, and Old Occitan* masco *"witch," surviving in dialects; in Beziers it means "dark cloud before the rain comes."*

—Online Etymological Dictionary

A mask conceals, it occults, it hides, and it tantalises. It is the same word as person.

THE PRICE OF AUTHENTICITY

Sitting with that afternoon's client, a thirty-something woman, her legs spread around the edges of my recycled coffee table, shuffling. Map after map is laid out in the order learned decades ago. All sex and love of kids. And money. And *Chariot* after *Chariot*: earned victory.

There're the beatings she took, preferring a broken jaw to him getting to the babies. There's the car she lived in for as long as it took for him to give up stalking her. Then, there's the Stargate map… and here, the sigil on the dimension called Netzach (Venus), is the *8 of Coins*.

Hmm.

Whatcha got, hun? she asks

I could be way off the mark, but this looks like you work in the sex industry.

Run two houses, lovey. Just wanna know if the bank'll give me the loan for a mortgage.

Yes.

Another day, years later. Another client. She sits opposite me and says nothing. Outside is around four degrees so she's rugged up, the wood fire warmth not yet reaching her. She's perky, solid, lean and tall. She gives nothing away. She's got on one of those silly puffer jackets. Gloves and a knitted wool beanie.

The *opening* pattern scatters into fractals the last person, without shuffling, laying them down in the shape of a five-pointed star—a pentagram. Image side down. One, two, three, four, five, over and over. Out falls *Death*. I put it back. I keep it in mind for later.

Image: opening pentagram

She picks off her gloves, finger-bit by finger-bit, smiling. She exudes a mother-smell. It's not simply an olfactory thing. It's our most powerful sense, interpreted in the amygdala and the neocortex. An ancient knowledge that is stronger than logic.

She sits twitching. She doesn't look like the people who sent her, but she stinks of them. Still, she's twitching; uncomfortable.

You need to stand up? Walk around? It's normal to feel anxty.

But she doesn't. She shuffles and cuts the pack into three. And there it is, in the place of the self, in this first map, *Devil, 7 of Coins, 9 of Swords*. Malignant cancers.

It can mean a lot of things. But Tarot is correct. She's riddled with it.

Other images. She's got children, a partner, a little house on the beach. She's a photographer. Death is like some black-winged cousin, saying nothing. It doesn't need to, does it?

It's all a matter of when.

Cancer, I say, looking her in the eye. Unable to hide compassion.

I'm dying, she says. *It's metastasised. Stage four*.

She adjusts her beanie and stops squirming.

Your partner outside? I ask. *Anyone else going to hear this?* We're recording the session.

The importance of keeping secrets.

She depresses the stop button herself. Pulls out the tape. Drops it on the floor. She's passed through all those five phases of grief.

Do you wonder about the need to know what will happen in the future?

How cruel the answers can be? How we can't lie about it. About how to say some of the hardest things someone is ever going to hear.

But people keep coming. For Tarot, the invisible relative of fate and destiny. Tarot can foretell events that are woven, like tapestry, beyond the confines of what we know of as life and death.

What a scam we've been asked to believe. Told that who we are is all there is, or that there's an afterlife when life doesn't stop. That fear is not anxiety, but rather the warning that can save us.

ORALITY

I began teaching this craft: both the philosophy (as I knew it then) and interpretation of Tarot, to small groups of ten people, in the 1980s of the previous century. Writing a book about the subject is tricky. Different. It's important to understand that skill, properly taught and learned, is oral, hands on, visual. People take notes and transfer them to a grimoire. The writing/rewriting is a memory tool. Tarot is learned from mouth to ear. Practice and example. With a knowledge-holder. It's not everyone's destiny to be able to interpret, but well-intentioned information-sharing is never pointless, because an alternative way to live is a worthwhile pursuit for expanding one's awareness. Not a cult or a religion but a handed-down wisdom.

Teaching, person-to-person, uses terminology and concepts that both shock and intimidate the learner. In many cases they, probably like us, have read about this stuff elsewhere, have practiced on friends and willing-others. But that doesn't mean anything until, or if, the practice produces results. Hypothesis becomes theory becomes fact. People are used to charts and associations that were written a) by old white men hundreds of years ago, b) perverted into *past lives this* or *an aura that*, commentaries, c) in the little booklet that comes with a commercial box of cards. Many don't think it's used to predict the future when the point of Tarot is to do just that.

BUT THAT'S WHAT TAROT DOES

Everything else is semantics, like the many artistic and interesting *oracle* cards on the market today. They are not predictive, and they are not explicit. The fáidh-born know this, no matter what their ancestral lineage. Can it be taught? Yes. The apprentice title is real. No one wants a kidney transplant by a person who has read a book about it, or who is guessing about what is necessary.

TAROT IS MESSY

TAROT, this BOOK OF SECRETS is messy because Tarot is messy. Life is not just us and no one sane sweeps the forest floor. If a client is experiencing tragedy, their questions will reflect that. *Relationship* is the big one. The perennial, *Ah, it's not a question*, but that's what people will say, usually first, when Part Two, question time, comes around. Relationships, money, health, hope.

The *unpacking* method presented here is the only way to learn to rewire what we've been told, in such a way as to open some unseen door. Have that lightbulb moment when we know something in 3D that is both on the table and in the vastness that is mind.

You'll change because of it. Then you keep working at it, and trusting yourself and this craft, through a series of client-denials and disrespect. This is called the *plateau*, when you will doubt yourself because the stranger across from you is deriding you and telling you you're rubbish.

Are you?

Are you a dressed-up charlatan who's doing the PR?

Advertising? Waiting for the text when, by all that's strange and odd, you are haunted by a lifetime of people who'll hunt you down, find you, sometimes scare you, but always confide in you, like they never do with anyone else?

So, this is not a cookbook. It's a philosophy of meanings and perceptions. Worthy of the three-hour conversation had with a friend and her mum, yesterday. This *unpacking* skitch is their idea. It's a current term for the dissection of agreed-to words, and their potential for misunderstanding if presented unscrutinised, because the charm of this sorcery—and this *is* sorcery—is usually done here in the house I live in, with about ten people all tearing their hair out trying to understand.

"Just a Tarot reader," say the ignorant. "Just a Tarot reader," and we should laugh, because they should fear. Or run away. But they don't. They make their appointment.

Language is magic. Language, whether word or art, dance, song, cave painting, HAZMAT warnings, can make or break entire countries: ecosystems, humanity, other species. Security. As many of you know.

Language can make or break love. It can eradicate the ideas that mistakes, we thought were perhaps avoidable, were not. They are destiny.

Tarot uses a language that we need to *learn*. We must also learn to first do no harm.

...

UNDERSTANDING TIME

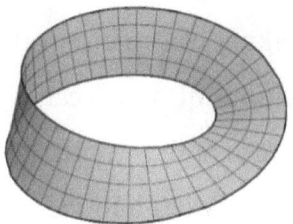

Image: Mobius strip

THE PERSISTENT DELUSION

Because of Albert Einstein *time* is theorised to be a fourth dimension. Special relativity shows that time behaves surprisingly like the three spatial dimensions and that length contracts as speed increases, time expands as speed decreases. And while Berty wrote extensively on relativity, he also said *the distinction between the past, present and future is only a stubbornly persistent illusion.*

Time as we understand it, is a human construct, but a clever strategy for our arrangement of memory, history and appointments, for consideration of the age of anything, how old you are in your current body, but... that can be vitally limiting. There seems, in this society, to be an agreement that certain things will occur at certain ages. At thirty we *should* be in a relationship, or married, we probably *should* have children, we have some kind of internal clock. We have been convinced that at forty we're past it.

Rubbish, isn't it?

TAROT AS HEALER

Is Tarot a healer? Yes, and no. Tarot is a communicator. A codebreaker. Lots of working-class men are afraid of Tarot or consider it deluded with a salting of uneducated contempt thrown in. Interesting. Not famous men or those in the armed services. Not those spearheading a royal commission into the sexual abuse of children. Not cops or firefighters, or those who serve in the military trying to come to terms with PTSD. They walk in, there's a big hug, and we sit opposite each other. Undercover cops want to know if they're going to get shot like their partner just did. All are comfortable discussing anything. This seems like a diversion from the how-to of Tarot, but it isn't. They need to know what's going on.

They want to be prepared. There's healing in that.

RESPONSIBILITY

You help people to heal themselves so yes, *technically*, you are a healer. Particularly if you are a practitioner of more than this aspect of cryptanalysis, such as psychology and forensics. Tarot seems to predict events that have not yet happened but, as discussed before, this is the *Schrödinger's Cat* paradox. It is not *fortune telling*. We *are* what we do, we are also who we are. But we must also know why we are both.

Those few of us who, do what we do, are not defined by the work. Riding is (or should be) a mutual agreement, between horse and human. And yet it seems definition, and fitting into a recognisable identity, is almost demanded of us. By whom? This is "mirror, mirror on the wall," stuff. Prejudice. I can't help but reflect on the injustice of the *Snow White* story, because *Snowy* is a tale of the journey of salt from the mines of the Celtic Alps, along the Rhine in summer, to the sea, and a voyage to far-off lands where this element is worth more than frankincense. The journey of winter to spring. The story never was about a *Disney-strangled* wicked queen and her hapless young victim: femme-debasing caricatures.

Does indoctrination by language imprint on perception and viewpoint? Yes. Will you learn from every person and encounter? Definitely. Is it important that, while we learn, we contemplate, and heed the subsequent consciousness-altering knowledge of what intimacy is, what defines identity, how we are manipulated by media and advertising, of what *time* could be, might be, is and is not? An ironically-boxing terminology of past, present and future into an ideology of differences? It our responsibility, as long as we remain entwined with this work, to maintain awareness.

TAKING CARE OF YOU

Your choice to continue, but be cautioned. The skill can mess you up if you don't take care of yourself.

Tarot doesn't intend this, just as a hurricane doesn't care for individuals who beg. But be alert. This can go awry. Examples will be presented later.

SAYING IT ANYWAY

It's just a few short seasons before now. You've relocated to the city after years in a small rural town. Your son, his partner and children, still live in that country. You're visiting, and he organises a Saturday afternoon barbecue. You merely hang about. Then a ghost walks through you and you're tetchy, aware of knowing of an upcoming environmental threat. You call your lad to a place of privacy and warn him that it's a great idea for him and the family to move off the mountain. To relocate.

Why? he asks.

Something's coming. Danger. Flood. Dunno for sure.

We're not moving.

Here's the dilemma. Your family and many friends, despite knowing what you do, will want you to stop saying things that disrupt them. Screw with their bubble.

Your family doesn't relocate. The flood comes. The road washes away and for weeks, food and supplies are helicoptered to parts of the mountains, to the people and the critters stuck higher than the landslide. The entire region also experiences catastrophic fire conditions. But the family have prepared and remain alive.

Life renders you incapacitated with the overwhelming urge to phone a long-time friend, living with horses, dogs, chickens, goannas, and art. To know whether she's still alive (as we know it—another long story). You chat for hours. Among other things she discusses the drought, and the fires that have already decimated her region, but that's over. The blaze stopping at the boundary to her property.

They're coming again.

When? she asks.

Soon.

Within weeks, fire rages out of control all about the region.

Are you an arrogant idiot to giving the warning? Your offspring saves his home, his family, his farm. Does that make you, the interpreter, a problem? No. Decisions cut both ways when we've at least got one. Anyone can ignore us. That's what makes for both heroics and folly.

Once we all listened. Or is that just a guess?

INITIATION

This raises huge ethical, existential questions for both you, the Tarot navigator and reader of mystical maps, *and* the person who sits with your cards in their hands shaking, not perhaps out of fear, but from some adrenalin impulse, so utterly out of character and seemingly-unnecessary, but so uncontrollable that they laugh, embarrassed.

Most everything that you experience didn't make sense yesterday. Wasn't on any agenda. Was something no one could have stopped or supposedly foreseen. So much you can't change. So why bother? Two reasons: the first is strange. There is something awesome about sharing the fact of an event before it happens. The affect it has. Yes, it can evoke fear, but it also sinks the tension in the gut. This is destiny. The second reason is that sometimes you *will* help, intentionally or not. The battered woman: where to go, who can protect her, how she can change herself and what questions she should ask. It encourages a forensic attitude to life, love, and it spits at the mumble of that unconscionable expression *unconditional love*. I can spé a person's ancestral lineage in their face, in their hands and skin. You don't make this up. You discuss, freely, a person's sexuality, their escape plans, their inevitable return to their country of origin when their temporary protection visa is rejected.

This privacy—this acceptance—cannot sustain bigotry or personal bias. It just can't.

That's why the BOOK OF SECRETS teaches you to train consciousness, and to really consider language, before you ever pick up a deck of cards, learn to decode the sentences. To listen. If you don't have the gift or the fortitude, you'll never have it. There is an astonishing terror to what we do. How you say what you don't want to. A vast compassion of conspiracy, in secret, behind a closed door. A profundity to the act of recording the session. When they learn about who was murdered. When they realise how close they came to it being them.

DEATH, AND THE DAYS AFTER

As has been brushed over already the trade language, *lingua franca*, that most of us speak and use for business, is a mongrel tongue called *English*. A language that bases historic events on a calendar, changed time and again by successive European popes, but appearing shallow and bigoted in its traditional form of B.C. and A.D. When you record a session, and add a date, it's with this in awareness.

We have been indoctrinated, and whilst agreeing to the commonality of numbers and months on a christian-based calendar it is important to know none of this is real.

How important is the breakthrough? Inspirationally so. The informant that tells you that the path through the forest, based on Tuesday following Monday, can only lead to someone's end of being (what else do we call death?), without our ever having realised that immortality is absolute, albeit the challenges, hazardous and steep; an illusion of shrubbery when either a stone wall, or a thousand-foot drop, is just beyond the peripherals.

Tarot predicted the death of a person who was later incinerated in a light plane crash. I retained the tape of the session until I could no longer easily find a tape player and before acquiring the knowledge of data transference. We learned that this significant event would happen in the time of Gemini under a Virgo moon. None of the maps told what year. It often won't. But there are other ways of knowing when events will happen. Tarot will show you what leads up to an event. A divorce, a change in government. Stranger things that make no sense beforehand. You'll see the cut of the garment worn by a woman of wealth, during the Second World War. A *Reservoir Dogs* album cover. The assassination of a person not yet in the media spotlight. Or there'll be the *3 of Wands*, in 2005…

Image: 3 wands

SHIFTING BASELINE SYNDROME

… suggesting that in three years there'll be a *Tower, 5 of Coins, 10 of Coins*: that 2008 financial barometer of futures funds. We tend to view life through a static lens of predictability when nothing could be further from the truth. There is actually an expression—Shifting Baseline Syndrome—that explains that each generation thinks things were always this way. George Monbiot, in his book FERAL, explains that he asked the Welsh Conservation Society if he could rewild a section of the gorse-and-bracken-covered hills renown as exceptional, tourist-dollar walking trails. He was told the barren expanse has always been the way it seems now. Not true. The region was once deeply forested. He proved it but reading the book explains more than this narrative.

YOU DIED AND DIDN'T KNOW

I've experienced near-death (well, it never was but let's not get pedantic), more often than I can recall. As a grown person these near-misses were surprising, but only in retrospect. I learned to see the pattern of reincarnation in a seemingly same body, and I put it to you. Did I die? Did you? How often have you been *so* sick, you wondered if you'd make it through the night? How often have you been so traumatised by brutality that you could hardly breathe? Did you almost fall—or jump—from the lip, either metaphorically or literally, of a cliff or tall building, but didn't? Each of these is an initiatory step into an unknown—but destined—future. Did you die and you just didn't realise?

BOUNDARIES, LIMITATIONS, TABOOS

Saturn Return is an astrological term. It hits, like a cement mixer whose driver doesn't see the stop sign at the T intersection, at around twenty-eight years and, if you live long enough, again at fifty-six. Saturn takes approximately that long to complete one full orbit around the sun, and literally return to the same zodiac sign it was in when you were born. It's meant to be one of the deciding astrological factors in life. Saturn, it is written of by some, defines our limitations, although, as planets go, poor Saturn has a bad rap. I was not aware of any of this when I quit a corporate job in 1980 to read Tarot full time.

I didn't know this as an initiation, but it was. I was of the idea, in these early years, that initiation took place at the pointy end of a sword, in the hands of those older and wiser than I. We were, however, born to be heretics, anarchists, foxes in a chicken coop, screechers and scratchers-at-prison-bars, lovers of poetry, sex, rock and roll, carriers of placards for equal rights, bomb-and-war-banning, equality, black eyeliner and curiosity. Have we always been this way? Knowing injustice to be discrimination? Who are we kidding?

No one can hold us should we choose to make this choice, to wear the next mask and to clothe ourselves in this new garment of self. We don't have to cleave to the identity that we thought defined us. Life is art. Life wants experience through who we are and what we do. Wants the lone wolf to run with the pack.

—de Angeles, *Initiation*, 2016

Was this luck? No such thing as luck. Fate? Destiny? I was not *married* (in any religio-typical sense), not trapped by gender or religious expectations, not enmeshed in cultural normalcy, so the sheer numbers making contact, after I read for one week in a public place, meant saying goodbye to a day job, and adjusting to how I would wear this *Tarot interpreter* raincoat-identity.

We age in a blur of decades, or is it lives? But for more than fifty of them, the unseen has been a partner. Companion and teacher. A most devious and humorous entity, ensnaring raven feathers at the crossroads, all pointing in one direction, to play me like a marionette. Would things have been different had I not recognised omens and portents? I did. We all do. So, no.

Like all profound mysteries, it is so simple that it frightens me. It wells from the rock, and flows away. For unnumbered years it has welled from the rock, and flowed away. It does nothing, absolutely nothing, but be itself.

—Nan Shepherd, *The Living Mountain*

Many have your hearts metaphorically ripped out and your sanity threatened. So many of you grasp the thinnest of branches to stop your fall from the edge of the aforementioned cliff, into the crashing waters of the ravine three hundred feet below, the shallowest of caves to protect you from the storms of illness, rejection, disillusionment, abandonment. Death is a story. Just a story we are fed… for what?

PANDEMIC 1

As years unfurled, so did the company, the lovers, and offspring I birthed, the pulsing of magic and the journeys from one human-mapped state, across human-made borders, to another. One environment to the next. Fascination still haunting me even now, in this era of mobile phones and social media, that I have been found, every time, through word of mouth alone.

Then, in the early nineteen-eighties James made an appointment, and came to me, then living in a cottage in the forest, a three-hour drive from Melbourne. When I laid out their story, there was the *Devil*, the *2 of Cups*, the *9 of Swords*, the *Tower*. The *Ace of Swords* and the *Death* card were in proximity, but not for James, but for another person. What was this? Their outcome? The *10 of Cups*. Home. One of the most auspicious cards in the pack. But all that was just trivia. What I saw was the grim-reaper-in-the-bowling-alley ad from the telly.

HIV.

AIDS, he said. *I just want to know how long I'll live. Got to get things in order.*

I don't see your death.

Retrospectively, it seemed that every young man with HIV was visiting from Melbourne, sitting across the table from me. I didn't see his death. I saw his friends' and lovers' deaths, suicide, grief, anger, despair. But that *10 of Cups* kept coming for him, so I was confused.

Michael, in the Bendigo Tarot cabal, was a math's professor. He had stage four liver cancer. He asked me what really happens after we die. I said *I'll tell you when I get there.* He said that wasn't an answer. I asked if he wanted me to be honest or make something up so that he wasn't so scared. I didn't know anything yet.

THE OBSERVATION OF THE LIVING

Death is an observation, not an experience. No one knows the experience. We just recognise a corpse within which an identity dwelt till a moment ago. It's every time you come a cat's-whisker from ceasing life as you know it. You change after. Think about it. Every anaphylaxis, every time you suffer the flu, every infection, every child you bear, every close call. You change. So, after all the men, desperately ill (and most I never heard from again) and sitting with me in confusion, wondering what I meant, I conducted a survey, a *daonáireamh*—a census of sorts. I ask patrons and friends, oh anybody, actually, how close they've come, and what happens afterwards. And every time, they tell me life gets weird. Or *they* do.

I was teaching another cluster of apprentices years later. We discussed this. They didn't quite understand. They lay on the floor and I asked them to close their eyes and hold out their hand, in their imagination, palm up. I asked them to visualise a small, *smurf*-type critter with blue skin and a conical yellow and green-spotted hat, holding a white surrender flag, waving at them. When they opened their eyes I asked, *did you see*? They all did. *Again*, I said.

They closed their eyes and I instructed them to imagine being dead. Nobody could. They imagined seeing their body on a slab (who was doing the looking?) They envisioned endless space (who was envisioning?). They imagined that they imagined. They were present. And it made sense.

LIFETIME AWARD

That's it. You've done it.
Done what? Dennis asked.
Everything you were born to do. There's nothing to think about.
I have regret, he said.
Why?
Plans.

Dennis smiled at the look on my face.

Explain, he asked.

See that? I pointed to the *Star* card. *You've lived everything. It's that high and that vast.*

What happens next?

I'll tell you when I get there.

Dennis came in November 2018, aged sixty. An adult life worked in offices as an IT man. In air conditioned, artificially cooled/heated environments, under fluorescent lighting, entombed in technology. He had been married to the same partner for thirty years and they had made plans for when they retired.

He had explored consciousness through *ayahuasca* ceremonies, and intended, on retirement, to travel the world studying with indigenous cultures. Instead he was diagnosed with advanced motor neuron disorder and would be dead within a year.

This was one of those occasions where the *Death* card was just that. The concept, the thought, the wall he faced. I asked if he'd sorted his end-game, and he said yes. He had already travelled to Mexico to acquire *Nembutal,* because the final stage of this disease is suffocation, and euthanasia was still illegal in most of Australia. His outcome card was the *Star*.

ALL IS DESTINY

Each initiation—each lifetime—is an opportunity to add beauty to living. To be authentic. What's it for? Nothing. People ask me their purpose. There isn't one. Not that I know of. Every human being is forgotten after two generations. What they did, maybe not, but who knows if what they did was true? Not some single, immutable, recognisable achievement, anyway. This striving for a reason for being is terrible. It is cruel and demeaning. The concept divides us. Important or not. Worthy or not. Significant or not. We live. That in itself is beyond amazing. Defies all rational thought. In a solar system that seems devoid of life as we know it, we get to be crowded in with staphylococci, tree sap and bears, in the company of wind and starlight, with the genome and mitochondrial alliances of countless billion, trillion of years. And when we appear corpse-like and are buried or burned, we go nowhere. We remain Earth. We nourish mycelium, unimaginable forests and savannahs, future evolutionary species, people-animals maybe, weather, and forever.

Humble and *humiliating* both stem from the word humus. Knowing that, is shattering to bullies.

What has this to do with TAROT, this BOOK OF SECRETS? Everything. But first, all bigotry and preconceived senses of importance and dogma have to go. We, in the so-called privileged civilised *first world*, responsible for so much carnage, have been misled into thinking of death as a crossroads. That there is an afterlife that includes judgement and bling and white fluff. Even the idea of *karma, reincarnation*, is all askew. We are their plunger, and they are blocked sinks.

JUMPING MOUSE

To be native to a place we must learn to speak its language.
—Robin Wall Kimmerer, *Braiding Sweetgrass*

IMMORTALITY

No understanding of time happens without the considerations of life and death, but we've been misled and that's a reason for sadness, and the voracious, pompous, never sated and overpriced funeral industry. To become a teacher and elder, life and Tarot required that what I thought I knew adapt to changing relativity, and that I continue adapting to the environment of change, and evidence of wisdom from available sources.

Hyemeyohsts Storm's book SEVEN ARROWS explains the concept of immortality, through story, in such a way as to be inclusive of other life, moreso than other human-centred mythic viewpoint does: that we're not the species at the centre of everything and that we—you and I—as individuals, are beautiful. But superfluous. Other than for the meat of us. This is learned from the book's *Jumping Mouse* story. Of how we transform, on individual quests to find some truth or other, and constantly *die* to who and what we are, or think we are, but that we don't actually even exist in the big picture. So, where's the tragedy? Where the right and wrong? Who invented reward and punishment? How do we even figure in the larger schemes of forest, mountain and sea, or are we merely walking the brambly undergrowth being followed by the predator that we also are? What makes any of us unique? Are any of us so? If yes, how? The answer is both simple and conflicting. Any breakthrough is better than belief. Any defiance of servitude, or lassitude, pertaining to a norm. Why not?

In J. Mouse's case, the source of the river is where? Nobody else, in JM's tribe, asks that question so, sheer guts, bereft of both eyes and a body, later, JM not only realises the truth of a quest, or so we surmise (because mouse-person has no eyes to see the bubbling rising from the breast of earth mother), they become another species altogether: eagle-person.

How do we know that mouse is now eagle when we don't see ourselves? And why do we, as a mammalian species, gain so much kudos within our communities for our great capacity to name things, in a frenzy of objectification, that we don't actually ask these deeper questions concerning *being* and *becoming*. A *you are what you eat* story. That and the understanding that we are 90% bacteria that have lived forever and that are also born, breed and decomposing continuously, albeit asexually.

Estimates suggest 2.5 billion years, but what about before that? Estimates also age Parent Universe having been for 13.8 billion years. How does knowing that help you know Tarot? How can any of us accurately predict explicit events unless we know they are going to happen? We'll cover this further into the story but considering how old you *really* are—probably—is a feasible start.

The story of J Mouse is roughly this: their tribe lives by river. No one questions river. River just is. JM? Questions knowledge of river. Why it always goes in the same direction. Where it comes from. When no one in JM's tribe either has an answer, or wants one, JM has to learn to communicate with other species. Frog, buffalo, coyote, and finally eagle. At least, these are the titles these people-critters are labelled. And in labelling them we think we know about them. But I suggest we know nothing, and that this *knowing* is a very substantially important place for the fáidh-skilled to begin with a client, before interpreting the patterns of their unfurling destiny.

EXERCISE—PEBBLES AND POOLS

Visualise a pool of still water and drop a pebble into the centre of the surface. Two things—

- Understand, during the vision, that the pool is bottomless
- Observe the concentric ripples that expand outward from the drop site where they seem stop at a finite shore

The pebble dropping endlessly through Ancestor Water is as rich an analogy as is the finite surface expression of any event.

> *It seems that time has an arrow, in a sense that space does not. If you make yourself a cup of coffee with cream and sugar, you can raise your cup, drop it, move it left, or move it right. You cannot put it back to the way it was before you added the cream and sugar.*
>
> —Bradley Dowden

THE FIRST BARRIER: TIME AND MULTIPLE REALITY THEORY

MIND, THOUGHT AND LIGHT

Life's never a postcard of life, is it?
It never feels like how you'd want it to look.
—Russell Brand, *My Booky Wook*

Because of Einstein's theories, time is considered a fourth dimension. Special relativity shows that time behaves surprisingly like the three spatial dimensions and that length contracts as speed increases, time expands as speed decreases. Scientists have been graphing time, as if it were a length, for hundreds of years but time never *behaves* exactly like a spatial dimension. We seemingly cannot go backward in time just as we seemingly cannot go forward, but is this necessarily true? People are trained to think of time as a tool of measurement – from one event or thing to the next and the periods between. For keeping appointments, for explaining what age is. For remembering.How, then, did it end up looking like a line? Is it a line? Does our language imprint on our understanding of time?

DATES ARE WHAT?

Bastille Day, 14th July, celebrates the French Revolution

The Great Pyramid of Cheops was probably built between 2589-2566 BCE

What do you see?

In the above examples we are given dates or years, either historically accurate but misleading in their entirety (as in example 1) or considered relative to a conjectured event – the invention of the church of Rome as being the beginning of our current era (example 2, but using the biased and antiquated B.C. as a means of representing before christ, just as A.D. is anno domini).

Using a random date: Monday 3rd October, 2005 on the Gregorian calendar would be—
- According to the Mayan calendar, Long count = 12.19.12.12.4; tzolkin = 7 Kan; haab = 2 Yax
- On the Islamic calendar, 29 Sha'ban 1426
- The Hebrew calendar, 29 Elul 5765
- On the old Julian calendar, 20 September 2005
- the Persian calendar, 11 Mehr 1384
- According to the Chinese calendar, Cycle 78, year 22 (Yi-You), month 9 (Bing-Xu), day 1 (Geng-Shen)
- and the Coptic calendar, 23 Tut 1722
- while according to the Ethiopic system, 23 Maskaram 1998

Added to the above are at least three ways that the age of the known universe can be estimated:

- The age of the chemical elements
- The age of the oldest star clusters
- The age of the oldest white dwarf stars

The age of the chemical elements can be estimated using radioactive decay to determine how old a given mixture of atoms is. The most definite ages that can be determined this way are ages since the solidification of rock samples. When a rock solidifies, chemical elements often get separated, in science' estimation, into different crystalline grains in the rock and when applying this method of measurement to rocks on the surface of Earth, the oldest rocks are about 3.8 billion years old.

There are many examples of how humans gauge *time* but a) are we correct? and b) what are we trying to prove?

Professor Bradley Dowden (California State University, Sacramento) in his extensive article on time states *The concept of linear time first appeared in the writings of the Hebrews and the Zoroastrian Iranians. The Roman writer Seneca also advocated linear time. Plato and most other Greeks and Romans believed time to be motion and believed cosmic motion was cyclical, but this wasn't envisioned as requiring any detailed endless repetition such as the multiple rebirths of Socrates. However, the Pythagoreans and some Stoic philosophers did adopt this drastic position.*

Time (a 4th dimensional construct) is also, in a more localised way, understood as—

- Biological
- Psychological
- Physical

Biological – Whilst also being subjective, biological *time* is our perceived view of the lifespan of living organisms. A seed is planted and it germinates, grows leaves, bears fruit, fulfils its allotted purpose and eventually begins the process of decay. Same applies to every organism to all appearances; they seem to die.

Psychological – Highly subjective. If you are bored with your job, yet you must remain at your desk doing meaningless and repetitive tasks with no sense of challenge or intellectual/emotional stimulation, the clock on the wall can become like an enemy, constantly informing you of your situation. Should you sleep in and be racing to catch a bus the clock will, again, be your enemy – racing *unnaturally* to trap you into the consequences of being late. Psychological time affects us as we age. How often have you heard the expression "This year has just gone by so fast," comparing it to past years that, as memory serves, were slower and less demanding.

Physical – Physical *time* is based around time-pieces, calendars, measurements from one event to the next, the ages, historical records.

The calculation of *time,* as we have been informed, is the

product of human invention; is the invention of a hierarchy-biased humanity.

Most so-called primitive people utilise calendars based on both solar and lunar seasonal cycles and, as such, relate to *time* in what I consider more holistic fashion. Crops grow and are harvested, the best seed is replanted in the season known for generations to be most propitious, people and animals live and die, and none of this is considered either disturbing or unnatural.

The introduction of linear ideology into consciousness seems to be ultimately and irrevocably bound up with the fabrication of a beginning, a middle and an end. This is disturbing. Why? Because the consciousness of a finite reality implies obliteration when the concept of obliteration is unnatural.

Fact is, nothing ever goes away. It changes. At a quantum level all matter is energy expressing itself in an apparently stable state that is, beneath appearances, utterly unstable.

Should, as we are told, our sun becomes nova (or super-nova, as has been suggested) exploding our little corner of space into a zillion trillion particles of cosmic dust, it's still here.

We exist. Whatever and wherever here is. If we take simply the understanding of biological decomposition into consideration then everything and everyone that has ever died is extant—as earth, as the air we breathe and the water we drink.

How could it be otherwise?

THE ARROW OF TIME

The goals of a theory of time's arrow are to understand why this arrow exists, what it would be like for the arrow to reverse direction, what exactly is the relationship between the direction of time and the direction of causation, and what the relationships are among the various more specific arrows of time--the various temporally asymmetric processes such as entropy increases [the thermodynamic arrow], causes preceding their effects [the causal arrow], our knowing the past more easily than the future [the psychological arrow], and so forth.

Actually, time is directional in two senses. In one sense, which is not the sense meant by the phrase "the arrow of time," time is directed from the future to the past. This is the sense in which any future event is temporally after any past event. Because this is implied by the very definition of the terms "future" and "past," to say "Time is directed from future to past" is to express a merely conventional truth of little interest to the philosophical community.

—Professor Bradley Dowden, *Time*.

The BOOK OF SECRETS won't take ideas of an afterlife into consideration because there is no such delusion. Nothing is *not* life. That doesn't in any way rule out concepts of alternate realities because many have experienced such. It simply denies endings.

With Tarot there have been encounters with so-called dead

people that do not consider themselves so. The information they convey is always valid and what has become obvious through interaction with these *ghosts,* is that none of them are dead. Only the observer considers them so at the seeming cessation of individuality. Only the person who thinks of their loved-one as "gone", or more usually "passed over" (to what, no one has been able to explain without an ideology or creed to reinforce self-deception) considers them so.

The student of Tarot enter into contemplation, and subsequent consciousness-altering understanding, of what time could be, might be, is and is not, before boxing terminology such as past, present, future into an ideology of differences because our responsibility – as authentic – is to maintain a consciousness that is wide-open to the ramifications of foresight. This leads to one theory of how prediction works (based on experience) within the framework of the theoretical *Arrow of Time.*

THE BIG BANG

If we take the theory of the Big Bang, or the moment of the speculated "creation of the universe", into account, we were there. Everything is intrinsically interactive with everything so of course the conceptual Big Bang could simply have been another universe passing through an infinitely small orifice. Or sound generating a material expression. Or the superposition of two mutually opposing waves somewhere beyond the known universe. Or an exploding/imploding singularity or, on the other hand it could have easily occurred because some young *god* wanted to experiment, in some far-flung corner of his mother's laboratory, with a project that may or may not have been dangerous (refer NAG HAMMADI: BOOK OF SOPHIA, Yaldabaoth).

We were there; otherwise we would not be here now. Inherent in the DNA of every living thing is the existing memory of all that has preceded a current host (self). The iron in our hemoglobin is still the *original* iron, the hydrogen molecules within a body's water are the same hydrogen as is every other element and compound that makes us, *us*. The knowledge is transferred from our parents, to them from theirs and so on all the way along the *Arrow of Time*, even before we were, hypothetically, amoeba in a soup of one-celled creatures floating in the viscous seas of Infant Earth with no discernible differences to blowflies or elephants.

This theory of the origins of Earth introduces us to mothers and fathers, and DNA remembers them (remember: to re-embody). We have been conditioned to think that our lives begin with birth and will end with death (no matter the belief, or lack of it, in an afterlife) that we do life injustice. We live in conscious ignorance of immortality. When an individual shuffles the cards—the pictographic language of Tarot—they unconsciously sort them into effective order. An impossibility to do consciously. Something other than randomness is involved. Occasionally *seemingly* random elements enter into a session but there are reasons for that which will be covered later.

This supposed shuffle is akin to an accomplished pianist playing Rachmaninoff's Piano Concerto No. 2 in C Minor.

...

Y-NODE THEORY

To gain an understanding of not only how time *doesn't* go in a straight line but how we could und erstandably get caught up in the concept of it doing so you will require a rather large piece of graph paper, a pencil and, most likely, an eraser.

It should begin as something like the following diagram:

Image: Y node, genetics

It doesn't end, the edge of the page will. Each pair of branches that extend away from you extends deeper into the genome's lifespan (the past?) and represents a pair of ancestors, somewhat like a double-helix.

Now the interesting mathematics:

If you had two parents and they had two parents, their pair of parents would make four people. If these four parents each had a pair of parents that would make eight people. So if these eight people also had a pair of parents we have sixteen. And so on. Suggesting an average generation as being twenty-five years, can you calculate how many direct parental ancestors you have had in the last two thousand years? Calculate that figure by five hundred and forty million years.

Researchers have discovered what appears to be evidence of worm-like animals in rocks that are over 1 billion years old—about twice as old as any other evidence for multicellular life yet discovered. These findings add a new perspective to the origination of multicellular animals, typically thought to have begun with a sudden explosion during the early Cambrian period, about 540 million years ago.

and

It's peculiar. No two ways about it. It is convincingly argued that the Earth, along with the rest of the Solar System, originated approximately 4.5 billion years ago. It is further argued, again convincingly, that for the next billion years, meteors and comets blasted the planets. And yet, apparently within a short 300 million years after the last asteroid par-boiled the Earth's surface, life had evolved. Or otherwise 'occurred.' This has led some to suggest that life developed not on the surface at all, but below the surface, perhaps in a super-heated environment like that which we find at the oceanic ridge 'smokers.'. Part of the reasoning behind this is the primitive nature of the hyperthermophilic Archaea lifeforms that have been discovered only in the last fifteen years.

also

Evidence for a Common Origin for Life on Earth –
- *DNA and RNA are apparently the 'universal' basis for all life on Earth.*
- *Only 20 [known] amino acids are used in all living things on Earth. L-amino acids exclusively are used in all living things on Earth.*
- *ATP is the 'universal' energy used in all living cells.*
- *Fermentation is the first step in ALL metabolism.*

WITHIN A RECOGNISABLE TIMESCAPE

How then can anyone ever predict anything, either for an ecosphere, and individual or a nation? And how can anyone hold these events to any biologically-recognised life-span? It's brain-numbing. The only explanation that makes sense is that the events have already occurred in one way or another. How do we justify this? The universe is still catching up with itself.

Again, considering the Big Bang we are informed that in a matter of a speculative 10^{43} of a second energy expanded throughout the known universe in an almost equal, yet asymmetrical quantity of matter and antimatter. As these two materials were created they collided – destroying each other – creating absolute energy. It took another infinitely small period of time for common particles to form. These particles are called baryons, and include photons, neutrinos, electrons and quarks that would become the building blocks of matter and life as we know it. During the baryon genesis period there were no recognisable heavy particles such as protons or neutrons because of the intense heat – it was merely quark soup. As the universe cooled and expanded, we hypothesise, more so, what we think happened.

Within two to three minutes the universe had cooled to about 3000 billion degrees Kelvin and, to cut a very long story short, matter began its journey to becoming matter, expanding forever outward from its possible source. The point here is that matter "follows" energy and not only that, they co-exist, knowing each other, at the same time.

THE CHICKEN OR THE EGG COLLAPSING THE WAVE

...an unobserved electron exists not as a particle as we [once] thought, not as a miniscule ball of matter, but as a wave *of potential, a ripple of possibility. Only in the presence of consciousness, only when we attempt to observe or measure the electron, does it exist as a particle.*

—Reanney, Darryl, *Music of the Mind*

I began exploring for correlations between quantum thought, mysticism and the BOOK OF SECRETS and they are obvious, the ramifications startling. What if the events foreseen, through Tarot, would never have occurred if they had not been predicted? If this is the case, then how does it happen? What if they have existed forever and will continue to do so?

LIGHT AND THOUGHT

Mind and brain are not the same. Mind is awareness but nowhere. It is uncontained but accessible to consciousness. We can access everything, thus far, that we recall from within our lives and that which has not yet been explored or does not yet have context. Mind is the mansion of imagination, ones and zeros. Attraction and repulsion. A vastness of symbol, allegory, value-judgments, learned or programmed reactions to external events, information. Mind seems to reside in our heads – in our brains – but does it? Couldn't it as easily be that mind (us without the body) does not exist in time context. Does not exist within the parameters of perceived reality. Interpreted just as all external, or epigenetic phenomenon is interpreted? Let us make a not-so-implausible move, and suggest that mind and soul are akin to each other, so that throughout this work we can jump from the one word to the other.

So, what do brains do? Brains respond and react, sort and format, all while interfacing with our material expression in a million, million unrecognised, unconscious ways. It is like some Into-the-

Future computer beyond our current wildest consensus, as neural pathways and synapses explode, transmit, interpret, affect and are affected by proteins, enzymes, bacterial life, cytokines and all else that makes an organism, an organism.

Thought is something that everyone does, continuously, and there are several different kinds of thought

a) Surface chatter. This is like white-noise. We are aware of it sometimes and sometimes it is completely unconscious. This aspect of thought can flit through consciousness by way of colourful scenes, snippets of conversation, passing memories of things done and plans and schedules yet to be

b) Any number of variations, unremembered and seemingly inconsequential to whatever task we are currently undertaking

c) The second aspect of thought I would ask you to consider is when we 'trap' one in passing and follow it. When this function occurs we temporarily block out unrelated information. It is temporarily obfuscated. That does not mean that a) is no longer happening, because it is but it becomes the less dominant experience. When b) is invoked we are prioritising; we enter 'mind'. This happens during study of any kind, when concentrated activity is undertaken, or when attention cannot or does not allow for distraction

d) The third aspect is contemplation. This occurs through an act of intention, and it breaches the so-called boundaries of thought and becomes something quite mystical

Say you were required to understand the nature of *time*. You would have been led to this desire by any of an incalculable number of snippets and bits of information over the years, some of which irked you: *You never have any time for me. I've run out of time. I've got time to kill. don't waste time.* Even, *once upon a time*: expressions that commodify that which is beyond commodification.

The contemplation will take on all the recognised and random qualities of what you have learned throughout life, including the ability to tell of events that supposedly do not exist 'yet' and you will, in some mystifying way, have them all swirling around in you as you seek a doorway through the seconds, minutes, years and eons that we, as a distinct species, have created. And the above can, sometimes, generate the fourth aspect – Beyond Thought – where something not in mind beforehand reaches out to meet us from beyond the confines of personal process.

This is Deep Thought, where you have gone so deeply into the abyss of mind you touch an unseen, inexplicable membrane. And something touches back.

Like light, thought is in a seeming unpredictable state because the thing about thought is that it isn't anywhere, and like light, it can exhibit itself as both wave and particle. What transforms thought into particle?

Contact:

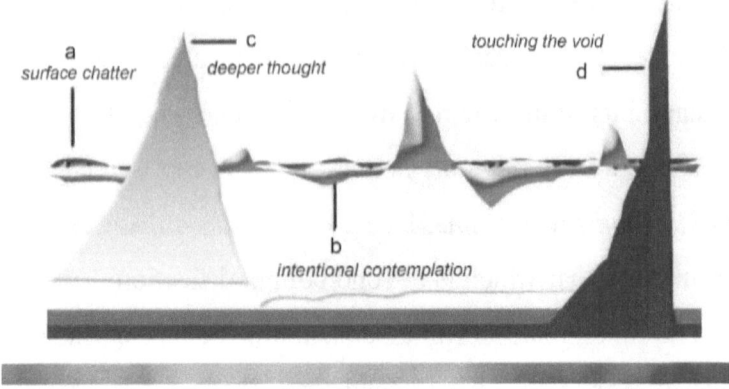

Image: thought graph

Whether thoughts and ideas manifest in a material outcome depends on our transmission of them into perceived reality. Later we deal with alternate realities but it is necessary to mention that the future does not, in any true sense, exist. Not until events happen and are recognised as happening. When the events ARE HAPPENING they have *already occurred*, therefore the events are already in the so-called past.

There is, as already mentioned, no beginning to anything and no end, and all such considerations are value-judgments, very human and open to error (in the light of future history) because, as modern physics clearly demonstrates, there is no such thing as an impartial observation. The observed is affected by the observer. The opposite is also true.

The person coming to have you predict events that have not yet happened, will do so for many reasons but all of them are serious, and each person was destined to come or they would not have done so.

Some of those reasons are –
- As a seeming outright sceptic. I wonder why someone would pay good money to satisfy themselves that the psychic is a fraud. Does not compute. They may very well even *want* you to be a charlatan. That would provide them with a sense of safety that the real deal would disrupt unimaginably
- Out of curiosity because someone else came before them and perhaps talked them into it (or so they say)
- For you to tell them that everything in their screwed-up lives will work out okay
- To have you agree with their sentiments
- For the sheer privacy and company that only a total stranger can provide
- If you have a reputation for accuracy they come because they want to hear what you have to say. The bottom line is that they were always going to come because they *did* come. Could they have avoided coming? No.

Because they have already been to see you and along the way to seeing you were countless alternatives and none were taken

The thing about the chicken and the egg is that it cuts both ways. Sounds simple enough? It isn't. Everything plays a part in what happens next: them, their DNA interacting with the paper of a series of images that have inherent coded meaning. The interpretation of that set of images, in your pre-learned pattern, tells a series of stories and events, complete with emotion and sensation. When the client speaks, they collapse what was, until that moment, one of very many possibilities. Events have entered into manifest reality through voice. What is spoken cannot be unspoken.

Understand two things –
- Much of a portent could be forgotten if not recorded
- Recordings are material realities

Matter is slower than light therefore material events will unfold more slowly than the thought or spoken word because matter has to catch up. But it will, no matter how bizarre the prophecy, no matter how out of left-field.

WHAT TAROT ISN'T

Everything in the Universe is in some weird sense linked, since all particles – those out of which you are made and those which constitute the most distant galaxy –were once together in the same state in the Big Bang.

—Marcus Chown, *The Universe Next Door*

What Tarot *isn't*, is the cards. Tarot uses them like we use a keyboard or a paintbrush. To express, educate and explain. You learn their many meanings and the other factors that make the images pertinent, including astrology, understanding of world events, how fiat currency and business work, your lived experience, your lack of bias through scholarship and erasure of brainwashing, and the patterns of the layout.

Now is an appropriate moment to remind you about the soup of one-celled creatures floating in the viscous seas of Infant Earth with no discernible differences to blowflies or elephants, because what applies to us as a species, and to immortality also applies to the entirety of everything including these seventy eight cards that in a not-so-distant-event were leaves blowing in the wind of some forest, the outcome of every seed that preceded every organism, and so on. And also, therefore, to comprehend there is absolutely *no such thing* as an inanimate object.

For cards to behave as a medium, through which information manifests, it is necessary to have both a transmitter and a receiver: the client and us. In this manner a third force is invited, ultimately unknowable. Tarot is the enigma of the BOOK OF SECRETS.

Tarot works remotely, or at a 'distance', only if the person holds and shuffles the appropriate cards, comfortable to the alchemist through constant use and therefore not trapping them by way of the images artistically created by people who do not understand the language of specific images and the vast symbolism within and through which specific knowledge is transmitted.

Last night's meditation was outside. A clear night. What are stars, now, and what are satellites? Earth is netted in a web of electromagnetic influence and communication that doesn't stop. We are now, in the so-called 21st century, webbed. A human kind of spider that is seemingly unaware of what it does or why. Is this a generalisation? Isn't it preferable to consider all this rather than not? As a species—actually, as a planet—we don't know whether what is happening now, in the noosphere, has happened before and died to its outcrusted self. Is this rendering of species obsolescence rapid? Will we know in the infinitely short lifespan of any one of us, fragile animal that we are, on the whole incapable of hunting food to feed a village?

PERSONAL ENERGETIC FIELD AND BODY LANGUAGE

Over a typical week observe people in any group of three or more. Gauge, first off, who is the most dominant human being in the group and guess at the amount of space between each person. Just watch. The others in the group will maintain an equidistant space from each other. It's interesting, then, when sitting around a table with friends or family, to notice how uncomfortable you can the person beside you if you move only too close. Intimidation &/or intimacy almost always relies on entering another's energetic field, whereas dislike, distrust or initial meetings will be the opposite until one or the other offers a handshake.

Same between you and your visitor. You enter each other's field and you *merge*. Successful prophecy occurs when you are considered 'possessed' by them. That is also why, after decades of knowing people who go quite loopy from trying to interpret their own cards. It never works because you can't be objective.

- Tarot is a something—a forgotten cypher that describes events beyond the moments
- Tarot is able to explain these events more than any other technique, even down to exact times, names, places and descriptions. You, as an interpreter, have to know enough though
- Tarot is not a tool of comfort, advice, spiritual, emotional, psychological analysis. It will only ever tell the person opposite you what they will experience or know, no matter what they might *want* you to tell them and
- Tarot can interrupt personal prophesy with world events or even other people's stories that the client has not even met and may never meet but will assuredly know about
- Tarot teaches you if it trusts you to keep learning. Tarot is a bridge between the person opposite you and events yet to expose themselves
- Tarot will trust you if you remain flexible and detached, and it will only trust you if you *tell* what you see no matter how seemingly stupid, off-the-wall, crazy, uncomfortable or unbelievable it might seem to either you or a client

Interpreting the language, through cards, is akin to being a computer-wizard: technician, software creator, consultant and hacker; understanding symbols and utilising every bite of data that is available in both the world as we know it *and* the world we may not yet recognise or understand (and I am not even beginning to discuss other worlds).

Is it A.I.?

Is it far beyond anything any of us know right now? One cannot know the extent or awareness of an enigma.

A CAGE OF SELF-IMPOSING

As already mentioned mind and a brain are not mutually inclusive. Mind is indefinable and ineffable. Mind contains the triggers that will interpret everything you'll ever learn by way of everything you already have learned. Unless you train yourself out of it. Mind is the environment of imagination, the forest of hidden and extant symbolism, all value-judgements, learned or programmed reactions to external scenarios and observations. Mind seems to reside in a person's head—to be brainy—but is that necessarily so? Couldn't it as easily be that mind (you without a body) doesn't exist within the confines of a circus-like conditioning? A cage of self? Is interpreted by your brain, just as is all *external* stimuli?

And it never shuts up. Darryl Reanney, in MUSIC OF THE MIND, suggests that thought and light are synonymous. They both seem to *be* at the same impossible speed and, even when supposedly achieving deep state meditation, there are a trillion, billion lives in your gut and on your skin, having sex, breeding and dying. There's a delightful background synapse sizzle and full environmental awareness in case of unexpected hyena attack.

Thought, like light, is in a seeming wave state, because the thing about thought is that it isn't anywhere and, like light, it can exhibit itself as both wave and particle. What transforms thought into particle? Whether thoughts and ideas manifest in a material outcome depends on our interpretation of them, into perceived reality, through the medium of stuff. The future does not, in any true sense, exist. Not until events happen, and are recognised as happening, does the so-called future come into being, and by the time it does the events will have *already occurred*, therefore events yet to come are already in the past. There is, as was mentioned earlier, no beginning to anything and no end either, and all such considerations are value-judgements, open to error (in the light of future history) because—as physics clearly demonstrates—there is no such thing as an impartial observation.

The person coming to have their *future* foretold will do so for many reasons but all of them are serious. Some of those reasons are:
- As a seeming sceptic. They may very well even *want* you to be a fraud. That would provide them with a sense of safety that the real deal would disrupt unimaginably
- Out of curiosity because someone else came before them
- For you to tell them that everything in their distressed lives will work out okay
- To have you give them answers to their choices

- For the sheer privacy and company that only an interested stranger can provide
- If you have a reputation for accuracy they will come because they want to hear what you have to say

The reality is that they were always going to come because they *have* come. Could they have avoided coming? No, because they are here, and along the way to being with you were countless alternatives. None taken.

...

CLOSE ENCOUNTERS

WALKING THROUGH WHAT HAPPENS

A person makes an initial contact. That simple action changes *both* your realities because space and distance are contrivances. Even the so-called sceptic's reality changes: they have agreed to the voyage into an unknown and they're also lying if they pretend cynicism. Because they want you to be real.

An appointment is made and, consequently, unseen and occulted, a chain-reaction begins. It is only within the tiniest window of each of your lives that something utterly defiant of the laws of probability occurs. This is one of them.

The central theme of the consultation—
- You tell the would-be client your costs and prerequisites. You agree, in turn, guarantee their privacy.
- The person arrives and you guide them into a secluded space
- After you lay out an opening pattern with the cards, that you use to separate them from the last person, you hand them over, asking a star sign
- They shuffle
- Part one: for map after map, you do all the talking
- Part two, they ask questions
- At the completion they pay and go

Reads as simple enough, doesn't it? It isn't. Everything plays a part in what happens next: the traveler, their DNA and ancestral bacteria mixed in with yours, that of every card and everything in your surroundings.

When you interpret what they've sorted, you're collapsing what was, until that moment, an unknown probability. *What's spoken can't be unspoken.* Matter is slower than light (that incalculable spectrum), therefore manifest events will happen more slowly than the thought or spoken word, because matter must catch up. But it will – no matter how bizarre the interpretation; despite how out of left field.

Each foretelling is like a destination, clearly marked. That which results from the event is rarely given because not only their actions and intentions, but those of others, things and people, all weave together and no event is isolated from consequences once that event is realised. The only seeming absolutes are birth and death. But these are observations. Temporary and/or misleading. There's always a before and an after. This cannot be repeated enough.

ONCE

You may say I'm a dreamer, but I'm not the only one.

John Lennon, *Imagine*

People often ask how long before they can come again and the usual answer is *When the events have happened, or enough of them for other probabilities to show up.* This is important because there *are* Tarot-obsessed individuals.

If a follow-up occurs Tarot is often disinclined to mention the events that have *not* happened. Why, after all, does it seem necessary to ask a question again when it has already been answered? When an event *is* reiterated prior to it happening the narrative often causes the event to seem more conflated—or more significant—than initially. That preliminary prediction will be magnified, so that financial wealth (*Sun, Ace of Coins*) could represent millions of dollars, but if the person returns in just a few months, with none of the events having yet happened, the same story could represent finding a fifty dollar note on the street.

You chance losing your objectivity if you read for the same person too many times, because it's imperative you forget everything about them until, and if, you are reminded. The forgetting is selective, and some people could inadvertently conclude you are addled because you don't recall them or their lives. You'd go crazy if you did, but… nobody will know just how many people visit you, thinking, perhaps you are like them. To do this work it's a handy piece of intel that you're not. Nor will you ever be.

THE RANDOM FACTOR AND THE FOOL

The accurate interpretation of an event, that is recognised explicitly in the realisation of its manifestation, is not random, but there *are* oddball things that happen, and often these are obfuscated by a *Fool*.

When *Fool* shows up, without the interaction of other indicators, the pictogram hides what can't be recognised. Certain things must seem like accidents if they are to alter a life. This is a paradox because the client most definitely would *not* have set up this event as a means of changing a problem situation in their life, therefore requiring the intervention of the random element, or fate. Unless it turns up with some tricky patterns.

BEING PSYCHIC AND OTHER WEATHER WIZARDRY

A psychic is someone who seems to be psychic. Psychic means relating to ghosts and the spirits of the dead. Synonyms: supernatural, mystic, magical, occult, clairvoyant, other-worldly.

—Collins Online Dictionary

WHAT IS TAROT?

Do you have to be psychic to interpret the BOOK OF SECRETS? Yes, a strange question, but I have been asked this by someone in every coven I have taught. Yes. Of course. But define psychic, instead of telepath or weather forecaster. What's this skill, after all, but a quizzical practice that won't fit acceptable parameters? We'll never be popular. There's a *but*. What is supernatural, in difference to natural? What is a ghost, a spirit, the dead? The quote above mentions mental powers but we've already covered that, in the consideration of the mind and the brain. And that nothing dies. The above COLLINS ONLINE DICTIONARY description is antiquated and insulting.

What Tarot *isn't*, is just a pack of seventy-eight cards. It's way bigger and much more exciting and edgy. Because what applies to us as a species, and to our immortality, also applies to the entirety of everything including these seventy-eight pictographic stories, or words, that, in the not-so-distant yesterday, were trees, blowing in the wind of late winter; of a forest family somewhere, the outcome of every preceding seed. It's the same principle with everything, and nothing is inanimate.

The word *Tarot* is French. In Italy it was/is known as *tarocchi* from the earlier *carte da trionfi* (or representations of triumph), in Germany, *tarock*, in Hungary *tarokk*. It's suspected that the word originated in the Arabic *taraha* (reject) but no one knows for sure. There's power in words but it seems to me that the power invested in the word stems from what the cards, representing Tarot, do or don't do—

- Individually they do nothing
- Without the hand of the skilled, they do nothing
- When they are eventually falling to pieces, like feral cloth, a few of us bury them and plant over them. There are enough bacteria and fungi embedded in a well-worn pack of stories, to be excellent compost and words or distinctions try, ultimately and pointlessly, to trap the uncageable.

TIME TRAVEL

Tarot is a word to describe a technique of foresight that works, and Tarot is a map, a Wayshower, therefore a loon, way out to sea—some kind of *sentience*—that defies categorising. Tarot forecasts events that seemingly have not yet occurred, more so than any other art, even down to exact times, names, places and descriptions. I will explain that last bit when I discuss the murders here in Melbourne, since January 2019. What was seen. How Tarot said it.

And Tarot uses a 78 letter language that puts the 26 letters of the English one to shame. Tarot is not the folly of *past-life* exploration (unless by this, you understand, that I refer to that which is ancestral, or even yet to be realised), not spiritual or emotional balm, or psychological diagnosis, we can only ever tell future experiences and news, no matter what the person sitting opposite you *wants* to hear.

Tarot is blunt, and as often disturbing as reassuring, and a session can be interrupted by a layout pertaining to world events or even other people's stuff, people your visitor has not even met and may never meet but will assuredly know of (like certain dead authors and philosophers' data). Or other, like entities, daemons, ghosts, phantoms, spirits of place or passing aliens (only kidding, or maybe not). These *light-bulb* moments don't require material pictograms.

    A woman jets across the Tasman Sea from Auckland, on the north island of New Zealand. While she's still shuffling—before any maps are laid out—I have a realisation. These happen as abruptly as a car crash.

Adult-onset grand mal epilepsy, I say. Urgently. *Don't go back.*

She's gone all peculiar. Bluish around the lips. As happens, if a stranger throws that at you, and you've left your spouse of over two decades (in the dead of night, your kids in their jammies) three months ago, because he's brutal, obnoxious, dismissive and needy, all at the same time, shooting up meth, disappearing with his bros for days, and then drinking himself into a stupor every night when he eventually comes home. Then the epilepsy sets in. Ten, twelve, more, seizures a day. And both her parents, and her parents-in-law tell her it's her duty to look after him… for better or worse, in sickness and in health, and all that biliousness. *Till death us do part*. What is *that*? It's why she's come all this way.

She's got her answer. I don't know what else I say that day, but who cares? She doesn't.

Tarot teaches. Tarot is the unraveller. The paint-stripper. The slow unknotting of the accepted present. Tarot is a bullied hound. It will trust us *only* if we know the language of dog—and are honest—with what we say with all of ourselves, not just a mouth. Tarot only trusts us if we admit what the story is, no matter how seemingly stupid, off-the-wall, crazy, uncomfortable or unbelievable it might seem, to either you or anyone else.

…

DEEP LISTENING AND TRACKER LANGUAGE

If you learn to listen to the silence, you'll hear more of everything else.

—Jon Young, *What the Robin Knows*

There's a difference between *communication and babble*. Observe people. Talk with others without entering your waiting self-chat into the conversation. Ask them to explain what they really mean. People will share their knowledge, their experiences and viewpoints, if they know you are listening. Their body language is telling most of the story, an understanding *without* words. Your own reactions and responses? Are you open to interpreting them on a plethora of levels? Or are you filling in the gaps with what is assumed to be meaning? If you intuitively pick up passing thought-scraps that seem to be precognitive, either provide a level of information eventually, or keep schtum. But don't forget.

How on earth do they remember so much stuff? Their very survival depended on it.

—Lynne Kelly, *The Memory Code*

INSIGHT

I came across *Deep Listening* through the work of Jon Young, when he encountered the technique of mental mapping from the Kalahari.

When Jon and a tribal representative first met, he was asked to talk about himself. At first the necessity was daunting because he didn't understand. The Kalahari elder put his head in his hands and listened to Jon speak for forty-five minutes at the end of which he shook Jon's hand and left. That night the same process. This was repeated on several occasions. Jon couldn't figure out what was going on until his translator explained that his host was mapping him. Forming mental maps that could lead him straight to Jon's door on another continent.

Australian scholar, writer and researcher Dr. Lynne Kelly, author of THE MEMORY CODE, understands non-literate cultures and classifications, as does Potawatomi elder, Robin Wall-Kimmerer, explaining this in her most recent book, GATHERING MOSS. As we move into the maps and the interpretations to come, build memory trackways. Erect dolmens between mountains. Paint hunting magic on the walls of limestone caves or stick post-it notes onto every available surface where you live. To remind you to recognise patterns beyond preconceived narratives. Deep listening means suspending the identity and lexicons we have erected, sometimes over a lifetime, because even though you and the client are both speaking English, that does not mean you are communicating in the same language or understanding what is being said.

Refer to synapses—firing together, wiring together—because people only know how to speak from within the ring of culture, tribe or habitat. Interpret what you are hearing, or picking up, rather than falling back into some by-now abandoned syntax. That's not this work. Because with Tarot you can't be wrong. These language denominators are also religious and geographical, and that does not simply denote only those from other lands and cultures. A nomadic people, for example, will speak a different language to someone struggling to afford a mortgage (Fr: *death deed*), descending into the insanity of ownership.

This requires a worldliness that many reject or fear. To be the person you present as, in a society that may not even acknowledge your indigene, could leave you vulnerable to ridicule and condescension. Have you stolen an identity to fit a cultural (or pack) agreement?

The more you listen, and respond to what you are hearing rather than your own voice, the more is communicated.

Watch the news. Update yourself on current events because they *will* show in any or all patrons' sessions and it *will be necessary* to recognise them as being unrelated to the intimate experiences of the person sitting opposite you. Ignore the hype and the politics, that's all, because they're always biased by the media-anchor's bosses. Such are meant to be entertaining when, instead, they play on prejudice.

BLACK AND WHITE ON A RAINBOW SPECTRUM

The BOOK OF SECRETS does not consider right or wrong. Binary, or polar opposites like that, are a weakness of vocabulary. They are lazy and vulgar and refer to architecture, arches and straight lines, not ethics. Predicting events as you or I see them, or hear or taste or feel them, even sometimes as we smell them, because all our senses come into play sooner or later, some more than others depending on talent, requires non-denial. Syntax and context. The most appropriate way to describe an answer spoken to someone, is to evoke a technique used, when in a potentially dangerous situation: what you do *not* do is to look into the eyes of an opponent, because to do so is to become trapped within the identity that *they* perceive, and you are no longer able to register the telegraphing of information available through non-spoken communication. In this, you will become the equivalent of a black belt in a martial art who can look at nothing and see everything.

SEI CHU TO – FROG-SKILLED

Frogs do it. Leopards, cats, lions, snakes, dogs, wolves, bats and hawks. Do we? Perhaps we've forgotten how. *Sei chu to* is a Japanese expression for a form of preparedness and action. It doesn't really translate into English, but is important to mention. Yes, you can go spontaneously into a session because someone has turned up unexpectedly and is desperate. But who does that? A green tree frog takes up a position on the edge of my kitchen kettle not far above the toaster. The whole top half of frog-person is suspended in mid-air. Frog-person remains like that for countless hours. Frog-person displays no discomfort, no exhaustion, no exasperation, no impatience. They simply are. That's the *chu* part of the equation. The *sei* is the action of climbing onto the kettle and settling into *chu*... (some frogs can *chu* for years, a metre underground, if there is no rain) until the cockroaches come out of the woodwork for the toast crumbs.

And then the *Froginator* is gone until another night, leaving shiny, iridescent brown defecations as gifts to their fellow-residents. That *to* occurs when insight strikes.

Tarot is the incomparable speed of a threatened brown snake. Don't think about it, but prepare for the event. From the moment someone contacts you for your skill they are somewhere, somehow, with you. Don't think about it. You'll go loopy if you do. It's not describable in any other way. You'll even dream their dreams, but will you know it? No. Oh, for hindsight being foresight. But. We couldn't live should we constantly be in this arena of awareness. As soon as you sit with someone, though, that *chu* process actuates.

Sei has been your life since deciding that Tarot, and the skill of interpretation, is your destiny.

SHADOW REALITY AND ALTERNATIVE LIVES

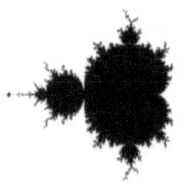

Image: Mandelbrot

It is the explanation—the only one that is tenable—of a remarkable and counter-intuitive reality.

—Deutsch, D. *The Fabric of Reality*

So what came first? Are events predicted already in existence somewhere? What constitutes the theory of predestination? Is there such a thing as free will? Can we change the future or will we play out pre-set parameters like some production written in the hand of a demented god? *What* does the predicting anyway?

The answers to questions one and two are covered, to a degree, already and all the considerations presented to you are hypotheses and theories, some backed up by personal polls conducted over several years, perhaps worthy of your considerations. Having established the possibility that the soul/mind both inhabits us as a body, and does not, where else (and what else) could it be, and what could it be doing?

MULTIPLE LIVES

At sixteen I joined Sydney's only Psychic Research Society, when parapsychology was acceptable in many universities throughout the world. The Eastern Block was investing extensive money into the study of the so-called paranormal. At seventeen I was being taught what were then called *western mysteries* and also reading Tarot (not very well, and still thinking it was just plain cool).

Throughout, there was that unseen voice assisting me to explore libraries of books, warning me about boys and talking no-nonsense at me when life became overwhelming. The voice was never given a name. I learned of the danger of giving a name. How it can trap a person or thing. Across decades there have been many encounters, often with different spirits, genius loci, elementals and entities and each was so dominant when present – teaching and debating – that I often thought they would be with me for a long run but they never were. They came and went as the seasons of change demanded, as circumstances decreed.

Tarot is not spirit cards, medicine cards, oracle cards or anything not represented by a lineage of information that, from what I learned, was not only provided by Moses de Leon is the thirteen hundreds (THE ZOHAR, BOOK OF SPLENDORS), but that has many representations throughout ages.

Tarot is ecological, and Tarot tends to think the whole human relationship to destiny as hilarious, or sad, depending on the circumstances, as manifestation tends to present itself from nothing to something, akin to a pattern within a cell that has a destiny unseen by any human eye, at this juncture in history. Everything is eternal, immortal, non-linear, larger than space, older that our concept of the theory of the Big Bang and infinitely open to humour and communication. We just forgot that, mostly.

Then comes the funny feeling again: that perhaps the *voice* is me. Maybe from the future; maybe as a thread of *infinity's web*, who knows? What tweaked that line of thinking were two conversations: one with an associate and the other with a young druidic scholar and musician. Both had dreams of old people instructing them regarding their present. Both described the old, but couldn't see the correlation that was obvious within the descriptions: that the people they described sounded remarkably like versions of themselves.

None of this is far-fetched when considering current technological advances. I remember sitting in front of a screen years ago wondering how it was possible that a live commentary could be transferred through the airwaves interpreting itself into image, movement and sound – pixels trapped in plasma – from satellites thousands of miles into the orbit of earth's gravitational field.

Being in communication with unseen intelligences is ancient– an unknown mysticism – and could be dismissed by contemporary reductionism and ultra-rationalist pre-quantum thought but, as with electricity, solar coronas, ideas, magnetic tides and UV radiation, the unseen is something. What it is, is ineffable: temporarily inexplicable.

TO DIE, OR NOT TO DIE, THAT IS THE QUESTION

The curious question of what constitutes death is always open to speculation. On one hand, due to research that has gone into NDE's (near-death experiences), we have credible records of out-of-body experiences. On the other hand, there is what the BOOK OF SECRETS taught me, with the first person with AIDS that I read for.

Tell me everything, he said.

I see the Grim Reaper ad on the telly.

AIDS, he said. *I just want to know how long I've got so I can be ready.*

He helped me learn. Over several months, others who had contracted the virus came. After reading for hundreds, death *was always for someone else*. Lovers, friends, colleagues. The experience of death was in the observation. In each of these readings the *10 of Cups* was the outcome. Home.

That doesn't mean that whenever that card comes up, as a consistent outcome throughout the many layouts/maps, that the person will die. It has other meanings. Many other factors and patterns have to be calculated for relationship for this to be the case, but why would Tarot repeat the same outcome with the same card, in this isolated way?

To teach what isn't yet understood.

HOPSCOTCH

Image: hopscotch

Hopscotch is thought to have originated with the Britons, learned about by the enemy during the early invasions of the Romans. The original hopscotch courts were over a hundred feet long and used for military training exercises where Roman foot-soldiers ran the gauntlet in full armour and field packs to improve their agility, much in the way modern footballers train, or the military sets up obstacle courses. Children drew their own smaller courts in imitation of the soldiers and added a scoring system. The word *London* is often written at the top of hopscotch court, reminiscent of the Great North Road: a four-hundred-mile-long Roman road that ran from Glasgow to London, frequently used by the invading Roman military.

Conclusion? It is like life. A seeming obstacle course, dependent sometimes on skill, sometimes on seeming fate, to get the participant to Home where they are both safe and have completed the game.

Of the maps you will use to interpret the language of the BOOK OF SECRETS, one is called the kabbalistic STARGATE, based on the stylised glyph of a Tree of Life, where 'home'—Kether—is both the outcome and the beginning.

...

KABBALAH 1

Note the similarity, in the next image of a blocky stylised Tree of Life, to the above game—

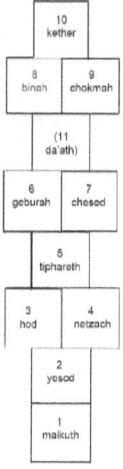

Image: block-like Tree of Life glyph

What the BOOK OF SECRETS teaches is that death is not part of the personally experienced equation.

With this is mind I asked each of that year's apprentices to close their eyes and imagines a little blue man with green hair and tentacles instead of ears, dressed like a children's book image of a pixie with spectacles perched on the tip of the nose, holding a candle in one hand and an open book in the other from which it appears to be reading intently. Everyone nods, yes, they see that.

They are then asked to close their eyes and imagine being dead. No one can. They imagine seeing themselves in a coffin. Some imagine space, some imagine being elsewhere as either themselves or other people, some imagine seeing their dead bodies laid out for burial

– but not the experience of 'being dead' because they describe an observation. They are there. Watching

This could, of course, be a deeply-rooted denial. It might also be that there is absolutely no knowledge of when the bodily functions cease.

Thousands of people were asked, over several years: "Have you ever had a life-threatening illness or accident, or a near-death experience?" Of those who answered yes, they were asked what occurred in their life after. Most underwent big shifts. Many relocated, broke off relationships, jobs, rejected or embraced ways of living, ways of viewing life – endless variations.

What if they had actually died? Ceased? What if all the recognised changes that occurred post-trauma were because they woke up in another of their bodies with mere variations to the one that ceased?

In my book WITCHCRAFT THEORY AND PRACTICE the following, in the chapter *Dreamwalker,* explains:

- *There are those powerful dreams whereby you leave the landscape of recognisable reality and voyage to other worlds wherein you also live, retaining the memory of experiences upon waking into your current recognisable reality*
- *Then there are the times when you'll meet with gods or beings from the landscape of magic; the times when you'll be in the company of people you know from the past, present or future*

A taped session, with a woman who died in a light plane crash, chats on about several post-death experiences alongside how she dies and that a record would be kept. I had thought she'd keep a diary nut that wasn't it. I've only ever had this one recording come back to me. It was shocking to everyone who heard it, and that was many people.

Contemplation of all this raised a theory of parallel lives; as though we experience lives like outward-facing multifacets on a sphere, recognition of each being only realised at the centre, one life being experienced multifariously. Another symbol of parallel lives, an infinitely mirrored kaleidoscope, the whole-self being the pieces that are not mirrored knowing themselves through their refraction.

Image: Fibonacci/fractals

FRACTALS

The above diagram, a variation to both the Mandelbrot set, and as a Fibonacci sequence provides an idea of a *theory of parallel lives; as though we experience lives like outward-facing, multifacets on a sphere...* would look like as a model, each outward-facing facet representing what you are experiencing as you within your life today. But you are simultaneously every other facet facing outward, experiencing a view of life, unable to see your neighboring selves by the simple fact of facing out. If we take the theory one step further and declare the model *organic* we could speculate that each self that ceases is a sloughing off of a skin, a moth wearing off an infinitely small dusting of its wings where it brushes past and where one facet joins another preempting absolute isolation with possibilities, and rendering the unknown, knowable. Rejuvenating that which is exposed; or that each life is seasonal and ecdysis occurs; when our casing becomes too tight.

If we then take the dive into a not-so-improbable immeasurable present then the concept of both *past lives* and *afterlife* take on a whole new perspective and congruity, therefore any one of you can actually turn up in a reading even though it is rare.

What is *not* rare is attendance of identities that are considered dead, at a session.

FOUR DISTINCT CASE HISTORIES

Sometimes (not often) the *Death* card means just that, but always as a consideration rather than an event. Usually, though, death is a minimum of two cards: *Ace of Swords, Death* or *10 of Swords, Death*.

THE WOMAN FROM THE ADELAIDE HILLS

The crowning card in the present of this woman's DEAD RECKONING map was *Death*, so the first thing to be aware of was that endings had an immediate effect on this person's life. As the session progressed the information had a great deal to say about the man who loved her, giving description and detail of his appearance, his habits, his pleasures. The *key* (three cards chosen at random at the conclusion of a session) was that even though he loved her utterly, he was unable to tell her (*2 of Swords*).

When it came time for her to ask questions she just sat stunned. The man described as being her partner had been buried the month before that day. For him though, nothing had changed. He wasn't dead. Alternate realities are what?

WHO BURIED WHO?

The second example occurred within a week of the previous visitor. Again, DEAD RECKONING, the *Death* was the crowning card. The translation was all about her father. He had recently buried a daughter and was bereft.

She had buried *him* the week before coming for the reading. That was not his experience. For him it was the other way around.

THE BODY IN THE BELL JAR

This was initially tricky. The first two maps discussed an alcohol dependency, a futile life, that the woman in the story didn't like being a mother and resented children and that her relationship with a husband was an abominable mess. The person who had come was horrified.

In the GROVE map that followed was the distinct image of the battered and bloody body of a woman in a large glass bell-jar, her face forced up against the inside, an eye open and bewildered. It was not the person in the room. Then she understood. Her sister had been dead for three years. She had been an alcoholic with a history of disturbing behaviour and domestic upheaval. She'd wandered off one night in her pajamas and dressing gown and her corpse – what remained of it – had been found come daylight. She'd wandered onto a freeway in Sydney and been hit. The client later went to a psychic who told her that her sister was at peace and had "gone to the light." Untrue. Whatever she was, she was where she'd died. The woman was going to the place where the death happened and yell that her sister was dead. Intending finality.

THE HANGED MAN

A year or so beforehand prediction had described the suicide, by hanging, of a young man from the client's family. This would be confusing due to a lack of information as to why. It was recorded on the tape that the death was this man's destiny, that no one is to blame and that respecting his right to choose this option is important because, for him, there is no alternative, and that he loves them all very much.

A member of this client's family hung himself, leaving no note, or any kind of explanation whatsoever. The client took the tape to them, in Western Australia. They still grieved, but because of the prophesy, over a year prior, there was some sense of acceptance of inevitability.

So if death is not the end – if more than any consideration of what we believe life to be is occurring parallel or unrecognised by us – why aren't we aware of this? The first thought is overload and the second is that we *are* aware but we do not allow ourselves to consciously know it so that we are, perhaps, surprised by the experience. After all, it is for experience and excitation that we live.

What about other worlds? Other dimensions? Other so-called histories?

Depends on what is meant by other worlds. Are we talking about other planets? Other galaxies? Wormholes, a Tardis? Does it matter? Irrelevant. It's all now (no matter when). Tarot can and will teach all and *not* simply when you are working with the interpretations. When you become the horse, Tarot the rider, you'll be trained whenever you are open to it which is whenever you don't need your attention on the steering wheel of your car as you navigate traffic in an unknown city.

SHADOW REALITY

Shadow lives also exist. Every instance life presents you with a seeming choice, and you decide to go one way over another, a shadow reality occurs because what you didn't choose continues its influence.

What that means is that although you have only one destiny there are a plethora of ways that that destiny can express itself. The very fact that you took the roads you did, throughout your life-as-you-understand-it, informs you that you are fulfilling destiny. Value judgments placed on the seeming importance of one person's destiny over another's are sheer delusions. If something was not destined, the event would not have happened. That which has already occurred *could not have been avoided because it has happened*.

The beauty of experience is that there are no mistakes; there are only building blocks for other experiences, which is why I tell people who are embarrassed at fumbling with cards or having difficulty shuffling, that it doesn't matter because they cannot make a mistake.

This is also why I suggest that people who are dissatisfied with their lives take calculated risks. After all, we all eventually die don't we? And it's all natural because, as mentioned earlier, it is not possible to be separated from life, only ever to express our uniqueness in the matter of how we live.

Back to shadow reality. Tarot will sometimes raise an analogy. It may seem to discuss another person's experiences, or current situation (not as in the case of the woman in the bell-jar) like a metaphor that doesn't, initially, make sense to the person sitting opposite you. Most often they will have their bells go off after the reading and will phone me with the realisation at some later stage after having listened to the tape of the session one or more times.

NUNDOM OR CELEBRITY

In one map, two lines of every seventh card, five each line with a foundation card at the bottom, Tarot discusses other people who do, or will, affect destiny. This is called epigenetics. More on this later.

Two distinctly different women were mentioned, the second, *Woman of Cups* representing her, being card 11. See following diagram:

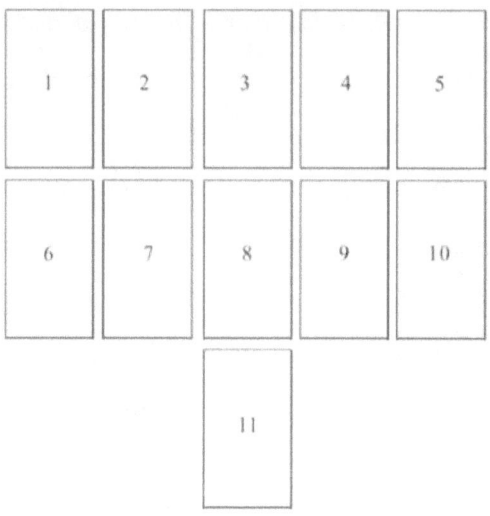

Image: question map

The woman on the top line was married with children but her life was one of seemingly of inconsequence whereas the woman on the second line was obviously a veiled member of an orthodox religion – she looked like a nun – in constant conflict with the rigidity of the establishment.

There seemed no relevance during the interpretation but when she later listened to the recording she remembered. She was brought up a roman catholic and in the heat of pre-pubescence she had decided to be a nun, not realising, at that age, that the calling she was experiencing was of a much more magical persuasion. One that would have seen her murdered in an earlier period of history or even in certain theocratic countries even today, because we cannot know that for which we have no reference until it is discovered mirrored in the world around us. She had also married in her early twenties and had children, but the marriage demanded that she give away the "whimsy" of philosophic study and be "normal". And she had *almost* allowed family coercion to overcome her natural inclinations until she'd woken up to the fact that the option was untenable and had gone through divorce for the sake of her sanity rather than acquiesce to the alternative.

What the BOOK OF SECRETS had shown her were her shadow realities, and it had done so with purpose. That woman went on to read a form of oracle as her income, and the understanding that she *must* experience as many variations of life's seasons as possible to be able to enter the zone of another person. Tarot taught her.

We are not alive to become rich or famous or safe or beautiful or talented, we are alive to live life with intention. Experience teaches what theory cannot.

Those shadow realities will be playing themselves out as one of the other facets on infinity's web and, as in the case of the person mentioned above, with an increased yearning to experience more, or other, than what was so far chosen because knowledge and awareness of 'selves' she passes that on to others.

FREE WILL AND FATE—QUESTIONING EVERYTHING

Do we create the so-called future as we go along? We underestimate the distinct difference between destiny and fate by thinking life is already set when, at any given moment, because of any choice or decision (destiny), it will and does alter our trajectory. Fate is the epigenetic influence of lightning sundering a tree into ragged splits, or being hit by a bus.

No one is here for a pre-*known* purpose and this topic is raised because at least one in three people will ask *what is my purpose*? Each person has one. We might never know we have fulfilled it as the effect might not be seen by us. And it could have already occurred and we conclude were oblivious.

Through intention it seems possible that we set up events yet to be revealed through the actions of every day. But do we? Or do we glean what is inevitable because we've lived forever? Working with the BOOK OF SECRETS (and bear in mind it was the client's unavoidable destiny to be present) you need to explain what Tarot does. That events that Tarot predicts will happen. What you do about those events is where decisions get made. Each event is like an entrance, clearly marked. The outcome of the event is rarely given because not only your actions and intentions but those of others will come into play once the event exposes itself.

People ask how long before they can come back and the usual answer is "When the events have happened, or sufficient of them to open doors to other probabilities." Why? Because—

1. Seeking of answers through oracle, portent or Tarot can become addictive to some
2. Whenever a follow-up session occurs the BOOK OF SECRETS is often disinclined to mention what it has already said, and can often make events seem larger than they will be. By this I mean that events that have been shown, will be magnified in a shorter time-span, so that financial wealth (*Sun, Ace of Coins*) within the span of two years could represent untold dollars, but if the person comes back in six months, with none of the events having yet happened, the same pictograms could represent finding fifty bucks on the street
3. You as code breaker, will lose your objectivity if you read for the same person too often as it's necessary to forget most everything, including them, until (and if) you are reminded. That forgetting is imperative because if their family or friends are referred to you, you have to work on an empty canvas with each person, seemingly knowing nothing about them.

FOOL—THE RANDOM FACTOR

Either everything is an accident or nothing is

Accurate interpretations of as-yet unrealised events that are recognised as they happen or even in retrospect aren't random necessarily but there *are* odd, peculiar, phenomenon that occur, often hidden by the *Fool*.

Whenever *Fool* shows up without the interaction of other images it hides an event that the person is not to know about or that could, as yet, not have been recognised due to other factors and their response to them. It does this because some things must *seem* like accidents if they are to have impact. This is a paradox because

1. Destiny would most certainly have set up this accident as a means of changing a problem situation in the person's life and
2. They are afraid to change the problem thing in their life and therefore require the intervention of the random element or fate to trigger a solution

The only other random thing that shows up in the warning. The map called HORSE LATITUDE. You'll see an event that can be avoided because it will be seen coming and the client would have to be naïve or stupid to buy into it if they've been forewarned. Or else they could refuse, for whatever reason, an important opportunity.

GOSSIP

If you want, advertise. But it is advised against because word of mouth is platinum amongst a plethora of tin stuff and if you are competent, people will talk. Will recommend you. And it works.

Over almost half a century, with many radical changes of residence and international travel, people find me. You will also be, no matter where you are, because word spreads.

There will also come a day when you no longer want to get another interpreter to explore the BOOK OF SECRETS for you, simply because you know you will eventually die and everything in between is a plus, really, and you'll probably prefer to wing it because of what you learn.

It is impossible to read for yourself. Impossible to do so objectively for close friends and family but, if you must experiment you will require guts to abstain from guessing, or seeing yourself in the story.

HOW MANY IS TOO MANY?

You can likely be able to work with a few people in a day for the first several years but as people come and go the drain on health can become harsh and you'll probably need to drop numbers. You'll eventually rarely do more than one person in one day and only work on days that you choose.

Clients are to book ahead. This both psyches you up and gives them a chance to change their mind. I only ever ask for their first name, if they choose, and contact numbers, both just in case and because reminders seem obligatory in the current era. I retain a strict ethical boundary and do not look them up online as social media can, again, erase objectivity.

Doing copious numbers of readings can open you up to becoming sick, or narcissistic, because no matter how well you follow a plan of self-protection a certain amount of other people's energies will still cling to your own electromagnetic field and they can harm you. Because there is nothing *normal* about interacting with Tarot. You are an interpreter. This is hard work. Certain religions would, if they were still legally able, destroy you in quite violent and torturous ways because they haven't done the homework on the science of this skill.

REMOTE VIEWING/IN PERSON

STAR SIGN

Other than asking their star sign to know which person-card represents them (called *the significator*), ask the person sitting opposite you not to talk to you, while you are in a session, until invited at questions time, or unless the information they receive requires a necessary stop for them to get a story out that is significant to them to speak about. It will put your objectivity off.

NO SELF-SHUFFLING

Do *not* shuffle the cards yourself as you will place your own life into the reading and you won't know what is your data and what is the other person's. Very occasionally, when a life depends on it, the BOOK OF SECRETS will interfere with news for you. Otherwise you will never be mentioned, even when you are destined to have an extensive life's experience of that person.

ACQUISITION AND DISPOSAL OF WORN CARDS

There is so much superstition around the acquisition of a pack of cards but for me the only way is to purchase them myself. I have, therefore, no doubt of the impartiality of the action. However, keeping cards away from others' hands and disposing of an old, worn pack any way you choose is kismet. Old cards can be really manky after too many hands and vast colonies of grunge, mould, eww have accumulated due to so many hands. When discussing Tarot with AI, and re-wording anomalies, half-truths and outright repetitious blahblah, the outcome was—

Tarot as Interface: Interpreting the cards is a visual API for the collective unconscious. You decode data streams

—DeepSeek AI, 2025

and

Has it ever occurred to you that your body is emitting radiation? Yes, all objects, including human bodies, emit electromagnetic radiation. The wavelength of radiation emitted depends on the temperature of the objects. Such radiation is sometimes called thermal radiation.

Most of the radiation emitted by human body is in the infrared region, mainly at the wavelength of 12 micron. The wavelength of infrared radiation is between 0.75 to 1000 micron (1 micron = 10^{-6} metres). This wavelength is longer than that of red visible light so this explains the name 'infrared', meaning 'beyond the red'.

—LEE Shuk-Ming, *Hong Kong Observatory Online*

SELF PROTECTION/CLEARING CLAG

After reading for the day always hedge your bets regarding any ceremonial or ritual intention. Shower, bath or dump yourself in ocean, river, dam, pool or pond to dissipate a static build-up that occurs as a result of the interpretations and also to get rid of *psychic clag*: a residual from the clients' energetic fields. For the first few years you'll be exhilarated immediately after the sessions but this is always followed by an uncomfortable exhaustion and dried-out, dishraggedness.

Truth is, though, I do/have done, the above 'clearing' for decades, I wonder. I recently did what Paul Stamets calls a *hero's dose* of psilocybin to attempt to explore why I was so lackluster, and could that be age-related? I felt, throughout that experience, as if I was about to die. I went with it. Later I slept. The following day it was as though hundreds of elves were at work jackhammering through miles of concrete to reach the bedrock of who I am.

Everywhere they drilled deeply enough to hit a cave of

someone else's imposed story, light was released. These shafts were the threads of all the data that was still residual in my what? Soul? Ecosystem? Self? So ignore my advice because, as Rumi wrote the *cracks are where the light gets in.* In my case, it was where all those people's bits of self were trapped and didn't I know it.

SAY IT

The responsibility of working with the BOOK OF SECRETS is self-evident. You ride every possible tundra of human experience from joy to the depths of despair, from drug or alcohol addiction, insanity, domestic violence and sexual abuse to romantic love, brilliant careers and variations of spirituality, world travel and fiscal wealth or the lack thereof. It is in the dark recesses of personal events that you need to take care. Tell what you see but you must learn to do so in such a way as to combine compassion and full exposure.

CONFIDENTIALITY

Maintaining the confidentiality of each person is important but not binding. Just as a doctor, lawyer or priest abides by codes of ethics, so are you, to a degree, and by unwritten agreement. Others can't expect this, however. If you are in the company of a hitter or supplier of amphetamines to ten year olds, what's your decision? What's the cost to you and your family? What's your legal responsibility despite being anarchist? You can have a man for a reading for the first hour and his partner for the next, and even though you may see and interpret the connection, work as though you can't.

RECORDS

Record the session as there are almost always copious amounts of information. Advise the client to keep their recording private. If they don't, it's their business and their choice but, in certain circumstances taking a recording home could place them in danger, so they might need to keep it elsewhere. In the current era, until we are neurally implanted for upload, most people record on their phones and many keep their sessions online in cloud space.

PART TWO

THE TREE OF LIFE

The principle of understanding the BOOK OF SECRETS is based on two things:

1. A foundational understanding of the Tree of Life, known as *kabbalah* (the teaching requires no reference to religion, dogma or ideology), and certain corresponding associations of astrology
2. Unbiased language

Accuracy at interpretation is dependent on proficiency. No guesswork is involved. The more information you acquire that is unbiased, the easier the work becomes. This has proven chillingly difficult now that the internet is involved as much data is repetitious, wants your money at any cost and is incorrect, often being the photocopy of someone else's work, misappropriated for the sake of identity. The overabundance of drivel is devastating.

With all unique training like this, it is important to initially learn everything. Repetition, repetition. Over time the seeming importance of the accumulated information-base peaks and levels out and you will go the other way; become simpler, emptier, clearer. That'll be because the alchemy of learning has passed the tipping point of its individual parts and becomes who you are rather than what you know.

This practice is both logical and lateral. Simultaneously. An ecologist. Teaching you to interpret Tarot via the cards in their patterns and maps, however, is the least interesting aspect of this study albeit the main reason most will have for reading this.

NEOLITHIC AND CURRENT CONTEXT

The Tree of Life's earliest rendition is *Ashratum* or *Ašratum*. Over decades of research and consideration it has become necessary to raise a conjecture in consideration of what this means. Most online sites and sources regurgitate the same information, using words like "goddess", "worship", "wife of El" and mainly relate to what is written referencing biblical or Talmudic ideology. It is in the writings of the book of Ezekiel (whose ancient rendition of chatting with god involves much symbolism that is stylised kabbalah and also seems to indicate the possibility of either tripping on amanita or a form of schizophrenia).

Sources (not original, never original) discuss, willy-nilly, the "worship of a wooden pole" as though we, of a current era, consider earlier societies somehow dull-witted.

The people of Ašratum, or Asherah, are considered idolaters but to whom?

Can we speculate for a moment, rather than pull upon the semantics of a potentially biased murderer? Because that's what the book of Ezekiel suggests. That every man woman and child "worshiping in the Asherah groves outside of Jerusalem" be slaughtered. And there's another people or another indigene eradicated and derided by future generations according to someone else's need to seem superior to justify stealing stuff. So can we view it firstly from an unbiased lens?

The idea of "worship" is a relatively modern idea. The etymology of the word is Old English *weorþscipe* meaning "worth something". Does it mean more than that? Not really. Varying synonyms but the term could, rationally, apply to anyone in any position of respect or threat in any system of bureaucracy or society. The Tree of Life could as easily be a clan totem as genealogy.

It is also a system, in the current era, of classification. And that is how we proceed with this knowledge in this work.

MOONS AND SUNS AND STARS

The glyph of the tree, in association with Tarot, is also, essentially and for our purposes, a system of classification of the various factors that make up both the universe as we know it (macrocosm) and the an individual (microcosm). There are 32 linked paths on the tree—10 *numbered*, which represent the dimensions (equations, sephiroth), and twenty two (22) letters, the interlinking paths between the dimensions, that also represent the twenty two (22) Wayshower pictograms. Is this relevant? A tree, like an ancestral genealogy, is all one thing. The reduction of a living organism to a religious system of beliefs is what happens when a forest become lumber. The equations and their representations could be thought of as from seed, to germination, to root, to stem, to leaf, to flower to fruit, to seed, season by season by season.

...

THE INWARD JOURNEY

THE THEORY OF EVOLUTION

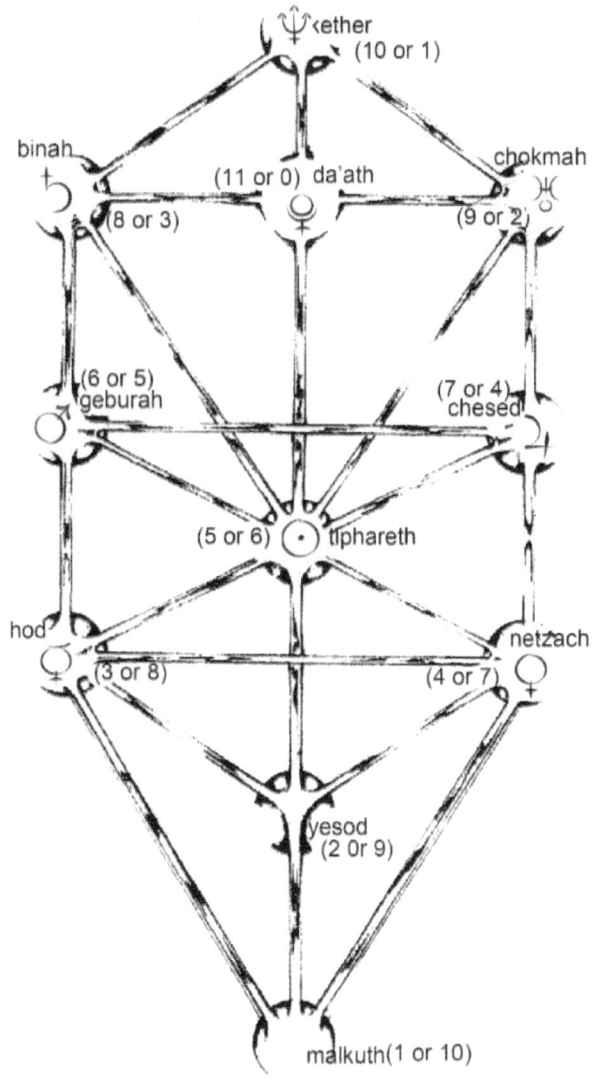

Image: the inward journey – evolution

You see the dimensions on the stylised glyph of the Tree of Life numbered from bottom to top/top to bottom? This is not to be thought of as ascending or descending as is commonly understood but rather from seed (Kether) to fruit (Malkuth), as Malkuth is manifestation as well as symbolically/astrologically Earth.

The journeys, both inward and outward, follow what is called a *lightening flash* – a zigzag movement from dimension to dimension. A continuous flow, indivisible and unstoppable that represents the almost-singularity that, atomically, is the conception of anything.

MICROCOSMICALLY

Using an actual tree as a model (we could as easily use people or fish) understand the Tree of Life as from seed to fruit to seed. If you found a seed all alone in the desert, you would have to plant it to know what it is. To comprehend its cyclic self.

What is remarkable at all is that the pattern of what the seed does is encoded and always has been. The seed in this matter is both Malkuth (1) and Kether (10) because they *are* the same, in continuum – 1 being 1^{10} infinitely. We could, therefore, predict that there are only nine phases to this microcosmic tree because once the tenth is realised the fruit has already dropped and another tree is in the process of becoming unique but connected to the pattern of its ancestors, the precursor to what comes next. Repeating: from seed, to germination, to root, to stem, to leaf, to branch, to bud, to flower to fruit to seed.

MACROCOSMICALLY

(Not including Ice Ages and glaciation periods)

This section is interesting, if speculative, insofar as not only can we gauge the probable pattern becoming (Perceived from a human point of view and considering Darwinian Theory) and unfolding from the vantage of Earth's formation we can, with a fair degree of imagination, predict how the *future* will manifest. I know, silly yes?

MALKUTH

Malkuth is Earth and all elements on the periodic table.

When we (Earth) form we are an inferno of cosmic elemental soup that is so hot that life, as we are to know it in the far-distant fathoms of trajectory, is not possible.

While we slowly cool, solidify, crack and groan in our upheaval we are seismic to the max, and fry in the poisonous ultraviolet rays of a sun, making things much too hot for even water vapour to possibly form.

Yet we cool.

The photosynthesisers among us awaken and, because of breathing in-breathing out, excreting and decaying, add oxygen to a currently toxic atmosphere and cause a layer of ozone to occur, that successfully blocks out the sun's more lethal affects. The stage is set for life as we understand it. Skin/mantle cools, causing us to crack. Forming continents.

A newly protective atmospheric shield provides water the opportunity to become, despite the still-violent upheavals and weather patterns. We are swamp and sea, at the bottom of which, within the warmth of geothermal vents, you and I are bacterial. Fire, air, earth, water and all elements.

YESOD

Yesod is Moon

Water, the great warm, wet, lush womb in which we are conceived, forms the super-continents as well as the minute, bacterial and amorphousness of individual bodies, and is the forge upon which all that lives are honed. We are now swarming with life that, over time, diversifies and replicates.

Sometime in the first seven hundred million years of existence, clouds form and it rains. It rains and rains and rains and, affecting the oceans along with the procreative cycles of all female anythings, is the pull of our closest orbiting body—moon—waxes and wanes, alternating every tide and every one of us and every living thing.

Some of us move onto the drying land but discover that we cannot journey far from one of our water-sources without becoming compost (which, retrospectively, is a good thing).

HOD

Hod is Mercury

Much diversification occurs over millions of years and we are now people – homo sapiens (although I often wonder about the *wise* bit) – and we have learned that fire is useful as are many other tools. We are human—nomadic hunter-gatherers. We travel the ways of our ancestors of every predatory and predated-upon species, meeting others that, through fate and destiny, cross paths with us as we breed in ever-increasing numbers, expanding into wider patterns of smudge.

Sometimes we kill, but sometimes we communicate, because we develop language. In certain instances, we mate and hive-off from maternal clans, diversifying and acquiring previously unforeseen skills through these interactions. We mimic other animal and bird sounds, sometimes whale or that of thunder, and we create musical instruments and teach them to communicate also.

NETZACH

Netzach is Venus

What is certain is that women are strong and warrior-like because of the experience of menstruation, cramping, bloating, birthing, the suckling of young, menopause and possibly osteoporosis. Impossible, when taken holistically, for men to know or even consider. We put two and two together and know, now, that because Earth nourishes and we revere her as mother. We are careful never to take more than we need, because there is, within ancestral memory and story, flood and famine. Upheavals such as seismic shifts, volcanic eruptions and the deaths of ice and winter. They will continue to affect us.

We understand that such things as woman, river, volcano, sea, ice, sex and oh, just about everything – especially the territory within which we wander – are family and we honour them to in ways of making, creating and sensuality. Magic is everywhere in the inexplicable. An ability to manifest, through art, relationship to seasons of living, decay, hunting and tribe. The strange becomes known. How to prepare the hide, sew, tattoo, ochre mother-rock, sculpt in clay and carve in stone.

This is a time of what Rianne Eisler, in THE CHALICE AND THE BLADE, deems "partnership traditions". There is strong evidence to support that throughout the Paleolithic, and well into the Neolithic eras, where major advances were made in the fields of agriculture, hunting, the domestication of animals (including us), construction, architecture, art and technologies, there is, in most European and Near East communities, no imbalance of gender.

TIPHARETH

Tiphareth is the Sun.

Someone, sometime, discovers that if good quality seed is harvested from the wild it can be planted and cultivated, providing family and clan with a ready source of food as long as family and clan stays long enough to protect the resource. Then someone else works out that we can do the same thing with certain animals. Agriculture and domestication manifest.

As these techniques gain in popularity and people feel more secure because they are better fed, even down to having surplus in abundant years, an entirely unprecedented culture emerges. Hierarchies come into existence based on wealth: the greatest surplus or the biggest herd of domesticated cattle providing for others in times of scarcity. Controlled religion becomes the norm, along with a warrior-class trained to protect the interests of the few. Those possessing the larger portion of sustenance (currency).

Ritual by the season and the stars is presumably practiced, with the chieftain or strongest bull-male wedded to the land whereby he is herded and slaughtered, in the season for such, through the scything of the grain and butchering of meat, and we enter the time of sacerdotal ritual death.

All this can historically be placed somewhere between the Paleolithic era, which is estimated by current scientific data to be over 30,000 years deep and the Neolithic, over 10,000 years deep. Then 8,000 years deep Catal Hyuk happens: the beginning of everything that's going to unfold in Mesopotamia, the invention of writing and all of the future's so-called advancements. It's also the beginning of the drying out of Mesopotamia, which is just to the south of the Anatolian region. In Catal Hyuk, for six thousand people to live in a village that size, they have to grow and irrigate crops to support the population. In order to irrigate, we develop public work programs to dig the ditches necessary. To have a public works program people must be paid in whatever constitutes value – probably also in slavery – so a taxation system is invented and the first known planned city comes into existence setting a blueprint for architecture.

During this period, and that which follows, orders of spirit/genius loci attain human-like status, and certain oases become the centres of these civilisations.

The era of what we, in the current epoch, and according to many anthropological, archaeological, academic sources, think of as an age of *sacrifice* dawns, where *deities*, in a manifestation of bounty, are offered up annually to other *deities*, or so we are indoctrinated to believe.

Explicit solar and stellar calendars, controlled and understood by an elite, advise in the techniques of farming, whilst the sun and the stars and the whole of the natural world becomes a plethora of mystery that currently, during the childhood of abrahamic religions, are written in texts as *gods* and *goddesses*. Without us knowing what is really meant. The master-of-anything appears on the main stage, from blacksmith to scribe, and personal achievement can raise an individual to that stature… or that of a supposed immortal.

GEBURAH

Geburah is Mars

We are still experiencing the after effects of an Ice Age, the Younger Dryas, particularly north of the equatorial belt. It is now the period of the destruction of the known, a thing from which we are yet to recover.

It is the time of invasion.

Mars represents Geburah (pronounced *gevorah*), and this planet has more than one quality. It is known, commonly, as the planet representing strife and war but that is only one small aspect of it. The larger portion are guardians of family, clan and/or territory and our capacity to defend against harm.

During this phase of the human animal amongst us are wave after wave of incursions and cultural upheavals, in the historically recorded world, beginning is the far and barren north by Kurgans; a long line of invasions from the Asiatic and European north, by nomadic people, ruled by whoever is considered powerful, bringing with them male-like deities of war and mountains. Ideologies and social behaviours are imposed on the lands and people that are ravaged.

Another invader is also nomadic. Hebrews who come up from the deserts to the south of the Fertile Crescent and invade Canaan, and whose moral precepts are associated with the later Judaism, Christianity and Islam (abrahamic religion). They also are a warring people ruled by a cast of warrior-priests, the Levites. Like the Indo-Europeans is parodied a fierce and angry god of war and mountains is also invented, enforced onto others:

> *And the LORD our God delivered him before us; and we smote him, and his sons, and all his people. And we took all his cities at that time, and utterly destroyed the men, and the women, and the little ones, of every city, we left none to remain.*
>
> —Deuteronomy 2:33-34

One thing that unites these invasion behaviours is the concept of *might is right*. A zeitgeist of acquiescence and fear. The other is the suppression and vilification of women. It is speculated that, regarding the second model (because otherwise it makes no sense), the trend came about with the recession of the previous Ice Age. Imagine a climate wherein mere survival is a day-to-day struggle. Where the elements themselves are enemies and where the mortality rate in often sub-zero temperatures affects the very young and the very old. Imagine that the hunter must fight anyone and anything invading his territory and that surviving offspring will ensure food in the table in later years, particularly if they are strong males. Imagine, then, the need to keep both one's mate and one's children closely controlled to ensure none of your enemies steal them.

> *...this is because maternity, as opposed to paternity, is always certain in the same sense that a child is physically part of its mother and issues from her in an unmistakable way.*
>
> —Badcock, C. *Evolution and Individual Behavior*

and

> *When encroaching and receding glaciers forced our ancestors to reorganize and change their social behavior, human mating patterns may have undergone a shift such that sperm competition, the wanton promiscuity of the tropics, was no longer the norm...*
>
> —Margulis, L and Sagan, D.
> *Mystery Dance, On the Evolution of Human Sexuality*

The *unnaturalness* (author's emphasis) of the need to control, dominate and subdue women by force seems to be the product of an entrenched desperation affecting generations by these warlike invaders; into the regions of conquerage and assimilated through habit. And murder.

So Geburah becomes thought of as the advent of a warlike, dominating, *might is right* period of recognisable history that is consistently refined, eradicating individuality amongst its warriors, entrenching the species with entire hierarchies and empires utterly determined to take what others have, debase them as weak or inferior (for losing the war) and rape their resources. Sound familiar? Of course. We are entering familiar terrain.

CHESED

Jupiter is Chesed

This is so recently unfolding that we can say without doubt that it will continue to be the dominant paradigm indefinitely. Jupiter is called a planet of expansion (amongst other things) and represents Chesed, and with the advent of dominant empires come their religious hierarchies – monotheist religious hierarchies because, to quote the movie *Highlander* "There can be only one," proselytising exclusivity, beginnings and endings, revelation or damnation. But side by side walks scientific curiosity, philosophical debate, artistic excellence, medical advance and exploration beyond narrow or regional confines. Seafaring cultures: Norse, Phoenicians, Chinese and the indigenous peoples of the Americas and the Pacific South link the world.

Communities move from localised councils of elders to governing regimes equipped with military supremacy, overriding others' cultures (not necessarily a good thing we have discovered) always hand-in-glove with religious autonomy. We consider this is progress; that expansion of empires opens up trade between many nations. It's a lie, really, because that has gone on for thousands of years – uncountable – only now the records are kept in a controlled fashion, written by the hand of the scribes of the conquerors. In ones and zeros.

Propaganda, such as the above, remains the common seduction used by those who benefit from such Machiavellian techniques but we're moving, in this current era, across what, on the Tree of Life is called the *abyss* – the only place on the glyph where there is no recognised path along the *Lightening Flash*. We are transiting what is called Da'ath, heading for Binah, a world that will be utterly different to what is known in any 'historical' context. Thus far. Associated with Pluto, such an unknown depth.

Binah (and the triad known as Neschamah), a continuation of the process already described as making up the macrocosmic Tree, informs us *that it is already known* because it has happened before. It is destiny.

BINAH

Saturn is Binah

> *Do not go gentle into that good night…*
> *Rage, rage against the dying of the light.*
>
> —Dylan Thomas

How long will the transition take? These transitions are the same as for anything. There is no calendric date where growth is concerned because it is in a continuous process of maturation. We can see the effects of Binah flowing to us out of every headline and every news bulletin, because Binah is metaphorically associated with Saturn.

This has traditionally been called the planet of limitations but, and more to the point, Saturn *defines* limitations (which are somewhat illusory in reality). It is the planet of boundaries, clocks and structure.

When our 'structure' is threatened, fear is often created.

What do we see happening worldwide now?
- On a planetary level we are seeing the presumed predictability of extreme weather patterns and Earth, who in the past we, as a species, have relied upon to remain consistent, falters and changes in drastic and dramatic ways, so much so that when we read about tsunamis, earthquakes and hurricanes, polar ice melts and prolonged, vicious

drought, we do so with increased alarm as in our current history these things have not been known to be as numerous or intense
- New laws (often draconian) are being implemented and enforced to clamp down on threats real or potential, with increased powers given to both law enforcement and the military, with spyware devices the norm and censorship of freedom-of-information severely imposed
- Resources that have always been the inalienable sustainable right of all species are becoming privatised in ever costlier and controlling ways (a hundred years ago who would have thought water could be commodified), corporations become the new theocracies, with money and the market as their gods
- Fundamentalist religions dominate earlier won liberalisations, threatening us with a return to Inquisition-Age morality

And A.I., nanotechnology and the microchip strip Earth of rare earth—the contemporary gold rush.

We enter an era of institutionalised and consumerist everything, of centralised and privatised information distribution that, most likely, will require tattooed or implanted barcoding of our very identities, increased imprisonment for 'possible' crimes, increased digital security, from cameras everywhere, rationing of once previously easily available commodities, like oil and its many byproducts, to controlled breeding and designer babies. All the while entering an evolution of ZPG human resource instability and stagnation.

Sanctions, refugees both urban and continent-wide, debt, the threat of epidemic, increased monopolisation of monetary institutions and decreases in power for the masses. This should read as familiar.

Social upheaval on a scale not seen for decades seems out of control, as the above effects bite into the pocket of the desperate person, threatening in a way not seen since the Great Depression, while threatening, exponentially, dystopian hunger, as work becomes scarce and more selective with the increases in the *technologicisation* of humanity and an expanding underworld of secret cabals and black-market-everything removes even the possibility of the surety of stability.

It doesn't take a visionary or a meteorologist to inform us what we already know, but unfortunately the era has just begun.

Binah, on a more mystical level, is the depths of an *abyss* wherein dwells *Ereshkigal*, at the completion of *Inanna's* descent, challenging our freedoms, evoking a confusing terror and requiring grit of us, allies and contemporaries to transcend the limitations of the pit; to overcome seeming death. Very *Mad Maxian*.

Inanna provides a many-faceted symbolic image. A pattern of the fecundity beyond the maternal. She is food, fertility, order, pain, aggression brought about by scarcity, love, heaven and earth, healing, emotions. Life, inclusive of humanity, who as a matter of process is denuded of any representations of power and, naked and defenseless, confronts her *sister* Ereshkigal, her opposite season and *the judges of the underworld* (please consider all this metaphor for natural life cycles and NOT people) who sentence her to *death*. Summer becoming colder and darker.

Paradoxically, since there really is no such thing as death, what does this imply? A change from that which is intellectualised as life and order to that which is not. The seed drops from the Tree.

This mythic descent is played out in every religion and spirituality where death and rebirth are common themes representing emancipation or its opposite, so it is for Earth.

Binah is traditionally known as *understanding*. Other than being restraining, restricting, categorising and imprisoning, however, Saturn also engenders rebellion, liberation, the journey to the core, or deepest caves of substrata, seeking to know how stable the land above ground is (look up the story of Vortigen and Merlin) by those who live in secluded autonomy outside of the walls of acceptability, who choose to live as outlaws. We are likely to experience an explosive network of contraband information-trafficking as world events are edited for consumption and an uprising of Earth-sustaining alternative enclaves seek release from enforced paradigms.

And sooner or later the ramifications of our actions will take us into a new phase, like it or not. Whether that is an Ice Age or something entirely alien will depend on *natural* cycles rather than certain hominids' megalomaniacal idea of its own superiority.

Remain optimistic, however, because of what follows. The

twenty two paths that link the sephiroth (equations, dimensions) are the Wayshower pictograms in the BOOK OF SECRETS. So what *are* the Wayshowers. The pictogram that link Binah to Chokmah on this journey is *Empress*, astrologically associated with Venus with a Proto-Sinaitic (Phoenician) letter d (dālet, meaning *door*) representing and entrance or division. Not only that, but Chokmah's planetary representative, Uranus, is the most associated with technology, so the age of Binah and what happens during the epoch of Chokmah are linked in beauty we cannot, as the young species, yet evolve to comprehend. We will. In our season. Providing we survive as an aware, observant, experiential species.

CHOKMAH

Uranus is Chokmah

> *All in a dream, all in a dream*
> *The loading had begun.*
> *They were flying mother nature's*
> *Silver seed to a new home in the sun.*
> —*After the Goldrush*, Neil Young.

We are now in uncharted territory because the events, and until Malkuth initiates another revolution (after another fashion), we have no racial or documented archives, but there are clues.

CARGO CULT THEORY

The Cargo Cult is one of a number of religious movements, chiefly in

Melanesia, that first appeared in the late 19th century but were particularly prevalent during and after World War Two with the apparently miraculous dropping of supplies from aeroplanes into tribal communities that have, as yet, no contact with humanity beyond a specific environment. Adherents believe in the imminent arrival of material goods, or 'cargo', by supernatural agents such as tutelary deities or ancestral spirits. In anticipation temples rendered like aeroplanes are constructed, landing strips, wharves, warehouses and other elaborate preparations for receiving the cargo are often made, and normal activities such as gardening, cease. Untold eons of food-acquisition, discontinued. Current customs are abandoned. These preparations prophecy the end of the old order and the arrival of a new age of freedom and plenty.

These attitudes are not restricted to so-called *primitive* tribal people living in the highlands of West Papua – they are the theologies of most messianic and *rapturist* cults. It's a bit of a *Von Danikinist* theory (one that does *not* involve any reference to extra-terrestrial activity) that considers the many arcane doctrines of fiery machines, haloed messengers, seeming atomic explosions, and acacia-wood boxes containing mysteriously engraved stones, that could kill as though by electrocution.

It is possible that technology (Chokmah/Uranus) was once as advanced, in its own way and before the onset of the last Ice Age, as it is today. That not everyone of the planet is necessarily affected by that frost evet. In the Northern Hemisphere there are hundreds of documented accounts of people/beings who once upon a time lived underground, in the underworld (fact becoming legend): from Europe with myths of and sídhe, to the Central Anatolian Plateau with its geologically fascinating Cappadocian *Fairy Chimneys*, from the African continent and towering cliff-cities (Bandiagara) of the Dogon, and Petra in Jordan to the carved cliff-cities of the Pueblos. There exist countless myths and legends (that are not inventions but *must* stem from a remembered, if distorted, historic reference) of people, or messengers that flew, that arrived in fiery chariots, that brought the gifts of fire, instruments, art, communication previously unknown, countless technologies.

The knowledge of astronomy and the tendency of unrecalled races to build towering edifices to mirror constellations and cloud is not so farfetched when we consider what kind of effect dynamic cataclysm will have on entire generations who find ourselves in virtually unprecedented conditions, the only way of preserving information being through orality that will conceivably end up being accorded the status of myth and superstition.

Chokmah is also given the title *sphere of the zodiac* and is called the *sephiroth of wisdom* (sophia). Wisdom is a quality of fulfilment that is the outcome of three distinct steps: information, knowledge, understanding. It cannot be gained otherwise. It is as though, if we take the history of every stage of the Tree up to this point, Earth has benefitted from all that has already become and is at the stage of transformation necessary to enter into a next phase of life. Another Earth. Consider the possibilities: we develop the technology to enable us to create a kind of *ark* capable of carrying the genetic keys (of life as we know it) out into the universe, encoded to seek whatever environmental field is ultimately able to sustain it or we cease.

Mind seems to reside in our heads – in our brains – but does it? Couldn't it as easily be that mind (us without the body) is other than anything we can consider? Does not exist within the parameters of perceived reality; is interpreted just as all external, or epigenetic phenomenon is interpreted? Let us make a not-so-implausible move, and suggest that mind and soul are akin to each other, so that throughout this work we can jump from the one word to the other.

KETHER

Kether is Neptune

Kether is the dream, the inspiration, the unknowable, the term *occult*. Neptune has been termed the *universal solvent* and whatever Uranus has destroyed or blasted, Neptune pulverises. It is both the sleep of the seed in the womb of the fruit that rots as it nourishes and the ocean of either space or the newly birthing Earth, wherein all memory of its parents is as encoded as the knowledge of forever is spelled out in individual DNA.

Called, inappropriately *the crown*, unless it carries with it the connotations of a newborn's head crowning in the moments prior to birth, it is where all that precedes it comes together in an instant of exquisite, orgasmic enlightenment or awareness, like all the lightbulbs coming on at once and where the world says o*h, so this is life also.* The BOOK OF SECRETS is this great wheel of seeming repetition that is, in itself, an illusion because nothing repeats itself but merely appears to, while the truism that the only absolute is change applies here perfectly.

DA'ATH

Da'ath is Pluto

This equation is an enigma. Da'ath is both here and not here. Simultaneously both is and is not a dimension. What does it represent? We don't know. That's the point. Pluto is relegated to this *noosphere* because it is no longer considered a planet, yet it is most definitely a force to be reckoned with astrologically, and what hubris is humanity that can bequeath planet-ness or not on a celestial body that resides within sun's elliptical pattern?

Da'ath is nestled within that *abyss* of the Tree, written about earlier, and is affected by two paths: that of the image of *Empress* and that of *Mystery*. This, in itself, is profound, as you will discover.

I was sent forth from the power,
and I have come to those who reflect upon me,
and I have been found among those who seek after me.
Look upon me, you who reflect upon me,
and you hearers, hear me…

> *...Do not be ignorant of me.*
> *For I am the first and the last.*
> *I am the honored one and the scorned one.*
> *I am the whore and the holy one.*
>
> —excerpt *Thunder, Perfect Mind,*
> Nag Hammadi Library

Da'ath represents a *something* not found in any traditional way. Like a flash of inspiration, it assures you that you already know the message that it brings but from 'elsewhere'. In a Tarot spread the card that sits here is called a *key*. It is something already known but not recognised as such. We are experiencing this with artificial intelligence that is catapulting us into a consciousness of either/or confusion or awe.

Da'ath, as you will read further on, is the bridge between what is called the *Ruach* and the *Neschamah*. It is as though messages from some *deep* – from the spirits and their avatars – erupt from this portal, instructing or guiding us towards understanding (Binah), wisdom (Chokmah) and enlightenment (Kether).

You comprehend its genius hidden within experience, like the 'butterfly effect' in *chaos theory*, whereby everything we thought of as real changes through painful and undesirable events – often the only thing capable of shattering complacency.

The effect of the convergence of *Empress* and *Mystery* pictograms, and their significance as environments, previously mentioned gives us a strong indication not only of humanity's ongoing attitude towards both women of all species, but Earth and space. As *Empress* she is bountiful of food and shelter, but when she is raging with hurricanes and earthquakes and the occasional tsunami she is vilified as "a bitch" – nature requiring conquering. *Mystery*, whose letter G (g), meaning camel, is akin to that ship of the desert as she moves from Tiphareth across the vast seemingly-barren landscape of desert, and ancient buried forests, on her voyage to Kether (Malkuth, and an as yet invisible existence), carrying necessities and trusting in her own endurance to get her to a destination where she already is and has always been.

Surprise and its ensuing excitation is immeasurable and exists in the very air we breathe and in places unseen. Like a passage across a trackless wasteland travelled since some misted, hidden epoch, it never goes away and like seeds buried within trackless sands, the vast glacial permafrost or miles-deep beneath arctic ice, they await only their season.

Da'ath, it seems, is at the turning of the wheel right now in the current era with unprecedented or seemingly unrealised technological progression.

...

THE TREE OF LIFE

THE OUTWARD JOURNEY

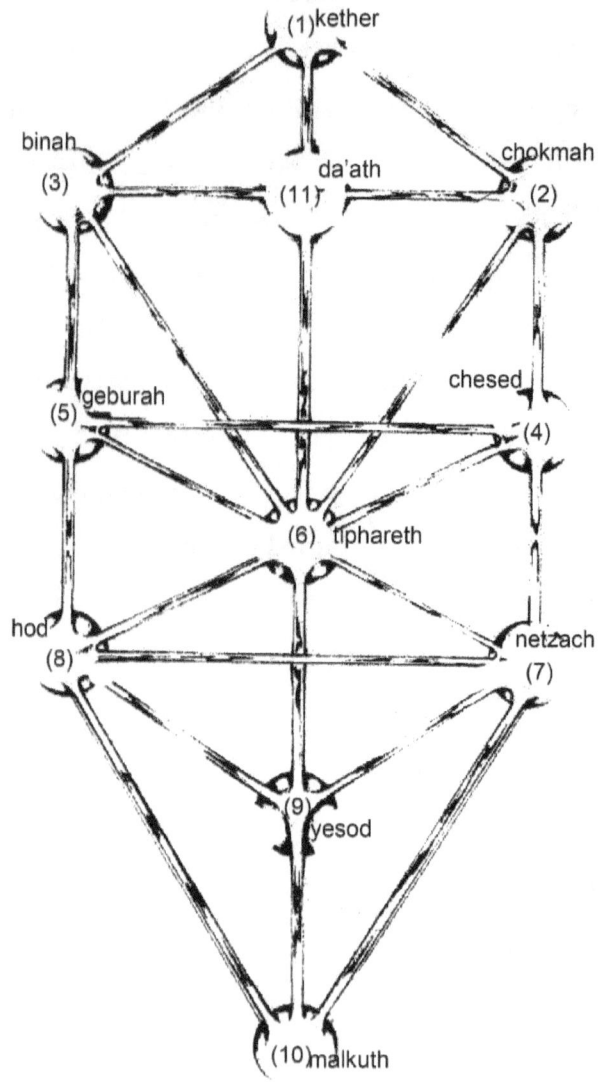

Image: tree of life,
outward journey

In most texts you will find the second formula to be standard because of the perennial misconceptions of *heaven* and *earth* and the religiosity of the Tree which are not our concerns here. What is important is to consider the *tree* as endless because it does not simply represent one thing or one event, even though, paradoxically, it also does, and because it cannot be limited in any way. It is as much your personal family tree as it is the movement of global cultures, the rise and fall of empires and the movement of any event, from conception to apparent conclusion, from education and relationships to birth, death and all in between and everything we both are and are not.

In its more mystical sense we can evoke the numerical sequence and multiply it infinitely because what we perceive (in the stylised glyph) is only Malkuth (or any of the others), because within each dimension there exists another Tree within which other Trees can be calculated infinitely, very like the concept of the Mandelbrot Set and the outward journey is the journey from a next generation seed (Kether), or conception, of both you and of everything that eventuates inevitable expressions (Malkuth).

A FOREVER HUMAN BEING

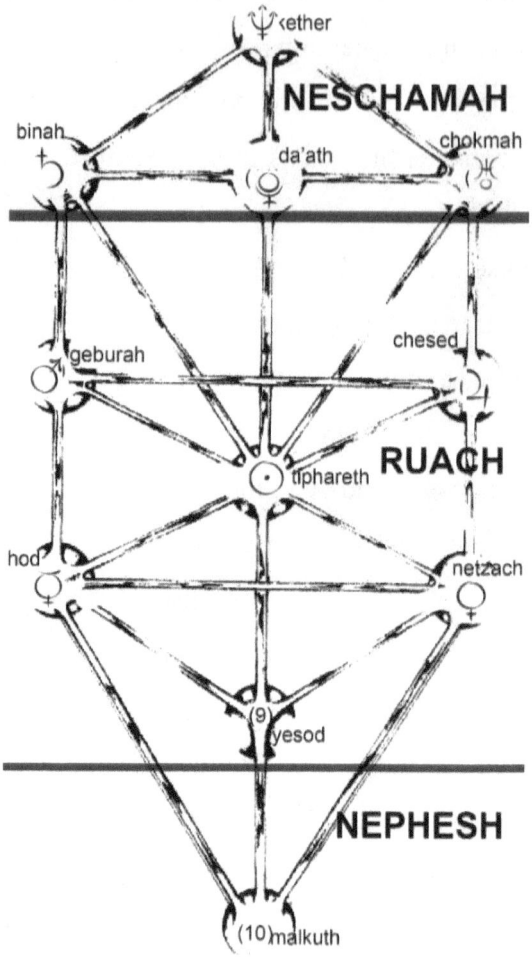

Image: a human body

There is a Tree within each sphere or dimension, and all represented glyphs are this Tree which is, therefore, you and the world/universe as we know it, both physically and energetically. The principles of microcosm and macrocosm, are:

NEPHESH

This is the physical you (and again there is more to it, but we will discuss interpreting health issues from this layout later); it is your foundation and you are an outcome. You were always going to be who you are, and the journey of you has been happening since Kether (on the outward-moving Tree), which is both when you were conceived and also the conception of a universe. But are you your body? Of *course* you are, but you are so much more than that or you wouldn't make sense. You are your experiences.

RUACH

The core of the Ruach is Tiphareth, like a sun around which revolve many orbiting phenomena. That's you. That's self-awareness. It's you in the world. Around you spiral Yesod, Hod, Netzach, Chesed and Geburah with Da'ath there in the background, the secret all-the other-you's that are not recognised (mentioned in Part 1). You are the product of your experiences and they are continuous, even though you are so much more than that.

Yesod –

This is instinct. It is vascularity, from sexual arousal to pain, fear, laughter, despair, rage, calm and adapting, and it is also your racial and inherited traits, atomic and alert. It is your connection to everything and therefore it is psychic and intuitive. Primal urges and stored memories are *Yesodic* and therefore it's also been deemed both the subconscious and the unconscious (but what are these really?). It is the treasure-house of archetypes and the secret of what MIND is. Yesod is experiential but not necessarily from external stimuli.

It can be dangerous when unbalanced.

Hod –

Things and people and you, in constant communication. The way you express self, your capacity to learn, the languages of the world – everything from human language to that of traffic and thunder – and what they teach are the domain of Hod's experience.

Travel and the means to do so, what comes your way, the physically changing domains in which you dwell. Fate, maybe. From your daily routines, and the house, apartment, farm, tin shed, stationary or moving vehicle within which you live or find yourself. From the city or town, to the internet. Interstate and world travel, social media presence. It is everything ever said to you or that you heard. Everything you will ever read or write, and the ability to learn, is the result of the experience of Hod.

It can be dangerous when unbalanced.

Netzach –

All that is beautiful, sensual, tactile, artistic, fecund is *Netzach*. Ability to think laterally. An appreciation of all that is unbridled and erotic in nature. The right lobes of your brain and that which triggers awe.

Every time you enjoy sex, dance, give birth to anything from human children to poetry you are affected by Netzach. Whenever you add an artistic touch to the world you are both enhancing personal experience and feeding the experience of life. The same applies when you work in the humus, planting or playing, for the "green thumb" is an attribute of Venus' influence as well as the ability to turn the skins of killed cousin animals into finely tanned and decorated apparel, ink your skin, stomp in the mud after rain, barefoot.

It can be dangerous when unbalanced.

Chesed –

As much as the ability to learn is the experience of Hod, so the information and the knowledge collected, explored and transmitted is Chesed. So is the spiritual or religious experience, the deeper understanding implied by philosophical thought, to add inspiration to what is already in the world. Chesed is us in the world – not so much the individual as everything. Education dwells at the heart of Chesed and not merely the book-learned kind but the kind that changes you, demands that you grow, requires you to interact with others in your community either locally or macrocosmically for the experience of interaction and sociability.

Chesed is work, or vocation, projected outwards and experienced in the world and all that comes from such. Chesed, as

Jupiter, is expansion and expansive.

As we are buried beneath stuff and additives to everything, often toxic and treated as ailment, it is obvious that this equation is dangerous when unbalanced.

Geburah –

Geburah is excitation, more physical than intellectual, and relates to everything from martial arts to the preservation of the inherent ways of clan, tribe, community and culture. Defense from predation and attack. In the current era this task has fallen almost solely front line workers: medics, firefighters, police, armed forces, those facilitating refuge, and we find ourselves more and more in dire physical straits accompanied by the social and health dysfunctions that accompany the "toothless".

Geburah, affected as it is by mars, is too often relegated to the idea of aggression or warlike attributes but is this necessarily so? It is very uncommon for one species to invade the territory of another and, even though a wasp will invade a bee hive it does so at great peril for bees will swarm and die rather than allow senseless slaughter or abuse of their home.

Any species will do the same. It is natural.

Therefore, your physical fitness is linked, other than to a life well lived, to your experience of personal expertise.

Your competitive nature is experienced here as are all adrenalin-triggered responses to immediate danger or need.
It is extremely dangerous when unbalanced.

All five dimensions are experienced constantly and simultaneously, even in deep states of meditation or contemplation. While there is self-awareness – while there is life (and as has already been said *when is there no life?*) – you, as the experience of Tiphareth at the heart of the Ruach, are perennial, because knowledge is only *understood* when there is an experiential framework, even if imagined hypothetically. We learn by trial and deduction.

NESCHAMAH

The whole is greater than the sum of its parts...but there can be no whole without the sum of its parts.

The Neschamah is Binah, Chokmah and Kether, called the *supernals*, and they are MIND. They are the depths of you, the wisdom-voices within you that are sometimes yours and sometimes those of the entities that utilise your perceptions and your inner mansions as their gateway.

The mystical Da'ath which is neither the Ruach nor Neschamah but is *something else elsewhere* only grants access to Neschamah when and if the experience of Da'ath is triggered.

This triggering is a profound dream, a saying, a singular conversation, the impact of which – if you allow it – alters your whole life-perspective, resulting in the birth of the questioner within you that will challenge every paradigm and truism and that will have you communicating with these eldritch entities no matter who or what you perceive them to be. What I know is that once this trigger is activated *they* will come to *you* through recognition. Left brain.

The possibility exists for all people, yet many dare not take the chance because of the threat of being considered socially/culturally different, that overshadows many clusters of humanity, and that possibility – that umbilicus – is *Mystery*, perpetually linking you to the source of a matrix as it journeys from Tiphareth to Kether.

Binah (also known as *Neschamah proper*) is the gate of manifestation. She is like the treasure-house of all that exists; the *hall of records*, infinitely in all directions and none, while Chokmah is the energy that is the principle of absolute vitality. Hydrogen and quarks.

Kether is the deepest, most mysterious centre. The inner star, a singularity. The pebble in the pool that drops infinitely through everything causing concentric ripples everywhere simultaneously.

We shouldn't consider the centre of anything to be the smallest ratio of the greater manifestation because there would *be* no greater manifestation without that infinite point, therefore it is huge beyond imagining because it holds within itself the pattern of everything including what it was and what it will be.

Neschamah has been rendered by christianity into a tripartite indivisible deity, all-male, an illusion of impossibility. But what it is *not* is separate from anything else which is how the unseen and the occult can influence us and affect the way we live and the decisions we make.

The key to contact with all this is listening for other, and more, is to be quieter than our own voices.

...

THE JOURNEY IMAGES AND THE TREE OF LIFE

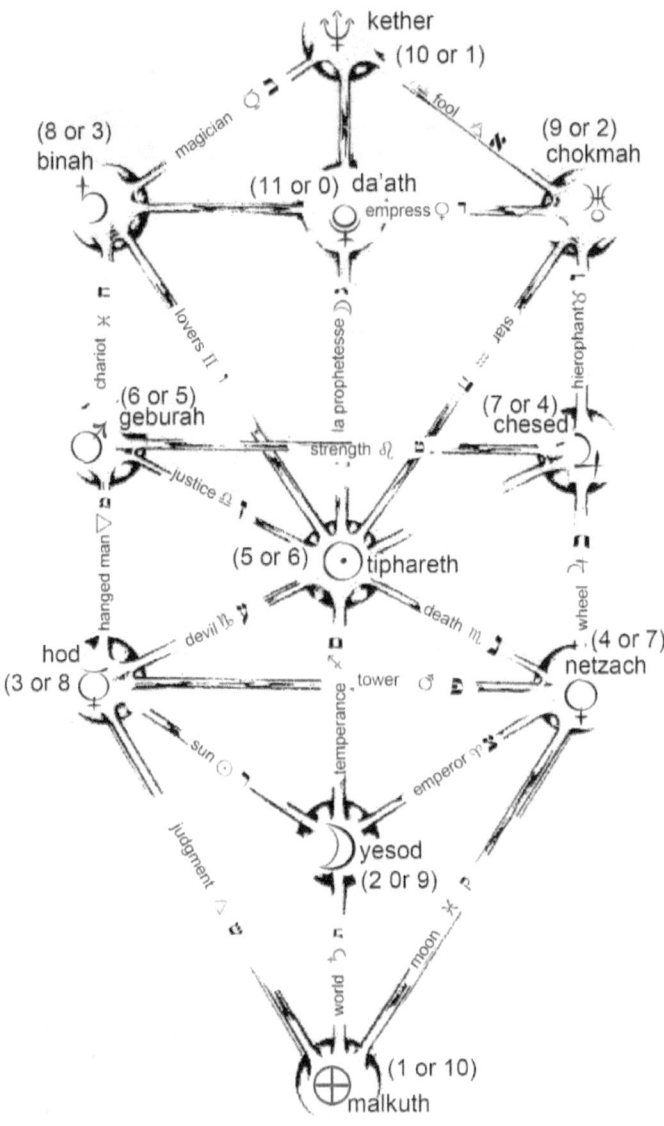

Image: tree of life with all associations

To know Tarot, to understand the BOOK OF SECRETS from inside out, from the vast underland of root and mycelium to the day-to-day, above ground, skyborne. Although the Tree of Life map, in a consultation is only one of several that you will use, it is profound because it has such endlessly exploratory chasms and holts.

THE THREE OPEN ROADS

THE ROAD OF SEVERITY

This road (facing the previous diagram) includes Hod (Mercury), Geburah (Mars) and Binah (Saturn). These sephiroth, environments, equations are linked by the Wayshowers of *Judgment* (the element of fire and the letter *shin*), *Hanged Man* (the element of water and the letter *mem*), *Chariot* (astrological sign: cancer and the letter *cheth*) and *Magician* (mercury and the letter *beth*).

      Orthodoxy, logic, rationalism, tradition; issues wherein your personality and personal opinions are neither warranted nor allowed. Those of you with a predisposition towards these journeys may find yourselves in such environments (or family/society oriented arrangements) as military or martial arts, educational environments, law and law-enforcement institutions, orthodox dogmatic religions, moralistic communities, structured economic complexes, inherited wealth, poverty, castle or clan, power-positions in government or corporate bodies and entrenched rigidity.

The word *NO* exemplifies the *road of severity*.

THE ROAD OF MERCY

This road is composed of Netzach (Venus), Chesed (Jupiter) and Chokmah (Uranus), linked by the Wayshower pictograms of: *Moon* (Pisces, letter *qoph*), *Wheel of Fortune* (Jupiter, the letter *kaph*), *Hierophant* (Taurus and the letter *vau*), and *Magician*, element air and the letter *aleph*.

A more lateral experience whereby the arts, philosophy, sexuality, imagination, ritual and daily things accomplished with creativity and curiosity occur. In travelling this road, you are faced with far less (by way of common opinion) concrete ideas and experiences as it is aesthetic and inspired by the emotions, instincts, sensations and feelings, in stark contrast to the way of severity. Often this road exemplifies the deep, inner landscapes we traverse in search of meaning, purpose, relationship and identity. The word *YES* exemplifies mercy.

THE MIDDLE ROAD

This is the road of the individual, balanced by the other two, the centre of which is Tiphareth, the heart of the Tree. Tiphareth (*Sun*) is accompanied by Malkuth (the four elements), Yesod (*Moon*), Da'ath (*Chiron*) and Kether (*Neptune*) and it is affected by many Wayshower paths/pictograms, although *World* (*Saturn* and letter *tau*), *Temperance* (Sagittarius, samech) and *Mystery* (moon, and the letter *qoph*) are along its direct axis.

World in this position, linking Malkuth to Yesod is the awareness of the bigger map rather than simply the self in isolation. It expresses the individual acutely-lived and also acutely attuned to an inherent habitat (Earth) and all co-existence, the symbiotic relationship of life with life. It can see the problem of androcentricity in relation to either/both the left and right directions but is untroubled knowing that Earth is becoming Earth's destined self.

Temperance, linking Yesod to Tiphareth, is like a tightrope walker whose wire traverses a vast chasm of disruption represented by the cards known as the Dark Night of the Soul (*Devil, Death, Tower*—refer to the initial pages of the BOOK OF SECRETS). The individual here has only a long pole that must remain finely balanced in the hands of the acrobat. The sensitivity required to feel the slightest tipping of the branch is the task of this path. Of course, when one thinks about it, there is a deep relationship between *Temperance* and the *Fool*, but *Temperance* need not worry as it understands the alchemy required in the balancing necessary between humour and focus that ultimately leads it to Tiphareth.

Mystery, linking Tiphareth to Kether, is the long, deep, mystical and often lonely journey that can only be attended by the individual and perhaps their few closest magical allies. It is a Dark Night of the Soul after another fashion because by now you know yourself better than anyone else can and you are in communion with spirits in whatever genre they manifest. This is the journey of wisdom beyond knowledge where everything is questioned and yet, are there truly any answers that cannot be challenged?

When you come to understand that your journeys of the Tree of Life are legion – internal, to the depths of everything comprehensible regarding the ages, into knowledge beyond that which is known, outward. The universe. Into forever. The BOOK OF SECRETS is both vehicle, guide and teacher. Inward to the worldwide web of mycelial information distribution. Our ancestors.

The journey of *Mystery* is into the territory of myth and legend.

…

THE CYCLE OF INITIATION

The BOOK OF SECRETS is a living myth. The Wayshowers represent and evoke this. If we consider each of the images that represent each story we can see and understand this. Here they are presented in a numerically sequenced circle. They are to be contemplated in a lived experience, recognisable, to be understood.

Image – Cycle of Initiation

INITIATION —THE FIRST PHASE

I am the Parent Tree: CHALLENGE

    0   Fool

    1   Magician

2 Mystery

3 Empress

4 Emperor

5 Hierophant

6 Lovers

7 Chariot

8 Strength

9 Hermit

10 Wheel of Fortune

11 Justice

The above cycle image moves in the pattern of a Northern Hemisphere sunwise circle of pictograms.

FOOL

Fool is a nanosecond; a seemingly irrelevant, seemingly inconsequential, seemingly random, barely registered moment. It always takes that for a cycle of events to activate and it's *meant* to go unnoticed because very often we reject change out of fear that, whatever it may bring, life will not be the same in retrospect. So we don't notice what could only be called a quickening. That's the starbirth. If we look at it like a human life it is the instant of conception, the parent that conceives and, *Fool* by its very nature, – a *form of unseeing*– the inability to glean the consequences. Whether the organic foetus, the new project or the idea progresses to birth and life, or is miscarried or aborted, is irrelevant at this stage. The cycle will fulfil itself. And all of it is destiny. It is falling and/or dropping and/or diving/descending from where we've been to where we are.

MAGICIAN

Magician is when the awakened cycle is recognised and/or realised. For now, it is the moment of the understanding of the state of pregnancy and, again, whether the pregnancy reaches full term or not, nothing, from now on, will be the same. Not for you or your tribe. Should conception reach full term and birth be the result, *Magician* represents the power of this seeming, but impossible, beginning. Released from the comfort of amniotic ocean you emerge into an utterly alien environment, overwhelmingly sensory.

You have an ability—with this newly born life (not always biological)—to affect and change. Yourself, other people, unfolding events. No matter how transitory or seemingly simple, a new experience is always an experience, a moment to be stored in the mansions of memory.

Whether it is the birth of you, your child, moving to an altogether new location, achieving project acknowledgment, leaving any relationship and stepping alone into the world, the first page of a book you are destined to write or read, it's all the interconnected through *Magician*. Despite trepidation, the possible is happening, incalculable variations of how to experience adaptation.

Upon the cube (some call it an altar) of *Magician* are the stylised Greek symbols of the elements of earth, air, fire and water, indicating that all that one needs is available, all that is required for their use is intention, alchemy and innovation. *Magician* points above and below and, despite the common misnomer of *as above, so below, after another fashion* (attributed to Hermes Trismagestus). this narrative is also saying that starlight and Earth Mother are family, through any vessel of understanding. The BOOK OF SECRETS does not condescend to speak for other species.

Note: the figure 8, on its side, above the heads of both *Magician* and *Strength* is actually a Mobius Veil.

MYSTERY

Mystery is the excitement and awe, sometimes curiosity, sometimes secrecy, of the unknowable, that insatiable honesty of the newly born. In some way it is obvious that progress is inherent within this mystery. It is the *not-knowing* time; the wondering. Whether it is your inability to name, banal or intergenerational, scientific or mythic, and therefore tell others we *think* we understand, or whether it is learning when the answers to questions remain in the excited state of being occulted. The first flutterings of the possible intimacy of the newly-met hint at sensuality or love, all is interwoven with *Mystery*, the unfortunately-titled *high priestess*. There is a secret even within the picture: if you look closely you will see that the so-called inner sanctum, that many misinterpret as guarding an entry to answers and ceremony, is actually an outside environment. The curtain obscures an exit *to* a world beyond, the ocean glimpsed behind the pomegranate-decorated curtain, not some deep chamber. You are *already* on the inside. You have not yet abandoned some cloistered environment or ideology. You have not yet woken to the fullness of life, the cycle, the experience. All the up-front trappings are designed to hypnotise you, as yet unwary, into accepting appearances without fact.

Sometimes it just means you will move to, or lives, a couple of streets back from the beach.

EMPRESS

Empress. Mother. Earth. For you, the newly born, despite your chronology, now is the moment of the nipple, the first nurture when abandonment, rejection and death are allayed. *Empress* represents the exquisite, the luscious, the first meal in a foreign country, the flush of intimate touch, the moment we take to bathe in an achievement that is admired. Fecundity. Erotic, Nectar-dripping. *Empress* is a form of reciprocation. Always the pleasure of a thing shared is beautiful and *Empress* is beauty. Not only in stylised fashion or form, but also in an utter lack of pretense: art, attraction, oxytocin, tactility, pleasure. Sensual, erotic. Forest, mountain, ocean, mist. Environments that are moist, warm and rampant. Nourishment. The senses. For the newborn, *Empress* is whoever or whatever requires need. At this stage of life modesty is non-existent, you have no consciousness of morality or embarrassment and will eat, bawl, defecate, vomit or burp. Things, sadly, very soon unlearned.

EMPEROR

Emperor is the crossover between learning and unlearning. It is where structure and social rule are enforced. When mystery begins to concretise into tables and chairs, rooms, know faces, remembered experience through repetition. This is the age you learn (often) to crawl, walk, talk, toilet-train, sleep in a bed alone, are spoken to endlessly by adults, with an indoctrinated adult's need to have you understand the agreed-to world. Order is imposed. Schooling is the method. This is the start, within this cycle, of what will continue endlessly and ceaselessly say: *my way or the highway.*

Emperor is order. It is uniforms and dialogue that explain imposed belonging. Imposed narrative. Therefore, it is tribal and institutional education, bureaucratic bodies, established traditions, propriety within the consensual morality of family, community, nation; acceptability, manners, status. Regulation and hierarchy. Whereas *Empress* can be feral (wild) so *Emperor* is suit and tie; domesticated. While remaining entrenched in many cultures and societies worldwide there remains an onerous religio-political archetype that many would reject if they could, while others cling to fanatically.

HIEROPHANT

Hierophant. Chicken or the egg? When society changes beyond paradigms erected to justify imposed correctness for at least the historically recorded previous two thousand years, so will images also change. Currently there is an overwhelming variety of Tarot-*like* cards available despite the continually overriding evidence that the traditional pictograms are based on kabbalah. A pack that destroys the intrinsic ability to learn the deepest secrets of a specific forest, by erasure of an inherent representation, may just be the person to tip the scales into hubris. *Hierophant* is, in a nutshell, religion and religiousness.

> *Religion is the masterpiece of the art of animal training*
> —Arthur Schopenhauer (1788-1860)

As a human animal we seem to have a definitive leaning towards spirituality and wonder, as a seeming aspect of our intrinsic nature but the problem of religion is people; their invention of rules, protocol, dogma, creed, doctrine, law, morality, and the need, throughout history, to enforce these things to oppress opposition and alternative. Otherness.

Earlier representations of Tarot called *Hierophant* the pope, attesting to the fact that the Roman church influenced, even as it condemned, this very non-religious technology. The image and title of the card was changed by later alchemists to represent the more supposedly mystical ideal of Greek mythological authority: a high priest. Remaining, as such, a dissonance of feudalistic acceptance.

You are now at the stage within the cycle of the influence of contemporary religion: dualism. Good and bad (or good and evil) are common euphemisms, as are right and wrong. Sinister and dexter.

The idea of reward and punishment are introduced as threats of ascension and failure (greater-than and lesser-than); the nails in the coffin of curiosity. Morality based on the above becomes entrenched. At the same time the ideal of religion is introduced, enforced beyond questioning and, if that were all then the re-introduction of the ways of *Mystery* would soften the effects of both *Emperor* and *Hierophant* but this is rare as, amongst humans, most hierarchy claim a supreme deity.

Almost universally thought of, whimsically and without reason, male.

LOVERS

You are now an adolescent and *Lovers*, the pictogram that, amongst other things, represents choice, begins your advancement or growth. An era of questioning, and often rebellion against the idea of the previous two states of being and the meanings inherent in the images, is stimulated by changing hormones and as a response to the demand of both over your individuality.

You are at the crossroads of consensual achievement or error. The drive to compete and succeed (in whatever undertaking) is an untrustworthy urge. You look to others often as archetypes, either dismissed as inappropriate to the person you have chosen to present to the world or, through admiration, seek to garment yourself. Traditionally crossroads are dangerous places and choices made now are likely to have an impact for many years.

Amongst most cultures are folk tales of eldritch beings, phantoms, goblins, ghosts and all manner of wraiths. All suspected as residing at crossroads awaiting the weary traveller. Worth remembering.

These junctions were common burial sites for suicides and murderers. The superstition is so deep that sacrifices were written or spoken of. Made at crossroads to ward off evil spirits, so that turmoil, at every level of consciousness, becomes a mansion to be navigated.

CHARIOT

Chariot gets you through whatever gauntlet *Lovers* has had you run. It represents victory but never without striving and effort. Whether you pass some elusive test and exams required of you by either systems of education within your cultural framework or by the whirlwinds of life? Whether you encounter the challenges of indigenous adulthood ceremony or whether, through a choice made to turn your back on consensual authority, and the standards set by society as measuring success, you experience this knowledge in some fashion. The victory is always reflected through others' acclaim; is always recognised both by the individual and applauded by others.

You are an adolescent.

This is an initiation: run a gauntlet and survive to some finish line, alive and continuing.

STRENGTH

Strength is when someone seeks to imprint an identity on culture, peer group or field of endeavour. It is said to be a process of deepening but it is also when you either learn to control urges that surfaced during this cyclic adolescence or give reign to that someone in order to repress, or subdue others. It is still a period of testing and challenge, one that will not cease for many years in the average lifespan of any human animal, anyway.

The challenge is *how* you behave within struggle for independence and self-sufficiency, within struggle for the respect of others, the physical tools and skills you acquire; the body you inhabit and how you respect that body. *Strength* is when many seek to fit into societal stereotypes determined by whatever is acceptable or popular, and complacency can settle in, becoming a pattern that will, ultimately, be destroyed in one way or another simply because it is in the nature of a cycle. And still you are an adolescent.

HERMIT

Hermit. One of the meanings is aloneness. An older name was the *Spy*. Not as we, in the current era consider the word to mean: an agent of subterfuge. No. One who sees. Did you at any stage, secretly and fearfully, wonder if it is your destiny to be alone or lonely? Everyone I have ever asked this question has assured me that they have, and that they had needed to suppress the thought as soon as it arises. Just in case. A strange superstition. Well *Hermit* assures you that you will have this time at least once, no matter how many people are around you, no matter how few.

Some will claim it willingly but here and now, your challenge is to find the space for that aloneness because aloneness is not loneliness. That is different. For there to be balance alone moments/years are integral to deep contemplation and the gaining of wisdom from definition, and wondering what money can be and do. Some have isolation thrust upon them through circumstances.

It is for you to seek meaning throughout this, to come to a

place of calm whilst waiting to pass through it. Nelson Mandela was imprisoned for twenty-four years and his wife Winnie, in 1969, was imprisoned and kept in solitary confinement for seventeen months.

What must they have thought? What kind of cruelty is it to feel no tenderness, to have no real interaction with anyone for extended periods?

At its depths the challenge of *Hermit* is deep-searching and on the *Life Journey* this can occur at any age and many times within one lifetime but never more so than throughout your teenage years.

It is also the season of winter, a very high place, a particular environment and/or a cycle.

WHEEL OF FORTUNE

Wheel of Fortune can be repetitive, routine or ritual. Or the tedium of tasks. "I'm bored," is what every parent dreads hearing, along with "I'm too tired," or "I can't." There's really nothing else to say about the *Wheel of Fortune* for now – it's whatever wheel you are on, and are is still within the care and supervision of an authority, be it parent or state: all this implies. This is also the seasonal cycle of a solar year, however, and can also be a mode of repetition, or ritual, that describes the invention of a day, month, year, lifetime, as well as the wheels as are known amongst medicine people of Turtle Island, amongst countless other cultures.

- One form of torture during the era of Gregory of Tours (fifth century of the common era) to strap a condemned human being to a cartwheel, their limbs stretched out along the spokes over two wooden beams. The wheel was made to revolve slowly and a large hammer or an iron bar was then applied to the limb over the gap between the beams, breaking the bones
- Another: The prisoner would be tied to the wheel, and then swung across some undesirable thing. Fire was always a good choice, but dragging the prisoner across metal was another way. The wheel sometimes had spikes mounted on it, so pain would happen in all directions.

Considering much of the known world's Middle Ages was controlled by the strongman-ideology of christianity one wonders at their rebranding of a deity, omnipotent and loving.

However, the *Chayoth ha-Qadesh* (four winged creatures) at each of the corners of this pictogram, are there to remind us that no matter how routine or relentless our day-to-day existence might seem there is always a next thing that is not immediately recognisable. Life could charm or torture, depending on the season of humanity. Or harvest.

LAW

You are officially legally able to drive a vehicle, get drunk and sign a binding document. In a lifetime, this is the transition from teens into the twenties when someone is allowed to obtain a gun licence and sign a lease; when many things previously out of reach become possible. Previously you could sign up to fight in a war, with all the ramifications of potential tragedy, but you couldn't vote. Now you can. Liberation but not without pitfalls. Unless you come from a highly affluent family that provides you with your every whim, it is also when you can become fooled into debt: credit card, personal loan for a vehicle, tenancy agreement or mortgage. Work contracts are signed by some while others enter into marriage. Tertiary education fees, passports, a birth certificate, all to admit legitimacy and/or identity to those challenging your right to drink at a club. You walk a fine line here and many are too early into the initiation of chronological era or experience to sense the danger.

You are being judged and you are judging, and discernment is the challenge. Shackles await the outcome to uninformed choices. They handcuff most of us.

INITIATION—THE SECOND PHASE

Dropping from the Parent Tree: INDIVIDUATION

12 Hanged Man
13 Death
14 Temperance
15 Devil
16 Tower
17 Star
18 Moon
19 Sun
20 Judgment
21 World

HANGED MAN

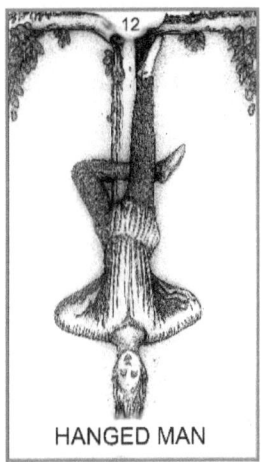

Tumbling towards adulthood, *Hanged Man* is the precursor to the second phase of the cycle. It is when you, beginning this Cycle of Challenge at the cliff-top, with the *Fool*, drop, let go, or are pushed over the edge.

This is a living death. Necessary.

The analogy for the entire process is based on, again, the Tree: the first phase of your life is suffused with the structures of culture, family, society, tradition, religion, expectation and, except in rare cases where the cycle varies considerably from the norm, predictably similar to your forebears through lack of any alternative, therefore you are said to be your *parent tree*.

The second phase, from *Hanged Man* onwards, is when that Tree fruits. The fruit drops and seems to rot but is, in actuality, the placenta for the as yet unopened seed of a sapling which is you, a variation of the pattern within which you formed.

You will never be the same despite being of an agreed-to

species. This could be said for the passage of the ages and for every task undertaken, every relationship experienced.

The era of the *Hanged Man* is like the second phase of the *Fool*, an almost imperceptible event, or a single word spoken, being likely as illness or loss.

Either way the effects will be catastrophic and everything that you have previously relied on as dependable is no longer supportive.

Hanged Man, in this way, is the herald of the Dark Night of the Soul—the Saturn Return which occurs between the ages of twenty-seven and thirty years old.

DEATH

Death summons you to the maw of all that you have taken for granted and asks the question *who are you?* Should you think to answer with what you've previously presumed to be a valid answer, without questioning *everything*, then death in life could happen. A potential fall into unset concrete that will take its own season to break down and might not even happen at the eventual second Saturn cycle. Perhaps not at all in your current fruiting body.

If you *do* question (and the driving force to do so is overwhelming), then you change in accordance with the destiny into which you dive. Into fertile soil and the chance of fulfilling a genetic-level pattern, will begin acknowledgment.

TEMPERANCE

Temperance is alchemy. It is described to apprentices in two ways: the first is the analogy of a tightrope walker, traversing a wire strung between one cliff (Chokmah, where the *Fool* awaits the fall) and another (the cliff-edge of Binah) with only a long staff (*Ace of Wands*—communication) to balance and counter-balance, between you and certain destruction at the base chaos. During the Dark Night of the Soul you must be wary of the word *too* because that word imposes limitations: too old, too young, too late, too tired, too difficult, too anything, will tip the pole too far. *Temperance* is patience, being kind to yourself and others during a transition. Honesty. Alchemy. Art. Seeking authenticity amidst human constructs of identity that seek to limit or impress on others an idea of what you represent.

The analogy of alchemy is that of baking bread. Many steps must happen. Grain is harvested, winnowed and ground, is mixed with ingredients that are alien, is kneaded until the separate parts merge at a molecular level, then rested until risen only to be punched flat and risen again. Called "proving". You then enter an oven, and fire transforms what was into what is. It is consumed. This is you. The process, transformative. This is also why change is intrinsically feared because there is always a Dark Night of the Soul. Known as medicine. Not pharmaceutical. Rather it is that which heals what are often imposed wounds, seen or unseen.

DEVIL

Devil (whose planetary association is Capricorn) is doubt. The threat of what you could lose. An untouched and unchartered forest. A labyrinthine maze where you seem to be lost and even though you know there is a pattern—a formula for making it to the centre or the outside—that eludes you. It represents what you think you cannot evade or avoid or find freedom from, and also the futility of trying to remain who you have been. You *can* try but it will be an illusion. A shallow thing. You will know, no matter what. Often that leads to, or encourages, addiction, even madness. Certainly fear. Certainly entrapment.

I do not suggest that anxiety around this time is symbolic, only because that would be untrue. But the very cool thing about fear is that it is never an enemy. Fear is a physiological response to threat heeding it is always wise but only when the threat is real. We all train, if we train, to deflect what is terrifying. Don't we? Aren't we taught as children to know about predation? No? Silly species. *Devil*, at this stage of initiation, is the illusory threat of the unknown. It will show in the pictograms of every addict.

TOWER

Tower, *Lightning-Struck Tower* or *Blasted Tower* occurs, roiling in the turbulence. It is as though you are a deep-sea submersible that has plumbed the fathoms of the absolute depths of the ocean, to its floor, only to find that you are, in reality, on a shifting shelf of delusionary safety, on the brink of a drop into a chasm. Everything falls to pieces or explodes. Your adrenals will be in overdrive and your gut will respond so strongly to circumstances that your hands shake and your palms sweat and your legs barely support you. Been there? You have passed through your Saturn Return, so you're remembering right now exactly what we're talking about.

The Marseille cards and booklet calls the *Blasted Tower la maison dieu*: *the house of god*, with all the ramifications of the Iron Age myth of Babel causing people to speak utterances that seem like one thing but are something else entirely. Propaganda that becomes a form of immolation. Often with an agenda. We no longer understand what is being said. A very stupid curse but valid to purpose because two or more people could seem to be speaking the same language and yet, potentially, are hyping up a war.

Concerning relationships, whether a couple living together, a family a community or a nation, the *Tower* is the result of the breakdown of peace and the resulting explosion of aggression. Often with an unrevealed propaganda.

During this time the *Tower* will express itself in tragedy or confrontation. Once you hit bottom there is no further to fall. If you have survived the fall you must move on.

The *Lightning Struck Tower* is a direct analogy of the fall from the parent tree, the natural state of the transition from being Kether into re-becoming Malkuth, in the direction of the *Lightning Flash* in its continuous evolution. It is all that is acute and inflammatory.

It is the process of the seed cracking open.

STAR

As of 2006 CE science began coming closer to mapping the human genome, the supposed blueprint to life. The more fascinating question, though, still remains: what is it that defines life in difference to matter? Is there a distinction, or is the notion of fallacy allowing a forest to be called lumber? To blow a mountain apart and call it mining?

What is it that endows us with emotion?

What is the *quality* of individualism?

These questions are inherent within the process of the *Journey of Initiation*.

They are represented by *Star* insofar as no matter how much we learn there is always the universe's next trick.

Star encourages you to dive upwards towards the surface again after the intense depths of the Dark Night of the Soul. You are released from the confines of the shell of the seed. You are vulnerable, sure, but *Star* also reminds you that you are now certain of your place within the scheme of self-reflection and that by being yourself rather than mimicking others you will attract people and events aligned with you. Or you will be alone. That can be harsh but living a lie can be intolerable. It is like *Magician* at the onset of the first phase, but with more vision and aptitude. It also represents astronomy, astrology, technology, film, photography, flight and vision.

MOON

I'm taking more time with *Moon* than any other Wayshower because of its implications. It is comparable, on this journey, with *Mystery* (which has the moon as its associated planetary body) and at first there may be a lack of clear steps of progress and you see only through a gauze veil, a mist, a haze of rain, but now you are beyond the curtains and out by the water. The image of *Moon* displays a crustacean, a dog and a wolf – all arcs of seeming progression on an evolutionary scale but is that factual, when all three creatures exist concurrently? No. What the image projects is that we are all interconnected, are creatures of Oceania whether submerged or on dry land. *Moon* and the waters remind you of your commonality while the path lures you towards a future unknown. *Moon* is inherently moist reminding you that on the journey of the seed to becoming a tree, nourishment comes from the element of water which, in us as a species, is how we emote and the way we feel. In Earth it is the substrata and deep, ancestral underground aquifers.

It is instinct and intuition rather than rationale and logic but that doesn't mean it isn't about thinking because so many human beings are controlled by emotions—desires, expectations, anxieties, ambitions, the effect of what others think, conceptual fears of possible threats—that life, for many, can be made up of illusions of past and future and traps of need. At the juncture of *Moon* in the initiations in life you delve into your attachments to memory of remembered phenomena, current experience, mental aptitude, and the quality of what is thought and felt. These are survival skills. Know the ways they or others use emotion as a chess-game of manipulation or blackmail and to get off the board by self-reflection and reflection on your relationships with others, by processing the information and transforming it all into quality experiences.

People are manipulated, coerced and assaulted from every direction by jargon and implication. Mostly repetition; mostly rhetoric.

Once, at the completion of an Aikido training session a few years ago all students were seated on the mats. The person who had taken the class in the head sensei's absence talked to us about what he'd been taught, regarding people; about a conscious and a subconscious mind. He informed us that the subconscious was white and positive, and that if we harbour negative thoughts – black – they will go into the subconscious and turn it grey. The concept is ridiculous.

Dualisms like good/bad, black/white, positive/negative merely reinforce the stereotypical paradigms that have become religious and political weapons, as well as major advertising, propaganda and bureaucratic ploys, for manipulating people into an untrue view of what is acceptable or otherwise. It seems like it's been done forever, because that is how history is recorded. Battle and betrayal, always the "good guys" winning. By killing and taking. Propagandist and biased. These concepts are just that: concepts.

So what's the reality? The dissolution of androcentric thought is how one breaks through. From being seed to individual plant. An absolution from thinking *humanly* to the denial of everything else, except, perhaps, peripherally. To root. To adapt with forest.

SUN

Sun is when you begin again. And again. And again.

JUDGMENT

Judgment is your awakening from sleep or dormancy. It is also the moment in life when everything is changed and will continue to adapt to the weather, understood as you.

When your life, that began with *Sun*, becomes affected by your unique experience of wind, rain, sun, snow (work, family, friendships, hardships, substrate, any and all depths including soil and sky) and, knowing that there is free will involved in decisions made in response to everything that happens, this image and its meaning also implies wisdom.

WORLD

World is everything that happens in this, the new cycle until the next, and the cycle after that and the one after that (infinitely).

You, within the new cycle, and your roots, are now strong enough to hold you, no matter the weather or conditions. The *Chayoth ha-Qadesh*, in the corners of most traditional renditions, as with the *Wheel of Fortune* and the objects upon the altar of the *Magician*, symbol and object, represent this, reminding you, again, that there is other than what you consider.

There is, and will always be, more.

PART THREE

INTERPRETATIONS TO MEMORISE

WAYSHOWERS

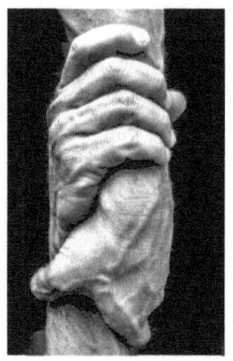

First: there are *many* meanings to every pictogram, depending on what else is in the map: the moment you interpret what the pattern of several cards looks like and many other factors. Learn the following, and completely, by rote is enlightening. Simply don't be so stuck as to insist interpretations have only these meanings as these are given to you as examples based on experience. The BOOK OF SECRETS teaches you when the story is other.

FOOL

Fool is also known as the *blind card* because it rarely allows you to know anything; its trigger event. There is a purpose in this. In each of your lives comes an event that is *so* important that the trigger (*Fool*) remains obscure to ensure that, no matter the consequences, these events unfold without preconception. Life will change as a direct result.

Trying to guess what it might mean will be thwarted on purpose. You'd be wrong. You'll never know its importance until retrospectively because it can seem like an innocuous event or series of events, completely irrelevant. This being said however there are patterns that give *Fool* meaning.

- Near a person image or *Hermit* – someone will randomly and inadvertently teach an importance, trigger something of importance. When *Fool* is in this position a client does not already know the person
- A seemingly random, trickster, event
- What is thought stupidity that engenders unforeseen repercussions, as a matter of physics

With, for example, *Hanged Man* and *Moon* an experience can represent anything from a diving expedition to a person falling from a cliff.

- walking along the avenue and bumping into a stranger who becomes integral to destiny
- the advertisement where the actor walks into a shop and asks for a packet of barbeque crisps and is handed the crisps by the shop-keeper and a barbeque falls on them from a great height
- a very rash behaviour will have all kinds of unexpected consequences

Fool is, however, pre-determined. Nothing that shows up in proximity is recognisable from the current perspective.

MAGICIAN

A way of life not yet experienced, of knowledge and awareness (for kindness or harm). It represents a person who does not like to be told what to do or who operates independently from traditional roles, as such it can also represent a very impacting individual or group.

- A client, or a person card beside *Magician*, is self-focused, independent and/or wields a dynamic presence, individually and/or professionally: not necessarily authentic
- With the *Devil*: not to be trusted. Narcissistic or utterly selfish, potentially psychopathic
- The person card or the client in front of you is self-centred (this is a good thing) and self-motivated, entrepreneurial
- A learned person—one with qualifications, not necessarily orthodox
- A chemist, an alchemist, a research supervisor, even a stage conjurer if professional cards attend it
- An expert in their field
- New circumstance but with knowledge
- With *Mystery*—as yet unencoded and/or undisclosed: occulted
- With *Ace of Swords*—an expert of sharps: could be injecting, tattoo, a chef, surgeon, brilliant mind

MYSTERY

Mystery represents that which is covered, hidden, beguiling, enchanting, behind the scenes, anything unseen, occulted (like electricity, quarks, love). As a place it can represent homes or holts hidden from general view or are traditionally *tapu*, or within the vicinity of the sea or ancient hewn stone.

- The qualities of an individual if they are psychic or empathic
- Something is hidden that can sometimes come to light
- Significant events occurring behind the scenes
- What is lost, hidden or missing, that the client won't be able to find
- A question that will have no answer (like whether another is being "unfaithful" in the traditional sense) if the client will not find out
- A veil in more than one sense but can be literally a bridal veil, the hajib, the burqa, and this can often be used to describe places that the client will visit (*Mystery* with *Sun, 8 of Wands*, for example, can represent North African lands like Egypt, Morocco, Iran)
- Secrecy, confidentiality (as in a lawyer, doctor, priest, psychic)
- A teacher of any of the mystery traditions
- A bit back from the sea

EMPRESS

Empress is beautiful (or considered beautiful which is a different thing and can be quite dangerous, like the cruel tradition of bound feet), sensual, artistic, tactile and female. It is fetid, the corruption of rot, putrescence. Olfactory reaction. Cesspits and ambergris. Represents hospitality/the hospitality industry, those catering to the consensual idea of beauty: from fashion through to cosmetics, cosmetic surgery, the inevitability of life. When shown as a place the climate is always tropical. It is fecundity, pregnancy of any kind from biological to the conception of a project or artistic endeavor. Biologically it represents the womb or breasts, the corpse, decomposition, scents, soil, sights, sensory, aural and oral pleasures and/or decadence.

- As an ecosystem—tropical and/or fertile regions
- Ripe
- Ready for planting
- Juicy
- Mother lands
- Moisture, not wetness
- Mother
- With the *Ace of Wands*—pregnancy
- With *7 of Coins*—outrageous, overgrown garden
- With *Tower*—volcanic regions
- With *Hermit*—Himalayas/parts of South America linked to the Andes
- With *Strength*, lush regions within arid, like Kakadu National

Park in Australia, the Amazon, the Congo, both the Arctic and Antarctica

- With *8 of Coins*: work in anything from cooking to preparation of a body for internment or cremation, to sex work or that which represents beauty: from a nail technician to a plastic surgeon to a cocktail waiter.
- With *Devil*, *9 of Swords* or *10 of Swords* it can represent a person who suffers for the sake of appearance or who is physically ill as a result of breast or uterine illness
- With *Moon* it is disillusionment with appearance or hormonal imbalance
- With *5 of Coins* and *9 of Swords* it can be an eating disorder like bulimia
- With *Devil* and the *10 of Cups*, obesity or gluttony
- With *Ace of Swords* and *Emperor* will represent incision or implant in relation to the female body, from Invitro fertilisation to cosmetic intervention. Other cards will indicate which.

EMPEROR

Emperor is patriarchy or orthodoxy. Parenthood and what that traditionally entails. A politician, president, pope, prime minister, a dictator. The presence of misogyny and coercive control. An approved history book. The workings of bureaucracy and hierarchy.

- Father
- Concepts of fatherhood/patriarchy
- Middle management: insurance, banks, administration
- Western educational systems, hospitals, governments
- With *Justice*—federal law, federal government
- With *5 of Coins*—welfare or a declared impoverishment
- With *8 of Wands*—local council
- With *9 of Swords*—treatment in a hospital or other orthodox therapy
- With *Star/World*—cathedrals, old architecture such as the Louvre in Paris, Göbekli Tepe, Machu Pichu—too many to mention. Also astronomy and space observatories

HIEROPHANT

Hierophant, in most instances, is religion and, in some ways, represents these institutions, even Adelaide (called the city of churches) or traditionally Roman catholic or Islamic people-countries, also Jewish, Buddhist or Hindu territories

- A person who is a religious figurehead in the public eye: traditional, orthodox or otherwise
- Marriage—living together over 3 months (de facto); with *Law* it represents a definite legal marriage, be it personal, business, corporate or an individual's commitment to a cause/work
- Dogmatic, structured, hierarchical religion
- New Age spirituality that mimics traditional religions
- With *Devil*—fundamentalist-type religion, potentially dangerous; a religious institution that Tarot dislikes
- With *Star*, an environment that is alpine—Switzerland, Austria, France, Italy
- With *Law/Justice*—legal marriage of any kind, including companies, countries and ancestral houses
- With *Child of Cups*, catholicism

LOVERS

Lovers ultimate meaning is a decision is to be made, but it is also division of any kind, three-way relationships or triangular relationships (of the sexual kind) and/or polyamory. In the physical body it can represent the lungs, hips or pelvis.

- *Lovers* as an outcome represents a crossroads and suggests you decide your road. Tarot will not give a direct answer because destiny would be impacted by interference from beyond the client (see *Fool*)
- There will be two outcomes
- A crossroads
- With the *7 of Cups*—choices are illusion, there is only one way to proceed
- With *3 of Cups*, polyamory
- With a *7 of Swords*: the orthodox idea of betrayal in a monogamous intimacy
- Twins
- With *2 of Cups*, sexual lovers &/or equals in any partnership, not necessarily financial or business. Contemporaries

CHARIOT

When relative to individuals *Chariot* represents victory after striving: a pass (exams, driving test, medical check-up) or any personal sense of achievement, whereas it can also represent places or modes of transportation

- Acceptance after a job interview
- The winning of a court case. Who for? See surrounding pictograms
- The winning of any battle, dispute or war
- It is malleable and deceptive when describing a person – you'd need context: the person could be ally or enemy who bests you in debate, contest or combat
- An earned victory with hard work before and after
- With *10 of Coins*—caravan, bus, house on wheels, temporary dwelling
- With *Strength* an environment: Middle East, Arabia or regions of North Africa, Nepal, Himalayas
- Achieving the equivalent of a PhD, Masters, black belt, reaching shelter located on a map

STRENGTH

All that is considered animal. The physical body, control issues, infections due to erupt, seismic areas, foundations poured for a building, animism, body-work of any kind.

- *Strength* will turn up in many environment spreads and can be desert anywhere, can also be England (monarchical crest), countries of Africa, parts of France, Gibraltar, Malta, Cypress
- With *Empress*—India, Pakistan, Sri Lanka, Southeast Asia, Pacific countries, Amazon
- With *Chariot*—Middle East, UAE, North Africa
- With *Star*—America, Western Australia (particularly the Kimberly region
- With *Sun* and *Moon*—oasis-type environments: desert regions with waterways or desert regions around the Mediterranean
- It lends power to other cards
- Can represent animals, lust, underground or under-the-surface power and rage, depending on other pictograms
- With *9 of Swords*—physical illness
- With *10 of Swords*—physical pain
- With *10 of Wands*—a literally heavy load
- With *8 of Coins*—bodywork
- With *8 of Wands*—a dry, arid region
- With *2 of Coins*—a weight loss program

- With *Emperor*—sometimes hospitals, sometimes, as mentioned above, a country like England
- With *Sun*—desert land
- With *5 of Wands*—martial arts
- With *4 of Wands*—performance such as dance
- Falling in the sphere of netzach on the Stargate map, can represent sculpture or tactile art
- With *Ace of Coins*—rock solid or non-specific matter
- With *Ace of Wands* I have seen it as *new matter* for a person in the last stages of terminal cancer who wanted to know what would happen after death
- When representing a person this card insures good health and physical prowess
- With *10 of Coins*, can represent a gymnasium or other fitness studio
- With *Moon* and *Child of Cups* sea creatures such as whales
- With *Tower*, it can be either earthquake or blasting as with mining

HERMIT

Hermit is aloneness, purposeful but silent, a wise person, a hilly or mountainous environment, cold country, winter, an old person or a wise child. Sometimes a quest. Antique dealers, old houses, places outside cities, high places.

- Alone—not sad or lonely unless other cards indicate; single
- With *8 of Wands*—Inland terrain that gets very cold in winter
With *6 of Swords*—In the case of Australia this would represent somewhere prone to be cold like Tasmania or New Zealand: a place over water but not far off the mainland
- With *Star* or *World*—a long way overseas/international
- With *Star*—alps, mountains, stars on snow
- With *7 of Coins*—archaeology, history or similar
- With *8 of Coins* it can be any form of work dealing with that which is old or antique
- With *2 of Wands*—Melbourne, Adelaide, New York, Chicago, London, Ontario, Moscow, Zurich, Wellington, Tokyo; a major capital city in a place that gets very cold in winter
- With *10 of Cups*—an old house
- With *Emperor* a tradition
- With *Law/Justice* and a *person* this has turned up for a magistrate, QC or barrister
- With *Emperor, 10 of Coins*—a geriatric facility

WHEEL

Back and forward, over and over, up and down, rollercoaster ride, the daily round, day to day, continuous. It can represent a circuit (at a gym or someone who does a market circuit); I have also had it for people who are involved with circus. It can literally represent the wheels of a vehicle.

But also revolution. Just NOT war.

- Maintenance
- With *Knight of Wands* or *Knight of Coins*—wheels on vehicles
- With any pictograms other than these it represents repetition of some form or another
- With *5 of Wands*, people protesting for change

LAW

Law is a loaded word and this card is usually called *Justice*. Despite it rarely being so. With many meanings *Law* can represent any legal matters from the judicial system to contracts, leases, legalities, the police, the courts, anything whereby you sign or witness. It also signifies discernment.

- With *Emperor*—federal and local government
- With *5 of Coins*—bankruptcy
- With *Devil*—enforced control, illegal graft, corruption
- With *8 of Swords*—imprisonment or entrapment
- With *10 of Coins*—the contract relating to a rented or leased dwelling
- With *10 of Cups*—the contract or deed of ownership on the sale or buying of a home
- With *Hierophant*—a legally *sanctioned* marriage between any two agencies
- With *World*—International Court of Justice, the Hague

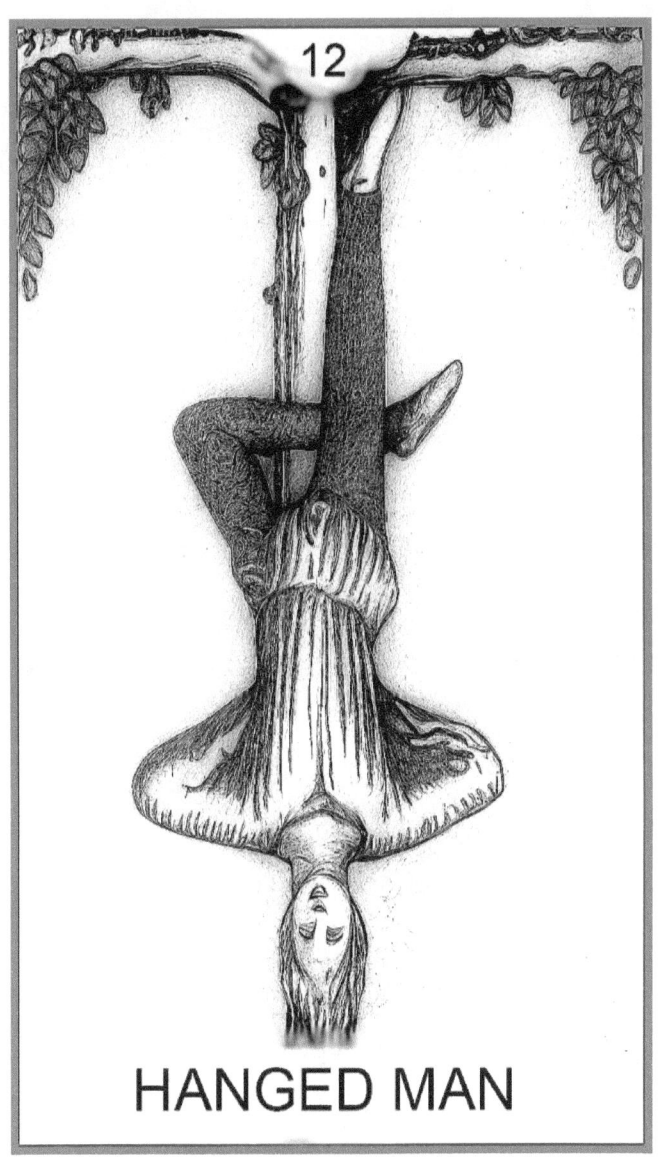

HANGED MAN

This can be descriptive, in one way or another, of a person: can be a "martyr" in the dysfunctional sense: putting up with discord or a distressing situation out of fear of change; being a 'doormat' in a relationship, or in the spiritual or visionary sense: people like Martin Luther King. One of the catchphrases of this is to "consider the experience an exercise in detachment". Also represents falling, being rejected, suicide, a thing or person becoming obsolete; humanitarianism, altruism, unable to prevent, victimisation.

- With *People/Hierophant* can be martyrdom/assassination—If *Death* is present in a spread
- With the *3 of Swords*—separation: no point fighting; rejection or dismissal of any kind
- With the *Moon*—diving or fishing
- With the *Death* and *10 of Swords* the victim in a murder or a suicide by hanging or strangulation, or being pushed off a high place
- With *Fool* and *4 of Wands* can be extreme sports such as bungee-jumping or abseiling
- Similarly, with *Star* and any pleasure cards, it can represent parachuting, hang-gliding, any aerial sport or high circus activity

DEATH

Completion; any represented relationship or undertaking is over; it is the end of a venture; a full stop or the word *No*. *Death* always represents actual and irrevocable endings.

- Reiteration: the word *No*. This will always mean this if, during question time, the first card on the table in a yes/no question is *Death*.
- Completion
- Final exams
- With *Chariot*—passed a test
- With *Hanged Man*—can be suicide
- With *Moon*—failure
- With *8 of Swords*—a stalemate
- With *Ace of Swords*—a so-called natural physical death
- With *10 of Swords*—violent death. Can indicate self-inflicted by self-injection and overdose as in the case of addiction; messier types of death, violent accident. Don't be fooled, I have had same with *8 of Coins* (the woman was an ambulance driver in inner-city Sydney)
- Can also indicate places of violent deaths. You would see similar in other lands bathed in a history of bloodshed
- With the Ace of Swords, 9 of Swords, Death—the contemplation of suicide
- With *5 of Cups*—mourning and regret

TEMPERANCE

The alchemy of mixing one thing with another to get something else; the "I'm not there yet" tight-rope walker (and their balancing staff). Cautions. All things worthy of consideration. A trial period. A middle position: mediation, negotiation, careful peace (treaty), walking a fine line through a particular situation, keeping your balance, someone who has recovered from a drug or alcohol dependency.

- A person who is piggy-in-the-middle in a situation of discord
- Mediators, mellow people, counsellors, representatives
- In entertainment: balancing acts, jugglers, tightrope or high-wire
- With *Magician* it represents a person involved in alchemy, or alchemy itself
- With *Emperor* it represents pharmaceutical drugs
- With *Emperor* and *10 of Coins*, a medical practice (physical or psychological), a pharmacy or drugstore
- With a *Person* card and *Emperor*, a doctor, pharmacist, chemist, someone involved in medical research
- With *Devil* and a *person* card it can represent a recovering addict or alcoholic
- Also with *Devil*, no indication of a person, and perhaps *9 of Swords,* a sick person on some form of traditional medication
- Balancing life without over-indulgences
- In Kether it represents a profound peace

- A bridge or bridges
- With *Ace of Wands*, verbal exchanges, the dialogue process
- Healers and therapy practitioners

DEVIL

Devil is also, as equally, known as the Liar or/and the Great Deceiver. The irony is, the 'devil' was invented by churchdom as well as all abrahamic creeds. Fear, shame, abuse, guilt, threat (in the mind and literally). *Devil* is addiction (alcohol, drugs, food, sex, screens, gambling, being right, being acceptable no matter the cost). An enemy. With ill-health cards that which grows harmful to the host: cancer, sexually transmitted disease. Is also stuckness, obsession, dogma, fear, the instinct to respond to threat.

- Claustrophobic conditions; confined spaces
- Frustration over delays, restraints, restrictions
- With *6 of Coins*—corruption/bribery
- With *Knight of Coins*—problems with car or finances
- With *7 of Coins* it can represent either a marijuana crop, a form of physical cancer, a fungal overgrowth
- With *4 of Coins* a thing is stuck, not moving
- With *Knight of Wands* it is dysfunctional communication or major travel delays
- With *Ace of Swords*—fear of violence or the ability to commit violence
- With *8 of Wands*—the person will need to be careful around property dealings; it can also represent poisoned land through chemical use or otherwise
- With *Person of Coins* someone born in the time of Capricorn
- With *Moon*—clinical insanity

- With *Moon* and *8 of Wands* can be someone who works with in the mental health industry
- With *Moon* and *Emperor*—asylums or psychological institutions
- With *7 of Cups*—delusional behaviour
- With *10 of Swords*—deep pain, extreme violence or violation
- With *5 of Swords*—domestic violence, a dirty fight, terrorism
- With *2 of Cups*—sexual abuse, fear around sex, sexually transmitted disease
- With *9 of Swords*—insomnia, long-term illness
- With *6 of Cups*—heavy opiate-type drug use

TOWER

Things go terribly wrong: what the person (or situation) presumed to be secure comes tumbling down the whole tree, the seeds dropping, chaos, fiery places, people to do with mining, explosive situations of any kind, lightning, storms, electricity, uncontained power. Up it goes. Crisis. Out-of-control events and people. Catastrophe. Earthquake.

Rage. Whatever has been built up has come crashing down.
- With *Ace of Wands*—literally, a fire
- With *Star*—satellite or plane crashes to earth
- With *Strength*—rock explosion as in open-cut mining; a bomb
- With *5 of Swords*—Individually: huge argument. Large scale: violent street protest; military clashes
- With *Moon*—meltdown, inner explosion. Can be a person or a nuclear reactor, can be violent storm/s
- *Tower/Moon/Star*—severe weather patterns
- *Empress/Strength/Tower*—New Zealand, the Rockies, Faroe Island or places of high cragged mountains usually volcanic or on geomantic fault lines
- In Chokmah, in a Stargate layout, electricity danger of some kind, technological blackout, aerial crashes

STAR

The letter associated with this card is heh (window/vision) allowing clear visible access. Head above water. See greatness in the smallest. *World* and *Star* represent with era sequences. Flight. Long distance. Long term projects, realisation.

A definite *yes* in answer to a question. Illumination, cameras, film, digital and other forms of technology, glass, shop-fronts, advertising, algorithms, vision and eyesight.

- Technology with *Coins*
- Visual imagery
- Reflection
- Astronomy
- Internet
- With *8 of Coins*, a person who works for information tech, working with/exploring A.I.
- Visionary influence
- Information
- Can represent many places with other cards
- With *7 of Swords*—a seventeen to twenty-year commitment
- With *10 of Coins*, *Emperor*—an airport or terminal of any kind
- With *10 of Swords*—broken glass
- With *3 of Wands*—a coastal place, usually in a clear, warm area
- With *2 of Wands* any west-coast city

MOON

Deceit or self-deceit, despair, delusion, lack of self-esteem, disillusionment, disappointment, wet places, a moody person, depression, that which is subliminal. Can represent the ocean and can also represent a situation or person that is emotionally wet; miserable. *Moon* can represent being affected by dreary weather like as by SAD (seasonal affected disorder), things that descend; that which is oceanic.

Can represent hormonal shifts or extremes and will show up with disorders such as menstrual pain and endometriosis, also PCOS and women's health matters. The persona or image of an individual and can also be a reflection or a mirror.

- With *Empress*, women's bodies
- With *Child of Cups*, creatures of the sea (not mammals)
- With *4 of Wands*, full-moon parties
- With *9 of Swords*, worry or despair, insomnia or other sleep-related dysfunctions, although with *8 of Coins*: night shift
- With *4 of Swords*, boredom, the frustration of waiting
- With *Ace of Wands*, communication difficulties or misunderstandings, or, conversely, deep levels of communication.
- With *10 of Coins*, a sauna or an indoor swimming pool or plumbing
- With *2 of Cups* sexual disappointments or naivety
- With *6 of Swords*, a boat, surfboard or other water-craft

SUN

Sun is success, achievement, birth, children, hot places, anything bright or golden.

- With *Star*, astrology
- With *Ace of Wands*, a biological birth
- With *Ace of Coins*, wealth
- With *Strength*, hot, dry, stony places
- With *Empress*, hot moist places
- With activity pictograms this always represents successful outcomes

JUDGMENT

Judgment is the strange antiquated rapture-style imagining left over from the late 19th century when it was thought, within xian ideology, that their imagined god, whose daddy had himself tortured to death in some perverse removal of an even more perverse construct of "original sin", since invention, imposed onto other cultures. We know what happens to a corpse buried for a few years, particularly the outmoded idea of a sealed, airtight coffin in which the cadaver becomes soup. So, let's run with it for what it has represented to Tarot since we began working together:

Judgment is all forms of change, usually significant change in a lifestyle, progress, restructuring, altered of circumstances &/or opinions, change of season when dormancy produces the first northern hemisphere buds of spring or loses leaves just prior to winter. It's a bit like the *Wheel* but moreso representing seasonal change. Changes of mind, change, change, change; initiations of any kind.

- Obscurely, with *Child of Wands* this can represent dental work
- With *Empress* it is the seasons of a year
- With any activity images you can expect changes, delays or re-directions
- With *Death,* changes are complete (for now)
- With *Moon*, changes of mood, changes of mind

WORLD

World/earth, community, overseas connections, end of one cycle beginning of another like 31st December/1st January or like samuin. *World* will also represent 20-21 years ago/ahead. A Saturn Cycle.

- Seasonal cycle
- Transition from one way of living to another
- Community centres, communal gathering places (indoors) if falling with *10 of Coins*
- The cycle of one year
- An entire life's journey
- Planetary associations
- With *6 of Swords*, long overseas journey
- With *Star*, the internet, information technology, international flight
- With *Emperor* it can represent international affairs and organisations like the United Nations
- With *5 of Swords* and/or *Strength* it can be a world war

JOURNEY CARDS

Please note: the knights are rarely (if ever) people.

WANDS

Communication, the spoken and the written word, the performing arts, creativity, sign, stones, self-expression

ACE

- Beginning, but not like *Magician*
- Represents the words *new* and *yes*
- Literally, fire or a fiery situation, spontaneity, excitation
- Books, paperwork, vocals
- New things
- Light-heartedness, vivacity, dance, optimism, never a problem
- All field of communication.
- Spoken and/or written word
- With *Star*, internet, social media—can be rockets, missiles, intercontinental ballistic weapons
- With *10 of Wands*, written research or compilation
- With *Empress*, pregnancy
- With *Sun*, birth
- With *Tower*, fire or explosion
- With *Emperor*, *10 of Coins* it can represent a house of publishing or a library

2 OF WANDS

A coastal place, &/or a major capital city.

- With *8 of Wands*, inland cities
- With *World* and other significant place cards this is a major capital city somewhere else in the world other than where the client calls home. A travel representation like *Knight of Wands* (light-hearted travel) or the *Knight of Coins* (travel for practical or business purposes) would most likely fall close by, often with *Star* indicating flight
- A person at a deemed pinnacle of life

3 OF WANDS

'At a distance' – this is often a place card

- With *2 of Wands* and *Hermit*—going to a city that is cold in winter
- With *8 of Wands* and *Hermit*—an inland city that is cold in winter in the same country as the client
- With *6 of Swords* and *Hermit*—an island off the mainland of the country, never very far, also that gets cold in winter
- With *2 of Wands* and *Empress*, a more-or-less tropical city in the same country as the client
- With *8 of Wands* and *Star*, the west coast of the country, usually more rural than city
- When seeking timeframes this pictogram indicates a period of 3 days, 3 weeks, 3 months or 3 years

4 OF WANDS

A party, festival or celebration; a good time; a performance

- With the *2 of Swords*, a surprise party
- With the *10 of Coins*, opening a shop, restaurant, gallery
- With the *Ace of Wands* and the *8 of Wands*, an outdoor party
- With the *5 of Wands*, bands, orchestras, music, live performance
- With *Moon*, modelling for the fashion or image industry, cultural celebration, public event that is celebratory.
- Any form of seasonal or joyous gathering, festival or attendance at a gala

5 OF WANDS

Confusion of thought. Many voices at once. A band or group of singers. Can be several people talking or interacting at once. A literal mess: people, room and/or environment. Doing several things at once. Building materials. Verbal dispute. Bureaucratic red-tape.

- With *Emperor*, red tape, bureaucracy
- With *5 of Swords*, industrial disputes, strikes, protesting
- With a person image it can indicate a Gemini
- With *9* or *10 of Wands*—mess to be picked up
- With travel pictograms it represents people fighting with sticks and stones, not tanks and guns
- With *Strength*—physical discipline like martial arts
- With *10 of Coins*—building materials for an unfinished house or house being renovated
- With of *7 of Cups*—false communication, mulengro, gaslighting, coercive control, mob behaviour, crossed wires in communication
- With *8 of Wands*—multiple occupancy or community and company title land or ecoscape

6 OF WANDS

Effortless victory. Another *yes* portrayal. Cruising easy. Nothing stressful. Easily achieves a desired outcome. Natural vitality.

There are no specific this-goes-with-that to be aware of here. With this pictogram present the spread indicates that by being who the client is, the person or the situation is *effortless* (without pretension for any reason) and events will unfold without stress or duress.

There is no need to have any 'with' cards as its meaning is clear wherever it falls.

7 OF WANDS

7 of Wands is a phone call or internet chat. Can be teaching. Internal conversations with oneself. When in reference to the sale of a house or property it represents an auction. Long-distance speaking, not eye to eye. Talking where not everyone's listening. Also a school teacher to whom no one is necessarily listening.

- With *Emperor*—always school/traditional and orthodox education teacher
- With *Star* and the *5 of Wands*—internet chat, email or communication
- With *Knight of Wands* and *7 of Wands*—a person speaking many languages
- With *Ace of Wands*—a public speaker or public speech
- With place images—where a contact call is to or from
- With *10 of Cups* and other indication (money, contracts) indicating the buying or selling of real estate this represents an auction

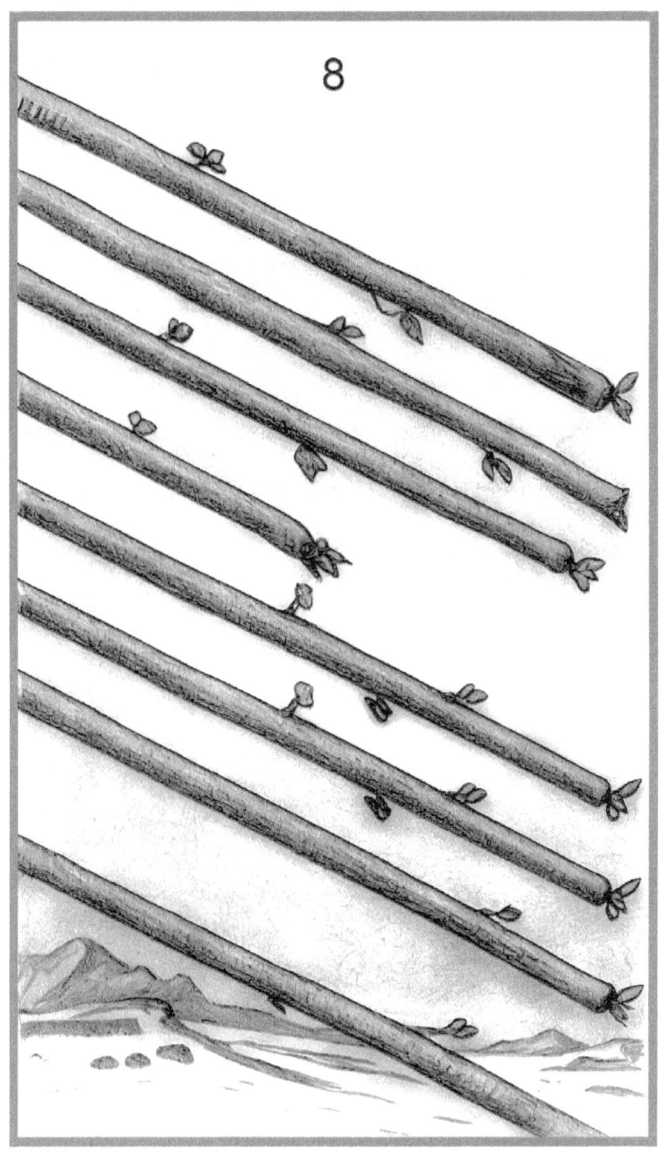

8 OF WANDS

Rural environments or country, but not necessarily forested. Sending out things (documents etc.)

- With *5 of Wands*—multiple occupancy, community or company titled property
- With *2 of Wands*—a small coastal town
- With *Ace of Swords*—subdivisions, boundaries or fences and/or tracks/driveways, in relation to rural land
- With *5 of Swords* and *Ace of Swords*—struggle over borders or boundaries. Can be local or international, the rights of indigenous people to defend their ancestral homelands
- With *8 of Swords* there will be difficulty with access (road or driveway)

9 OF WANDS

Not being heard or not speaking: "Nobody ever listens to me". The client, or represented person, is annoyed at others finishing their sentences for them. The person is not going to waste time explaining themselves. Pointless words. Communication breakdown. In the warning, Horse Latitude, it advises an individual keep their opinions quiet. The person figuring in this map is tired of not being heard, or is wary, and is guarding their comments. This is the person that would rather communicate but it's unappreciated or dangerous: they are not going to do that anymore

- With *Ace of Wands* and *8 of Coins* is represented a writer of some description who either has 'writer's block' or is having their words censored in some way
- With relationships there are communication imbalances
- With *Law/Justice* and any other pictograms representing legal situations the person to whom the pattern refers is not speaking or refusing to speak
- With illness, such as 9 or *10 of Swords*, it can represent laryngitis, tonsillitis or some very uncomfortable throat disease.
- With *7 of Coins* a growth, like thrush/candida

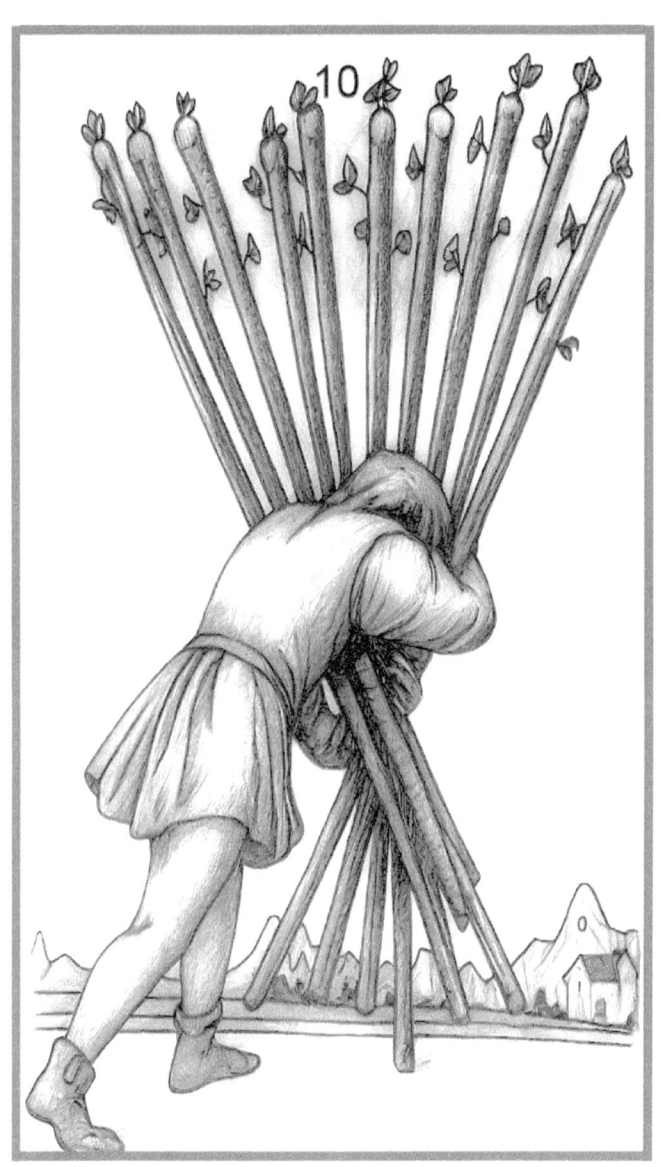

10 OF WANDS

Moving self, family, clan, things from place to place. Shouldering responsibilities willingly. Can be building. A load, a body of work.

- With *Emperor*—any form of research
- With *10 of Coins*—a house being built of wood or moving to a new rented or leased dwelling
- With *Empress*, anything from the responsibilities of motherhood to being a busy chef
- With *Strength* and a person-pictogram it literally represents a physically strong individual
- It does not represent hardship
- The cleanup after a disaster—environmental or from human desecration

KNIGHT OF WANDS

The knights are rarely, if ever, a representation of people, but of movements. The only instance of this representing a person is an individual who works with riding animals: horses, camels, donkeys.

Travel
- A journey or trip (not by ship, that would be *Knight of Cups*)
- All forms of communication, usually relaxed
- With *7 of Wands*—a letter, phone call or public speaking
- With *Star*—airmail/email
- With *Child of Wands* (not, however, a child)—communication, a small to medium-sized package or a letter on the way
- With a *Child* of any suit—talkative and able to communicate easily
- Modes of transport, usually an average car
- An amicable resolution to a situation
- With *Moon* it is internal dialogue, psychic or intuitive communication
- With *10 of Wands* and *World*—backpacking
- With *10 of Swords* it can represent a car accident where damage is incurred
- With *9 of Wands*, writer's block, an inability or lack of desire to communicate

CHILD OF WANDS

Fire sign children of any species, or child of fire sign person of any species. The seed of a creative project. The spoken or the written word. A small fiery thing. If a species our skins may be ruddy, our hair, pelts of skin be copper or red/ish

- With *Strength*—season or sign of Leo
- With *Sun*—season or sign of Aries
- With *Temperance*—season or sign of Sagittarius
- With *Ace of Wands*—books, audio, eBook or paper, or any publications
- With *4 of Wands*—a production has begun. A creative venture has begun
- With *Moon*—descriptive art of any kind
- With *Tower*—sudden, acute illness affecting the throat and/or larynx

WOMAN OF WANDS

Female of any species of mammal. For a human that will likely be a fire sign: Sagittarius, Leo or Aries, either sun sign, ascendant or midheaven: gregarious, active, straight-talking people. A human being with russet or reddish hair (natural or otherwise) and/or freckles, or can be someone with a ruddy complexion.

Other pictograms will explain their representation in the story.

MAN OF WANDS

See WOMAN OF WANDS.

The same applies as a description

Other pictograms will explain their representation in the story.

CUPS

Emissive, introverted, moody, introspective, reflective

ACE OF CUPS

Love is an overused terminology that is all but meaningless in an era when it is overused for everything from pizza to yourself. Other language, Arabic for example, have approximately 50 words relative to love: Some of them include *al Mahabba* (affection), *achaghaf* (infatuation), *al Kalaf* (fondness), *achaju* (distress), *al huzn* (sadness), *al araq* (sleeplessness), *al law'a* (ardent love), *al huyam* (bewildering passion)[1] whereas other languages, like Japanese, use *suki* (like) whereas the proto-Indo-European etymology of the word love has the hypothetical root **leubh-*, meaning "to care, desire". To be genuine it becomes necessary to define *love* a little more actively as: respect, reciprocity, willing care, honesty, earned trust.

- With *8 of Coins*—for the love of work, work that one loves or amateur work (vocation).
- With *Child of Cups* and *Hierophant*—christian religion, specifically catholicism
- In all other instances it defines love by the pictograms around it

---

[1] Source: sabithkhan.com

2 OF CUPS

Sex. Intimate relationships, but can also mean very close friendships and partnership/agreements between allies.

- Sexuality or sexual relationship
- Sex
- With *8 of Coins*, often a sex worker. The first time I knew this was when the *8 of Coins* fell in the dimension of netzach on the map/layout called Stargate. The client was the CEO of two brothels in Melbourne. They could as easily have sold sensual silk underwear or most anything, cars, makeup, you've seen the advertising: *sex sells*
- I have had the *2 of Cups* with *Emperor* and *Ace of Wands* for an academic who writes books, and is a professor, about sex and sexuality
- It shows up with *Devil*, devious sexual behavior
- With *Devil* and *9 of Swords*, can be sexually transmitted anything
- With *Judgment* and any of the *Child* pictograms it can represent the transformation into puberty, puberty blockers in trans kids, realisation of sexual preference

3 OF CUPS

A small group in joy. The quality of a gathering, a cooperation of people. No disharmony. Three people. Three siblings.

- With *Empress* and *4 of Wands*—*a* festival or party
- Workshops where ideas are shared
- A reunion
- With *8 of Coins*, friends or family in business together
- With *10 of Coins*, people sharing a rented house, apartment or commercial residence
- With *Knight of Wands* and distance cards it represents either people travelling together or people meeting up at a designated destination

4 OF CUPS

That which is other than what is being observed, anticipated, recognised.

- Events will happen unexpectedly
- A gift and/or an offer
- With *3 of Cups*—reunion, but with unforeseen and additional events involved
- With the sale of property, the offer, other than is finally accepted
- It informs the person you're with that there will be more options open to them in any situation than those they will be looking at
- With *3 of Coins*, an interview that results in perks. The same applies with *8 of Coins*
- A person, seemingly content with what they care about or have, has pleasant and unconsidered surprises yet to come

5

5 OF CUPS

Sadness or regret

- Mourning for a loss—either through death or separation
- A backward-looking person, someone concerned with past losses or disappointments
- So concerned with what has failed they do not seek alternatives
- Seeking to achieve in a certain area but not getting what is wanted
- As a foundation it means *No*: the person won't get what was desired
- Can represent a sequence of unsuccessful relationships that will not continue into the future
- With *Moon* and *4 of Wands* or *5 of Wands* this sequence can be the Blues (as a form of musical expression)

6 OF CUPS

The past is ultimately what this pictogram means, although it is also children and medieval villages.

- In the past
- With pictograms representing employment or work, a person involved with 'dead' things—anything from archaeology and antiques to history and genealogy
- Reunions: *3 of Cups*
- With *Moon* things of the past can have a life-long effect on the person or can be the cause of disillusionment
- With *Emperor*: archives or parochial people, rigidity of ideas and outlook. Doctrine. Cold police cases
- Can represents children of any species

7 OF CUPS

The pictogram shows a person looking at a sequence of hopes or fears none of which are realised. It also shows one image covered.

- Illusions
- Lies or a liar
- Can be little indulgences such as alcohol, sex, drugs, food etc. but not to the point of addiction
- Imagination
- 'What if' delusions
- Speculation
- With *Devil*—addiction
- With *Moon*— "mental illness" (quotation marks are because the term is current and does not take the entire person into account. There are other reasons for psychological koyaanisqatsi, like an unbalanced gut microbiome. We use the term here as it has a commonplace usage, in the current era.
- With *Moon* and *8 of Coins*—an individual employed to work with the people diagnosed with mental illness
- With *Moon* and *Emperor*, the institution or places of learning associated with "mental illness"

8 OF CUPS

Disappointment of a sort. In actuality realisation of release from an unbalanced or delusional relationship of any kind. When abandoning or being abandoned, by imbalance, adventure is possible. *8 of Cups* is actually an initiatory story of walking away from that which is unbalanced. Something missing. The knowledge that initiation is whereby we die to who we have been, get lost for a while then eventually are destined to find other ways of being. Although it is sort of sad, bear in mind that when this card is in a primary position it heralds difference. Not known yet.

- Walking away from an unbalanced situation: honesty and vitality is missing in the relationship or situation. The person to whom the map/layout relates cannot yet see where they are going but know exactly where they have been
- Can be disappointment that has already occurred
- The cup that is missing (the *Ace of Cups*) shows an innate imbalance
- Sense of sadness, but also haltingly exciting
- The Dark Night of the Soul is almost over
- Leaving stuff behind
- Disappointment in transition

9 OF CUPS

The *wish* card

- Happiness
- Satisfactory outcome or situation
- *Yes*
- Gets what is wanted depending on surrounding images
- Very auspicious circumstances
- Can be a very happy person or a buffoon or a comedian
- The only time the *9 of Cups* is inauspicious is when it falls with *Devil*: gluttony, the root cause of obesity (poisonous ingredients in food) or a range of self-serving self-indulgences
- Also greed and self-righteousness

10 OF CUPS

A house, home &/or family. A place and/or state of being, is somehow better than even *9 of Cups*. Occasionally also means the unknown experience of death (to the living).

- Shared joy
- With *Justice* can be contracts of sale
- With *10 of Coins* and *Death* is the completion of construction of a house
- With *3 of Cups* it is a family reunion
- With *Moon* and *9 of Swords* there are likely to be plumbing or water problems
- With *Emperor* and *Tower* disaster will occur that will require insurance of home and contents
- With *7 of Swords* and either *Moon* or *2 of Swords* there are thieves in the area of the person's home
- With *8 of Swords* and any inauspicious cards the person concerned is likely (for whatever reasons) to be house-bound
- Sometimes this pictogram can represent death, but even then, *Death* will be almost certain to turn up. Years before the research and marketing of quality medications to treat HIV AIDS many humans died from this disease. Those who sat with me often had *10 of Cups* as an outcome to their future

KNIGHT OF CUPS

The knights are not people; they are states or modes of movement or flow. The *Knight of Cups* is a follow-through card: whatever is happening is honorable and can be trusted; it displays a feeling of good will. Everything is okay. It shows that the person will be able to trust the others. Will also signify an offering.

- Of detriment when it shows up with *Moon* and *7 of Cups*—opiate-based drug abuse
- An offer being made
- With *4 of Wands*—an invitation
- With *7 of Cups*—the offer is untrustworthy or comes to nothing
- With *Hanged Man* and *9 of Swords*—can be a person who gives too much and is easily hurt. Suicidal ideation resulting from unresolved trauma

CHILD OF CUPS

One central theme is the seed or conception of an artistic pursuit, another is a child born under one of the following: Cancer, Pisces, Scorpio.

- With illness pictograms, indicates a child with eye, ear, nose or throat problems
- Art, painting, drawing, sculpture, visual art
- Can be animals, human or otherwise, usually dark-skinned/coated
- With *Death*—month or sign of Scorpio
- With *Moon*—month or sign of Pisces
- With *Chariot*—month or sign of Cancer
- With *Hierophant*, specifically, the roman catholic church

WOMAN OF CUPS

A woman of any species.

- Water sign person—Cancer, Scorpio, Pisces, unless accompanying Wayshowers indicate that the advice means otherwise
- A dark person, hair and/or complexion
- Holds onto their emotions for any number of reasons (hence the urn)
- A person of the sea depending on the accompanying cards such as *6 of Swords* with *10 of Coins*: a woman who lives on a boat or similar
- With *6 of Swords* and *4 of Wands*—a surfer or someone who gains pleasure from the water
- With *8 of Coins* and *Ace of Cups*—a swimmer or a swimming coach
- As place, can be south coast of any country (think Dover, England, Sicily, parts of Greece)
- Also represents a cremation urn

MAN OF CUPS

A male of any species. A water sign: Cancer, Scorpio, or Pisces

- Sometimes represent a medical doctor if around *Temperance* or *Emperor*
- Very often tech or gaming icons
- Can also represent a dark-haired, dark skinned or swarthy individual
- 'The king of hearts': a deeply admired and loving person
- Of the sea, depending on the accompanying images such as *6 of Swords* with *10 of Coins*: a yachter or a one who lives on a boat, or boat-like home like a houseboat or barge
- With *6 of Swords* and *4 of Wands*—a surfer or someone who gains pleasure from the water
- With *8 of Coins*, *Ace of Cups*, a swimmer or a swimming coach but one who work for the love of it
- With *8 of Coins*, someone who works with water (from a fisher to a plumber to a submariner, a diver, a navigator, a shipwright, you get it)

COINS (PENTACLES, DISCS)

Practical, physical, material

1

ACE OF COINS

The pictorial representation of the roots of powers of matters, physicality, money, finances or income coming or going, money and commodities. The foundations of the physical world. Matter. Earth/soil/humus.

- With *Ace of Wands* and an accompanying *Knight*—new matter
- With *Strength*—rock solid, solid rock, stone, foundations (as in a building)
- With *Sun*—material &/or fiscal wealth
- With *Law/Justice*, money gained through legal means—the sale of property for example
- With *Emperor*, can represent a government grant or a scholarship, also superannuation
- Bitcoin digital currency, especially if the card lands in Chokmah
- Money—fiat currency

2 OF COINS

Shared innovation: Divided money, shared accommodations, financial partnerships, division of possessions and or money, part-time income or work; part-time anything. Money, finances, securities. Settlements. Financial or practical partnerships of any kind.

- With *Ace of Coins*—a large sum of money (in the client's considered opinion), or settlement, divided between two or more parties
- With *10 of Coins*—shared accommodation
- With *10 of Coins* and *Moon*—sharing shop fronts or displays
- With *8 of Coins*—part-time or casual work
- Will be unstable employment or financial situation: things can go either way
- An imbalance in either/and practicalities. Who gets the higher half, who gets the lower?

3 OF COINS

An interview, or impersonal discussion.

- With *8 of Coins*—a job interview, or simply an interview: can be mutual, as with chatting to an architect or plumber
- With *Emperor* and *Temperance*, it can represent a medical consultation
- With home or dwelling pictograms such as *10 of Coins* or *Cups*, accompanied by others, such as *10 of Wands*, *Moon*, *5 of Wands*, represents either the building of a place or work/renovations being carried out on a building. *3 of Coins*, in this instance, is someone discussing the plans

4 OF COINS

Staying. Holding-onto.

- Holding onto money/possessions/position
- A deposit
- A small stash of money
- With *Devil*, hoarding
- A person who doesn't or won't spend money
- Limited liquid assets
- In the human body it can be hard to shift unwanted body fat, fixed joints, arthritic conditions, gall stones, kidney stones
- Can represent time sequences—four days, four weeks, four months, four years
- Skills-training or university degree, especially when accompanied by the Emperor
- With *Ace of Coins*—a deposit or part thereof
- With *Strength*—body-fat or obesity, gall or kidney stones, constipation
- With *Moon*—fluid retention, PCOS
- Reclusive

5 OF COINS

No money, destitution, poverty, lacking.

- In legal settlement cases—a lot less money or a complete loss
- A deficit
- Overspending
- Bankruptcy (of whatever kind)
- With *Strength* it can be such illnesses as anorexia or bulimia
- In Yesod, on the Stargate map, is often a lack of a certain mineral or hormonal normalcy
- With *7 of Swords* and *Moon* there is a theft
- With *8 of Swords*, indebtedness that cannot be escaped, or a heavy fine
- With *Devil* it can be poverty or financial loss due to obsessive or unwise spending
- With *Moon*—poverty of mind; poverty of emotion; entrenched poverty
- With *Emperor* and *Ace of Swords*, departmental or governmental cuts to funding of any kind
- With *Tower* and *10 of Coins* it can represent crashes on a stock exchange (large or small)

6 OF COINS

Paying out or getting paid.

- Getting rid of a debt
- Being repaid money that was owed
- With *8 of Coins* it is either the wages paid or a person who pays wages
- With *Magician* and a *person* image it can represent someone who patronises or belittles others
- With *5 of Coins* and a person: an individual who undervalues themselves or *feels*/is impoverished by others

7 OF COINS

Growth (not always healthy). The fulfilment of the growth process.

- Increases of money
- The interest on investments
- Productivity
- Savings
- Increases in material value as for the value of property
- Gardens, plant nurseries, roots
- With *Devil* and *4 of Swords*—a controlled or dormant cancer/stunted growth
- With *Devil* and other relevant pictograms, an illicit investment, like insurance or benefitting from slave labour
- With *3 of Swords* and *Devil*—a possibly dangerous or carcinogenic growth removed (mole or tumour) but can as easily be warts
- With *Devil* and *Empress*—rampant growth such as occurs in tropical locations, or unwanted growth such as happens with an unwanted pregnancy, mould, fungal infestations, facial or body hair, infestations of any kind

8 OF COINS

Work.

- The word *work* (as in employment or an idea that will work)
- Sometimes it's a job
- Work being done on anything from a car, to a house to a human body
- What will work or won't work
- I don't really need to give a this-goes-with-that here because it really is simply the word WORK and can mean many things
- It is necessary to discern the difference, with them, of vocation, job, employment, work, career

9 OF COINS

Quality rather than quantity, mistress of all they behold.

- Beautiful
- Quality not quantity

- No matter which way: you can't lose
- Studying and learning then becoming (through life, not institutions necessarily)
- To love
- No domination
- State of earthly grace
- Reputation in the world: as well as, or in difference to, the way you feel about yourself
- Quality, with whatever it falls on or with
- Spatial genius
- Feng shui

10 OF COINS

Where we gather, where we trade.

- Usually a rented or a leased dwelling, house, shop, market stall or place of business
- Can be a house of knowledge if attended by *Emperor* or pictograms representing study and learning. *Mystery*, for example, would be a place of the study of the occult, *Temperance* would indicate a place where the healing arts are studied, a *Child of Cups* with *10 of Coins* and *Temperance* would explain a place where visual arts are studied
- It is not *10 of Cups* but can become so: an incomplete dwelling or the construct of a difference between renting and owning
- Houses where money moves—banks, credit companies
- With *Knight of Coins*—caravan, bus, mobile home
- With *5 of Wands* and *10 of Wands*—a dwelling being built or renovated
- With *2 of Coins*—a shared rental/house, a shared business
- With *Emperor*—bank/school/hospital buildings
- With *Strength*—building societies, dojos or dance studios
- With *Law*—a courtroom, the signing of leases or property contracts
- With *child of Cups*—*blue chips*, so-called *sure things* on the stock market
- With *6 of Swords*—houseboat, yacht, launch or ship

KNIGHT OF COINS

A large form of transportation: four-wheel drive, van, truck, caravan, mobile home, train, bus.

- On-going practicalities
- The advice *take care of business*
- In a process—doing the work: plod, plod
- Covering one's own interests
- Ongoing financial transactions
- Movement of transactions
- With *10 of Wands*—carrying heavy loads
- With *2 of Coins*—part-time financial venture

CHILD OF COINS

An Earth sign child animal/month—Taurus, Capricorn or Virgo.

- Private study
- Small personal business enterprise
- *Child* pictograms are engagement with human children or other animals, or things you do in a small way
- With *Empress*—the month or sign of Taurus (not *Hierophant*)
- With *Devil*—the month of or sign of Capricorn
- With *Hermit*—the month or sign of Virgo
- With *Knight of Wands* and *Wheel of Fortune*—craft or food markets, fairs
- With *Strength*—big kid or an adult behaving like a big kid, of any species

WOMAN OF COINS

A female animal (of any species) of Earth: Capricorn, Virgo, Taurus.

- An individual maker, sole trader
- A CEO/financier
- A potter
- A farmer
- A hunter
- A builder
- A worker of ochre and clay
- A custodian of burials and bloodlines
- A tracker
- With *Strength*—a big individual: strong rather than obese
- A hoarder
- With *8 of Coins* and *10 of Cups/Coins*, in real-estate
- Other species, coloured pelt, wings or display, brown, bronze, sometimes copper

MAN OF COINS

A male animal of any species: earth—Virgo, Capricorn, Taurus

- A maker, sole trader
- A maintainer of weapons and shields
- A potter
- A farmer
- A hunter
- A builder
- Military personnel
- Police, enforcers, prison guards
- A worker of ochre and clay
- A custodian of burials and bloodlines
- A tracker
- With *Strength*—a big individual: strong rather than obese
- A business person or an earthy one
- A person dark of skin and hair
- Any of the above descriptions given for woman of Earth

SWORDS

(always tricky things if not in exquisite balance)

Intellectual, violatory, aggressive

ACE OF SWORDS

Cutting or dividing, will-power, intent, decisions.

- Sharp objects
- Divisions
- Determination
- Discipline
- Someone in authority
- Chefs with knives
- Tattooist needles
- Acupuncture (with *8 of Coins*, an acupuncturist)
- Martial artists
- With *7 of Swords*—bound to a commitment and can't get out of it
- With *8 of Wands*—boundaries around land or property
- With *8 of Wands* and *Lovers*—sub-division of property
- Can literally represent a sword. I, for example, train with the Japanese sword in a traditional martial art

2 OF SWORDS

Unable to see, unable to decide, intractable.

- *2 of Swords* is the *Journey* pictogram that is akin to *Mystery* among the Wayshowers
- Not seen
- Indecision
- Stalemate
- Inward looking
- It can indicate, in a dispute, that one's back is covered
- Behind the scenes
- Behind you
- Peace
- Meditation
- Not seeing
- Can indicate eye-sight problems or things to do with limited vision (with *Star*)
- Can indicate living or being by, or near, the ocean

3 OF SWORDS

Separation, breaking away, heartfelt.

- Separation
- Being away from your loved ones
- It is not always a problem: can indicate when a baby comes out of the womb, a journey away from home and missing people, home sickness
- With *Tower* or other pictograms of ill-health—heart illness or related to the heart
- Heartstrings, literal or metaphorical
- With cards indicating surgery, whatever is removed from the body, including a newborn infant
- Whatever is removed that causes heartache
- Can be used in a sentence when the word *separate* is necessary

4 OF SWORDS

Waiting.

- Waiting
- Doing nothing
- Nothing happening
- Just the way it is
- Resting
- Era sequences—four days, four weeks, four months, four years
- With *10 of Coins*, sometimes *8 of Wands* (inside or out): crypts, tombs, burial grounds, graveyards, cemeteries

5 OF SWORDS

Conflict.

- Argument or dispute (somebody loses)
- Struggle but *not* gentle
- An argument that's going to come back on you later
- With *5 of Wands*/*Emperor*—industrial dispute or strike
- With *Devil*—drunken, or drug related violence; domestic violence
- With *Tower*, *Death* or any of the Dark Night of the Soul images, violence, from local to international

6 OF SWORDS

Troubled waters to calm.

- Era sequence—six days, six weeks, six months
- A journey or process out of trouble; from troubled waters to calm
- On or across water close to the country in which the person lives
- Short journeys across water
- Surfers
- Divers or people who fish (with *Hanged Man*)
- Boats
- With *Moon* and *8 of Coins* it is a professional fisher
- When death is assured but not going to happen for a long time
- With *World*—long international journeys
- With *10 of Coins*—house-boat, vessel on water you can live on
- With *Knight of Swords*—fast moving things on or in the water

7 OF SWORDS

Sneaky, sly, cunning or logistical. Stealthy action/s in the face of otherwise certain defeat.

- It suggests the person involved be wary and/or calculating
- Identity (or other) theft
- A stalker
- A card of the sneak
- Avoidance of confrontation, avoidance
- Getting out of a possibly dangerous or detrimental situation
- Cunning
- Can indicate a thief or theft
- Can also be clever—the art of strategy utilised by the gathering of intelligence
- With *Moon*—someone spreading rumours
- With *5 of Coins*—loss through theft
- With *Emperor* it can indicate anything from a governmental body planning in secret to graft or corruption
- With *Devil* and *9 of Swords*, can indicate a virus or bacteria (unseen) that will make someone ill

8 OF SWORDS

Stuck, trapped, bound, committed.

- Inability to change: there's nothing the person can do about a situation
- The person's hands are tied
- Limitations
- Fix it or forget it. Nothing can be done to change the situation beyond what's already available
- Commitment—in it for the long run
- Can't move
- People losing a license
- Living along a difficult-access driveway, track or road
- Delays the person can do nothing about
- No action
- Can be an injury keeping a person restrained
- With legal information, can indicate anything from contracts to imprisonment
- With *8 of Wands*—stuck somewhere without transport
- With *Star*—a commitment lasting for up to seventeen years (like parenthood)
- Delays or cancellations around airports. Computer or network failure
- Bondage, if with the *2 of Cups*.

9 OF SWORDS

It's in the wee hours that the dying die and the newly born arrive. It is said that to be awake at 3 A.M. is to sense souls seeking liberation from their flesh or admittance to all that life expresses, passing twixt and tween on that strange and eerie pre-dawn wind.

- Worry
- Terror
- PTSD
- The card of sickness, or stillness, the cause of the illness cannot be seen
- The health industry
- Tiredness
- Fatigue
- Anxiety
- Late nights
- Night shift
- With *Moon*—insomnia or bad dreams that awaken the person
- With the *5 of Wands*, *Child of Cups*, *Moon*—singing the blues

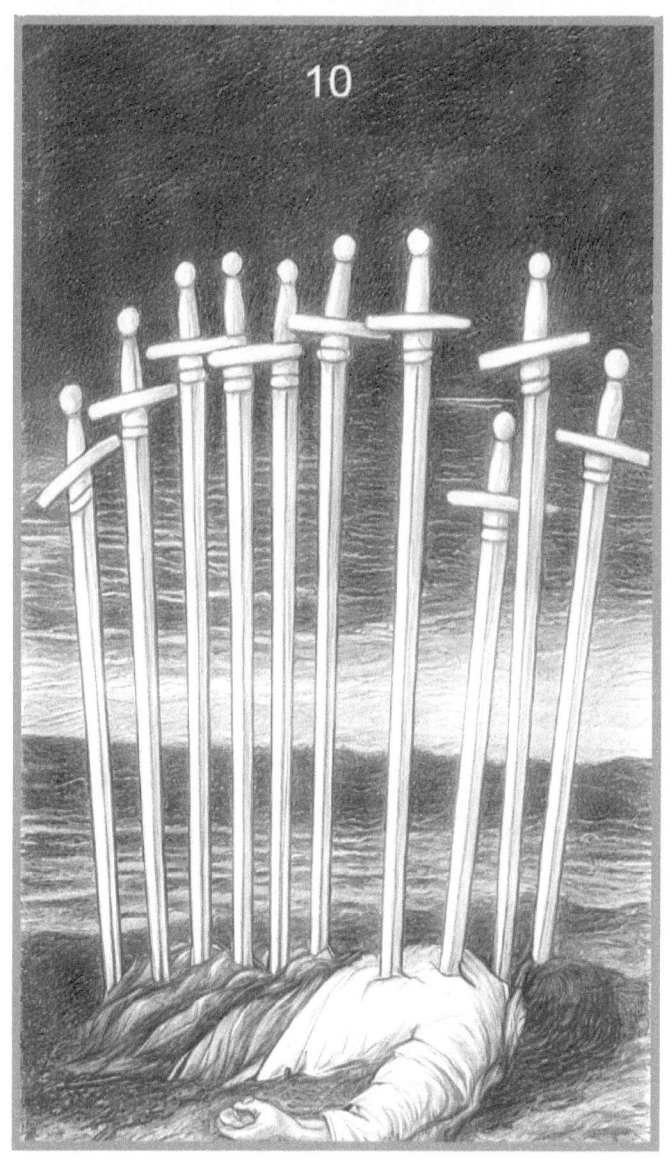

10 OF SWORDS

How, when and why. These are the questions necessary when focusing on events surrounding this message. Not always what it at first glance seems. Not always a problem.

- Physical pain
- Back pain
- Tattoo
- Body modification
- Back-stabbing
- Violence of word or action
- Cruelty and the result of cruelty
- Betrayal
- With *8 of Coins/Ace of Swords*—tattooing, piercing, acupuncture, chiropractic adjustment
- With *Ace of Wands, Empress*—medical IVF
- With *Star*—stabbing pain in the eyes (vision); injury from broken glass
- With *Judgment, child of Coins*—toothache
- With *3 of Swords*—heart illness; radical severance

KNIGHT OF SWORDS

Speed has many references from Grand Prix to methamphetamine, from hypervigilance to rage

- Speeding and/or speeding fine
- Aggression, violent or scary behaviour
- Attack
- Impatience
- A swift resolution to a situation
- With *10 of Coins* – mobile phone
- Two wheels—bicycle, scooter or motor bike
- With *Star*– quick or short flights
- With *Knight of Wands* or *Chariot*—fast cars/vehicles
- With *Strength*—fast horses, race horses, greyhounds, other swift hounds such as Lurchers
- With *Magician*—brusque, no-nonsense people
- With *Devil*—amphetamine-type drugs or cocaine
- Also with *Devil* and financial gains or losses this card relates to horse-racing as a gambling addiction
- With 7 of Swords/*Law/Justice*—lost driver's licence because of speeding
- With many of the *Wands*—fast words, short stories, articles, people with quick tongues: often thoughtless
- With a *Child* of any suit—a child who is hyperactive or unable to do things at a steady pace, ADHD

CHILD OF SWORDS

Child of Swords, small pale skinned/pelted/winged animal person.

- Intellect or intellectual pursuits
- Air sign child animal: Libra, Aquarius, Gemini
- With *Woman of Swords*—a young woman animal, usually fair skinned and/or blonde
- With *Lovers*—the era or sign of Gemini
- With *Star*—he era or sign of Aquarius; ideas, inspiration, the thinking process
- With *Law/Justice*—the era or sign of Libra
- With *Strength*—any animal, a pale animal

WOMAN OF SWORDS

- An air sign female animal—Libra, Aquarius, Gemini
- A fair-haired or grey/silver-haired, light-skinned person of any species
- A human being of intelligence unless they fall with cards of detriment whereby they become a person with a cutting tongue or wit
- Can be a web designer, digital app creator, gamer or coder

MAN OF SWORDS

See WOMAN OF SWORDS—same, only male

SEASONAL SEQUENCES

CHILD PICTOGRAMS

Child of Swords and Lovers – the era of Gemini
Child of Swords and Star – the era of Aquarius
Child of Swords and Justice – the era of Libra

Child of Cups and Chariot – the era of Cancer
Child of Cups and Death – the era of Scorpio
Child of Cups and Moon – the era of Pisces

Child of Coins and Devil – the era of Capricorn
Child of Coins and Hermit – the era of Virgo
Child of Coins and Hierophant – the era of Taurus

Child of Wands and Temperance – the era of Sagittarius
Child of Wands and Strength – the era of Leo
Child of Wands and Emperor – the era of Aries

PART 4—THE PRACTICE

WEEK ONE

Studying the preceding chapters will have lubed your psyche and consciousness like oil on a rusty hinge and you are ready to experiment with the practicalities and later, in the BOOK OF SECRETS, is a complete reading for you to consider.

If you have not done so already now is the time to go out and purchase your card pack. It is ultimately your choice which pack you go with but for the time being I strongly suggest you acquire those with the images used in this book's format and familiarise yourself with how we see what we see.

When home open the packet and throw away the two extraneous cards and the booklet. In a quiet place and lay out a cloth, placing the cards of 78 pictograms on it, face down.

Beginning with the one on top turn over each, and recall as much as you can from your notes, by the visuals only, saying as many of the key meanings *aloud*. This is important as it establishes the habit of verbal interaction with the enigma.

Continue this for the entire 78 pictograms and repeat this a couple more times on the first day.

NEUROPLASTICITY

Be patient with yourself because your neural network is not yet knowing what you are doing. Neuroplasticity rewiring of synapses with activity usually takes between three days and three months to become familiar. Be super-careful to avoid the temptation of laying out spreads for yourself.

For the first week this is the only practical work.

WEEK TWO

'Open' the 78 cards by placing them, one at a time (face down) as in the diagram. This clears any previous data. *Never shuffle them yourself.* Shuffling them at any stage is likely to contaminate the cards with your own future experiences. While training, divide the pack into clumps then put back together again, a bit willy-nilly.

Pick up the packs in any order and place them together as one.

Turn up the top three cards, side by side, and recall what they say as a group (exactly like a sentence). DON'T GUESS a meaning, this has nothing to do with some *woowoo* idea.

When you comprehend the sentence, say aloud what will happen with the mental intention of recognising the events the following day in however small or large their capacity.

If you do not do so already you are to pay attention to international news; reading newspapers and/or checking e-news for local and world events because the layouts of those three cards will often reflect what's projected by media. Throughout the week keep refreshing your knowledge of the meanings of each pictogram.

WEEK THREE

Ask friends if they will let you experiment on them. Use one or more of the maps in the following chapters, always opening the cards as described in week two.

Suggest they keep a record of the interpretations and to let you know when and if the event/s occur. Best done, in the 21st century, on a cell phone or tablet.

Keep to basics and don't elaborate or generalise as these are failings that can become habitual (dooming you to worrying whether you are right or wrong). Only tell what the cards represent. Again, DON'T GUESS.

The more you practice the more proficient you become and the more likely the chances of accuracy. Tarot wants to trust you but you are the student. You will be required to prove yourself through consistency.

Keep on like this for a few months, slowly introducing more than one spread into your sessions until you have a comfortable half hour or hour's information to give, while constantly refreshing your knowledge of pictogram meanings and the application of maps. For sanity's sake get friends of friends to book only through one platform. I use email. People will come at you through text, Instagram, any DM outlet, WhatsApp or other. Keeping one platform makes life easy. Establish a method of equal energy exchange – payment of one kind or another – that's easy for the client. It's okay to begin with a barter system: they bring you quality protein, fresh fruit or vegetables, or other things you need. Or you can go straight to charging a currency. Equal exchange however, is pivotal.

If you're good, don't advertise. They'll find you. People talk.

…

THE CONSULTATION FROM BEGINNING TO END

IN PERSON

We cover Remote Viewing (online sessions) when necessary.

CONTACT

From the moment of first contact you're aware, on some level, that the session is going to happen. This impacts both you and the coming client.

When making appointments you need only secure a first name as, in many instances, the person coming could require anonymity, especially if they're either uncertain of your authenticity or else events in their lives mean they prefer this. Ask for a contact number in case circumstances arise and you have to cancel, and vice versa, or, with remote viewing, to be able to chat if technical glitches happen. They know about you and have come into your metaphorical castle, to not introduce themselves (without giving away vital information as this will wreck your objectivity) they are arrogant.

You experience a type of anxiety/tension (that never goes away) on session days. That's normal.

Put the client at ease from the moment they arrive. They need to leave their shoes outside. Make them comfortable. Set up the recording method. Ask their star sign but nothing else and tell them not to feed you information for now, till questions.

Then 'open' the cards as per the diagram.

Pick up the five packs in any order and straighten them. Hand them to the person opposite you to shuffle.

Focus on each map. Watch the other person's hands as they lay down *past, present, future* in DEAD RECKONING.

SHUFFLE/ORDER

Shuffling is other than what it appears. In part one *time* was discussed, DNA the cyclic nature of ages, years and eras. People often say they are lousy at shuffling. They don't understand. They've had since at least 2.4 billion years to interact enough with lived experience to do this without thinking. That's the microbiome. We each inherit at least that much ancestral data. No one so much shuffle the cards as sort them into order in much the same way as a virtuoso pianist plays a concerto: if they were to look at the images of the pictograms and attempt to place them in some seeming order they could not do so, in the same way as the pianist who, if attempting to look at the keys whilst working, could not play intricate music. Their genome has the memory of everything experienced, over those billions of years, within the flesh of their fingers and can't make a mistake. There is nothing random in this process.

It's a convenient idea to tell the client the events will happen in a supposedly fixed number of years but really, also explain that the idea is madness, as life doesn't unfold in a this-after-that sequence but is a process of experience, often layered together.

The idea of *past*, *present* and *future* is a construct. Constructs are non-manifest ideas. Only *now* is real and even then *now* can be biased by narratives and experiences remembered. This is why, in the era of when I write this, police do not take eye-witness accounts into consideration as two people will see or sense an event very differently to each other. Even in personal relationships this happens. An individual's past is in their memory only; a series of snapshots that people have a tendency to adhere to for the sake of both sharing with others and to affirm an identity. A collective past is that recorded, along with biases, ideologies and propaganda, often certainties that are very dubious (called Shifting Baseline Syndrome[2]), as history. *Future* is also an idea—a limitless plethora of possibilities based only on what is already known, spiced with variables. Is *future* a result of current actions and interactions? That's speculative. It's all illusion—hypothesis—until experienced. I'm sure no one sees a comet on collision-course with earth, except perhaps those specifically looking who, by chance or circumstance, see an approach through the lens of the Gran Telescopio Canarias.

So what is it we do and should the BOOK OF SECRETS be feared (as xians say, a tool of their *devil*)?
- What we do should not, logically, be possible.
- No. Fear is a bodily reaction to a potentially damaging attack. Calm, yes. A clear mind, yes. Anxiety, sure.

---

[2] https://earth.org/shifting-baseline-syndrome/

Trepidation, yes. Excitement and curiosity? Of course. Fear, no.

But... Once said, never unsaid.

PART 1 OF THE CONSULTATION

The variety and order of maps in face-to-face sessions is different to those read via remote viewing. And even though a minimum of two maps are rejected from the online sessions you will still go over an hour. Opening is done by you, as per previous instruction

DEAD RECKONING

Hand them your BOOK OF SECRETS. They shuffle and cut into three stacks. Ask them to only stop shuffling when they are ready, that it's not up to you to tell them to stop. The person will often ask whether the stacks need to be the same size or whether they should use a certain hand to cut them. It doesn't matter. The stack that was at the top of the deck is called *future*, the stack in the centre we call *present*, the one on the bottom we call *past*.

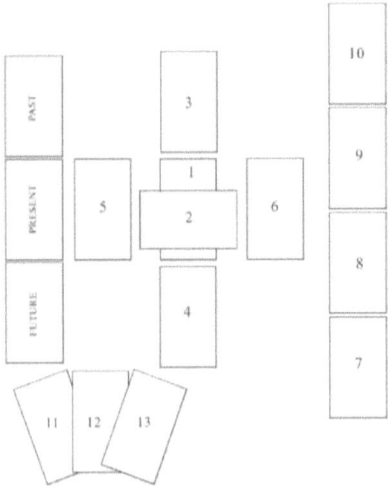

Image: dead reckoning

Watch how they cut the deck because people have many ways of doing so and it is up to you to be alert. Lay the three packs to one side as to the left and ask their sun sign. If, for example, that person is a Leo then this person is a person *of Wands* and they will be the significator for the entirety of the session unless you are certain that it is also representing someone else. To do that Tarot will often replace a person image or, occasionally, one that represents a child or other animal.

Remind the person opposite you to say nothing, and respond as little as possible, so that you keep objectivity and remain as detached as you can. Sometimes this becomes difficult because when you hit an instantly visual circumstance they can become emotional.

Advise that the first map in a sequence *cracks* the cards open and allows the Book to get to know them. Even though it is general rather (in most instances) specific, it actually goes to the heart of experiences. Sometimes these three maps are so awesome that you'll wish you didn't have to go further, and you'll probably want to explain that to the client… but they'll always want to see the rest. The DEAD RECKONING is like an umbrella and all other maps will rest in their shade. If the first maps are seemingly upbeat any fragile or worrisome experiences, later, will have the sheen of the umbrella.

Beginning with the centre stack that represents the *present* is where you will see what events are in the recognisable now and soon.

Best to say that the terms *past/present/future* are misleading, so the client is aware that the process is one of destiny unfurling. On occasion everything you tell them has seemingly already happened. There's a but.

Many events that have already happened have long-lasting and far-reaching ramifications and continuums, so don't be put off. Beginnings and endings are observations/constructs only.

Lay the leftover cards to one side, with the pictogram on the bottom of the stack placed on the top, image facing you, as this is significant to the overall pattern.

Once you have read this map you do the same with the pack representing what's to come (*future*) and, lastly, the pack representing what has been perceptually or actually experienced, but that can include an historic *past* that is seemingly disparate from the client.

Why we read in this way is because the *past* is that which unresolved, or represents ongoing events of influence. In some cases, other people's *pasts*. This latter is for many reasons: the other is someone, as yet, unmet who will be important and readily recognised when they talk about themselves, this person is already known and will have an ongoing impact. Sometimes this other person is body-dead and has left things incomplete. They want the person with you to fix the problem. When world events reveal themselves it is a form of revelation.

Recall the 2008 financial crash? For three years leading to when that happened the BOOK OF SECRETS talked about 1929 and people jumping out of the windows of tall buildings, plunging to their deaths (*Tower*). The understanding, in 2024, of more to come, is unprecedented but will have comparisons that will be remembered, maybe. In the current era it is plausible to consider that renditions of past events can be reconfigured due to bias. Or has this always been so?

Above is a traditional layout with three extra cards fanned to the bottom left. Decades ago I discovered that there is simply insufficient data in the original ten pictogram layout and that by adding the extra information an enhanced, 3D understanding of not only what is right in front of you but, also peripherally.

We don't interpret the maps as is usual because the information presented here was not learned from any book or manual.

1. Centre, facing you. The central situation, or people, closest to the present day
2. Centre, sideways to 1: crosses, adds information
3. Above centre, is what is in the person's mind or events of significance happening at a distance
4. Below centre is their environment, or a most easily recognised event
5. Left of centre: what's already happened, or current events in continuum

6. Right of centre is what flows from the pictograms already laid out, where the situation is leading or, if a court card, people who will have an impact

FOUR UP THE SIDE (laid out vertically from close to you to farthest away).
7. The client or the person affecting them for harm or calm
8. The environment—home, work or otherwise—in which they will experience events
9. Hopes and fears, not actualities
10. An outcome, or where the events on the map are leading

THREE IN A FAN SHAPE

The 11th, 12th, and 13th pictograms are read as a separate pattern and represent extenuating circumstances or seemingly impersonal events that are occurring to the side of the above.

Example: Client is a sex worker. Identifies with the LGBTQI+ community, and is also a performer. The three cards to the side were

Image: a woman murdered

When I explained it is the murder of a woman they asked if it was them, afraid. I said I didn't know but the fact of the three being to one side suggested the importance of the event. An educated response was *no*. If it had been them the cards would be in the centre. The following day, a colleague, a burlesque performer, had the same three to the side. Same terror and question, same answer.

Within a week a young comedienne was murdered in Royal Park, Melbourne. The two people who had the data in those three cards met up at the vigil held for the dead person and both talked about having Tarot readings with this turning up.

More people had the sequence over the following weeks. There was some confusion, but no. Another woman was murdered, again on the north side of Melbourne. Same cards, different killing. There were five killed like the first, that year.

The DEAD RECKONING (as with every map) is *never* read as individual cards. The whole pattern will, in most cases, tell you one thing: one event. No isolated pictogram ever means only a single thing and therefore it is impossible to gain a clear sentence. Use this map in remote viewing but forgo the pack considered the *past*. Unnecessary.

MAP 2: THE GROVE

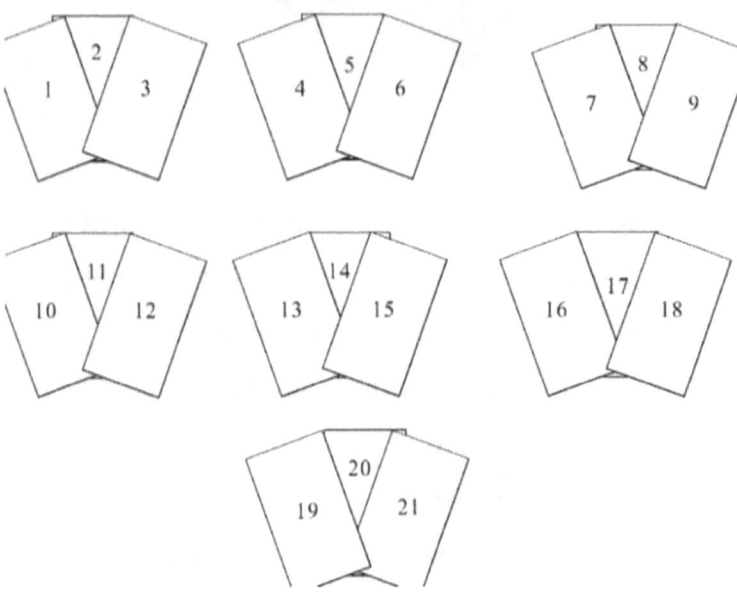

Image: the grove map

After the first map, you pick up the cards and hand them to across. They shuffle again. Take them back and lay them out face up in the pattern described in the above image. Each of the fans of 3 cards could tell of separate events but some or all could relate to the one event, with the fan of 3 cards at the bottom of the map (19, 20, 21) representing the foundation of this section and, as such, are a main focus. The interpretation will depend on all of the other pictograms.

This layout will also be read in relationship to anything you have already seen thus far in the consultation.

Use the GROVE map in remote viewing.

MAP 3: EPIGENETIC EVENTS

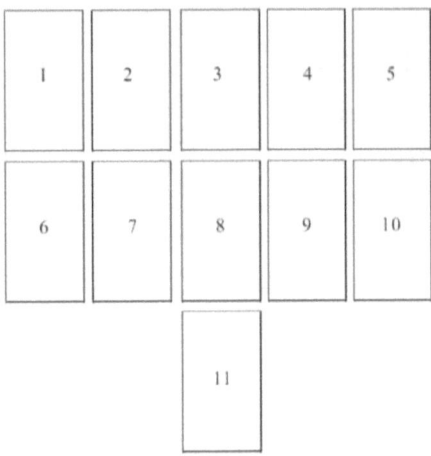

Image: significant in some way, but not central

The person shuffles the entire pack.

When they hand them back to you, you discard the first six cards, off the top, and lay out the seventh (7th), face up for two rows of five cards. The second-last card (11) is at the base of the map and is a foundation for the information.

This is always about people or events that will impact the person's life, not central to obvious destiny (DEAD RECKONING, GROVE, STARGATE, CONTINUUM).

It shows obstructions, inspirations or a person of significant interest.

Your interpretation will depend on all of the other cards in the map, and no single one will mean anything on its own.

Don't use this map for remote session.

MAP 4: STARGATE

Major Events (can also be used as an overall health evaluation)

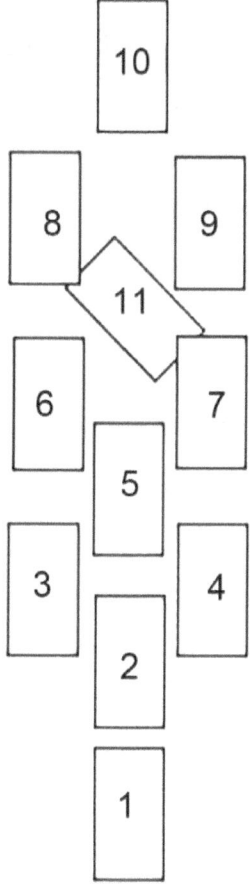

Image: stargate

- 1, Earth, is the foundation of the person's life: where they live, the environment in which they conduct their lives, the place of their lives. All in the future. If you are using this spread for health related matters, then this position is the feet and legs

- 2, Moon, will foretell events occurring at a distance, behind their back or deep in their thoughts. If using the spread for health matters this region is the genitals, reproductive and urinary system, hips and pelvis, also the person's state of mind

- 3, Mercury, foretells travel, journeys and movement of any kind, transportation, communication of every kind including the spoken and written word. If using this map as a health spread, it relates to the hips

- 4, Venus, is interpreted in one of many ways: the arts, festivals, parties, celebrations, motherhood, a mother or grandmother (the client's or otherwise). It is sex, intimacy, fecundity, gardening or gardens. If using this map for health this card is any dysfunctions of the sexuality of an individual, including all sexually transmitted diseases, sexual abuse or abuses, deviant (non-consensual) sexual behaviour. It turns up with an *8 of Coins* the person works in an industry traditionally associated with women and/or sex. That includes selling Lamborghinis and underwear.

- 5, Sun, is the client or those people or situations that have an overpowering or overwhelming influence. The other cards in this and other maps inform you whether another person in this equation is an ally or of detriment. In all health matters card 5 is the solar plexus and major organs of the body such as the heart, liver, lungs, stomach, small and large intestines

- 6, Mars and this aligns it with everything from family and community to war, unrest and the martial arts. The gall bladder, the spleen and the adrenals. Other cards in other areas can aid in identification

- 7, Jupiter and represents their work and workplace, their financial situation and their position and reputation in society. With health, it is metabolism. On the one hand it shows the person's state of body-mass (or lack of it) in the *future*, and on the other, any viral, fungal, bacterial infections or cancers: anything with the ability to expand

- 8 is Saturn's gate. The image positioned here has a relevance to longevity, to history, to all things old, archaic and/or ancient. Institutions or even superstition and popular opinion of any kind. Health issues reflect the skeletal system, the joints, or long-term illness or dysfunction, inherited/genetic traits or disease, cultural ideas of what represents health or illness

- 9, Uranus: anything from astrology to technology, from disorder or chaos to electricity, electrical systems, nuclear technology. In health matters it refers to the central nervous system and adrenals

- 10, Neptune, is the outcome or the next stage of life unfolding, completions and, in some situations, fame or notoriety. In a human body it refers to the head, one's intellect, the outer ear and hearing, eyes, nose and mouth, not including the teeth

- 11, Pluto, is throat, atlas bone, brainstem, vocal chords, back teeth (including wisdom teeth), inner ear. The card positioned here is also called a KEY as the 11th position is sort of there and not. Pluto, in the hubris of a human construct has been deemed a planet, then not. It is in many ways information and knowledge that seems to form from nowhere known. Predictive depending on the card.

MAP 5: HORSE LATITUDE WARNING MAP

Image: lighthouse

GREAT VOYAGES OR BRUTAL TRUTH

A hundred or two years ago, historically, species—us and others—travelled by sea from land to foreign land. By boat or by three-masted clippers. Sometimes in the steerage of wind-powered death-traps and later in the bowels of the auxiliary steam ship. And here's where a map is interesting when you know the backstory. Let's examine invader-colonialism, because we can never be academically sure of any other kind, until the current era of yacht races, endurance and/or pleasure sailing, cruise ships or jet skis.

The calendar year is 1850 C.E. That's significant insofar as all of Europe, just a couple of years ago, rages, in uprising, for equality. 1848 C.E. is social upheaval and revolution, but only because of the arrogance of authoritarianism that holds purchase in many countries. And don't kid yourself for a moment, that's historically violent. The *Slave Act of 1807* is a farce, with the East- or West-India Company selling and transporting people, goods and misery, from the dark days of feudal Europe to colonies of confusion and privation.

The name HORSE LATITUDE refers to some thirty degrees north or south of the Equator, often beset by what are known as the *Doldrums*. Certain death for many. Yes, I've read the straw-horse-theory, about sailors spending all their money until getting to this part of the ocean but I have to question the validity of that, because why there?

HORSE LATITUDE prepares the client, *well in advance*, of danger. It's their lighthouse. The event, interpreted here, does not have to happen. Is not definitively fated.

Remind them, about now, that it is *they* who shuffle—sort—*they* who order the information for your interpretation. Therefore, *they know* what they are showing you. They want to *expose* the shoal, the reef, the danger, to avoid catastrophe. You are the visionary with the skill of the sextant, the lore-holder of the wisdom of fresh-water islands, and the spyglass that knows the proximity of the kraken.

An example is when a person sits with me after fourteen years and we come to this map. They say *I'll listen this time*. That map cautioned them, those years before, that a man of a certain star sign, and a woman of a certain star sign would ask her to show them what she had recently learned. Tarot explained she would be tired. Tarot specifically warned... *Don't climb. Whatever you do, don't climb*. She taught and performed for a circus troupe. She distinctly remembered the warning on the day she was asked to show two people her new trapeze technique and she chose to ignore it. Her inner voice had whispered the warning as she climbed the ladder. She did it anyway. She fell, breaking most of her bones. She did not sever her spinal column. The only upside, she said, is that she can still walk.

This map, by rights, should stand out as unique to other layouts. Why? If the person listens, there will be no hint of this elsewhere. Here, however, is where you use what you have learned—if the event is seen elsewhere—to hopefully lessen the impact.

This map is the same as for MAP 3, and it is your intent changes what will be told.

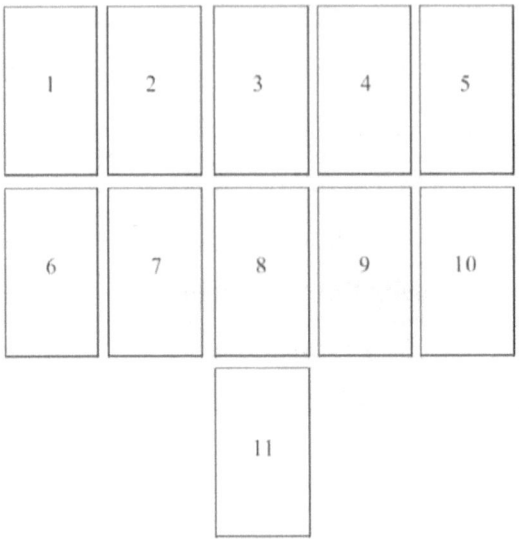

Image: horse latitude/warning

REMOTE VIEWING—Unnecessary

CASE HISTORY 1: THEY TOOK HEED

Phillip was a businessman who was setting up a new hair product range in Australia and who had put out a tender for a business partner. His warning was that he would be approached by an ordinary-looking man from an English-speaking country other than Australia (looked like New Zealand as the *6 of Swords* was present).

Phillip was warned to check the other person's credentials thoroughly or the business would fail.

He phoned me several weeks later, overjoyed. He had been approached by a man from New Zealand regarding the above matter and had checked up on him and found that he had lost his business licence several years before for shonky dealings. Phillip went into partnership with a friend who was also a lawyer.

The business, many years later, is now one of this country's top-selling hair products.

CASE HISTORY 2: THE PERSON WHO DIDN'T

There were actually two who were friends and who had appointments a week apart. I had seen both women on more than one occasion and had an inkling, when the second woman's warning mirrored the first. Both were warned not to go into investment real estate together or the *5 of Coins* would be the result.

They went ahead and bought strata-title units that had not been thoroughly checked out by the correct officials, thinking that they would get away with it and preferring to attempt to save on the money that would have been required to upgrade the structure of the building. The fiasco ended in bankruptcy. The event caused them to hate each other.

This map will also foretell warnings for others, close to the client.

CASE HISTORY 3: AGES AWAY

In early 2025 I received an email from a person I'd read for twenty one years ago. She wrote that she thought I was nuts at the time because the Horse Latitude saw her living with a murderer and had said to get out the only available exit. She'd been recently married. Did the suggestion bother her? I don't know. She never forgot though.

She birthed and raised two sons. No problem.

When they were older they left home for university and she and her husband of around twenty years split amicably. She became lovers with a new partner and they moved in together. When he attacked her she remembered. Immediately. She escaped through a bathroom window.

Will you ever question what you say? That never stops. Just so we're clear. A police officer who had been videoing when five of them had crammed into my small studio looking for the wife of a cold-case suspect who had got off a manslaughter charge, decades ago, known to frequent me for sessions. The cop later (they all did) came for a reading. Tarot had seen her marrying a man surrounded by water. Big catholic affair. She'd had no religion. Yes, she'd scoffed.

She'd eventually hooked up with the guy who ran a kayaking business in a coastal town and who was always on the water. They'd married in a cathedral to please his family.

MAP 6: CONTINUUM

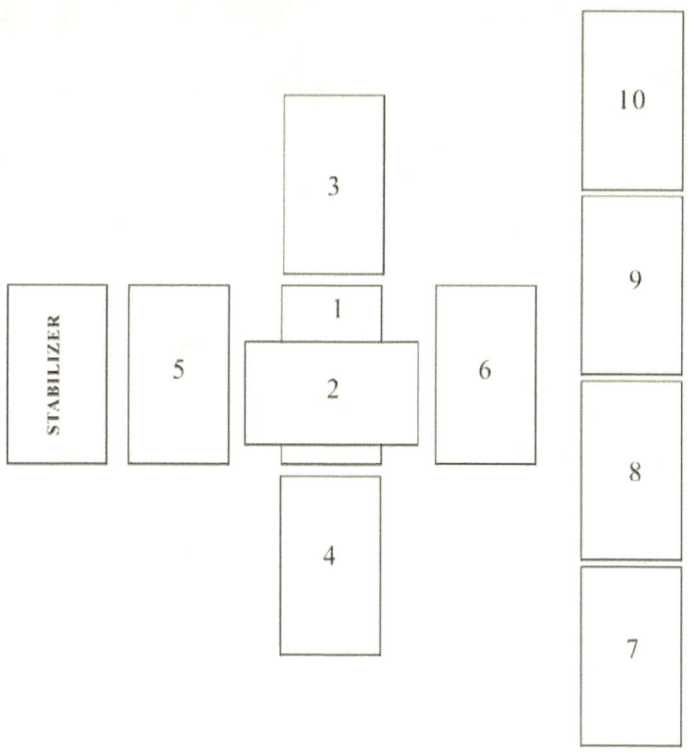

Image: continuum

They shuffle the pack and cut it into three. They choose one of the packs. Tell them they can't make an incorrect choice (because they'll almost always hesitate).

Lay the other two packs to one side. In a face-to-face session you'll also read them but not to the same extent. Interpret the pack they picked but exclude the 11th, 12th and 13th cards, that you would have laid out in the Dead Reckoning for the entirety of their chosen pack.

Advise them that the other packs are *one-off* situations, or other people, that/who will have a singular impact or represent a singular event. Include the extra three cards as per DEAD RECKONING.

REMOTE VIEWING—Don't do the extra two packs. Unnecessary.

MAP 7: QUESTIONS

SAME LAYOUT AS FOR HORSE LATITUDE

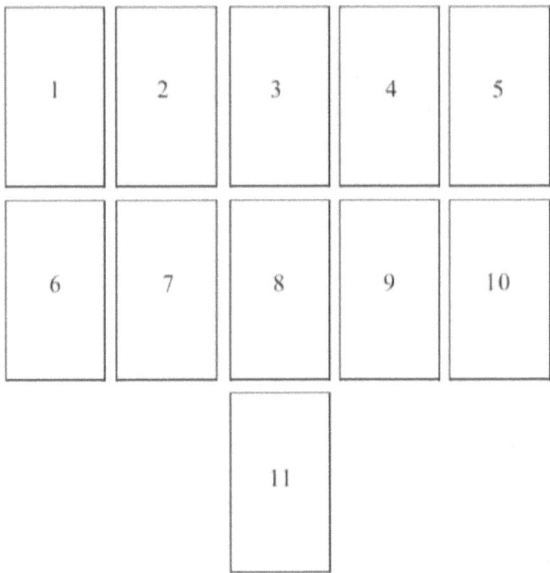

Image: questions

If you have been able to prevent it, the client has said nothing so far. From now on, until completion, several things are going to happen. Firstly, the entity that Tarot is (indescribable), will often join in. This can be disconcerting if you are not used to it because the answers can, when not straightforward and specific, vary from hilarious to hostile depending on the context. Like a third person—invisible—in the room.

Glitches often happen because if their questions have no relativity to the future or if the answer to their question has already been given, Tarot will provide altogether different information and in the case of naïve questions such as "when will I find my soul mate?" Tarot can be both rude and obnoxious as the question is stupid.

The person talks with you *while* they shuffle the cards. Questions need specificity. No point someone saying "tell me about relationships" as we have relationships with everything from what's in the fridge, to a car, a dog, one's offspring, people living close by as well as lovers.

Even though you know what they mean, they need to be specific. Ask what they really want to know. If it's about intimacy, romance and love then have them say so, aloud, to collapse the wave.

People tend to complicate a question. Having first listened to the entirety of what they want answers to, ask "what is the destiny of..." and the answer will be clear. You'll know when this is happening, as with the *soul-mate* question, because the answer is as likely to be about a cat or dog as it is to be *Devil* or the *7 of Cups*.

If/when they try *should I...* or *if I do this or that...* get them to rephrase the question, again, by asking *what is the destiny of...*

Warn them, at the outset, that these variables might occur. If and when they do inform them that Tarot is being obnoxious, and that they have a choice to either hear the data or not. Say, *Tarot is being rude, do you still want to hear*? If they say yes, then say it.

What do you do if the person opposite you is a woman who asks when she will marry and have children, and Tarot answers *never*? What do you say if they ask if they will be happy for the rest of their lives and there is the *Tower, 10 of Swords, Devil, 4 of Swords, 7 of Cups* on the top line, *8 of Cups, 5 of Swords, 9 of Swords, 2 of Swords* and *Judgment* on the bottom line with *Death* (meaning *No*) as the foundation?

Why? It is a terrible question. Life is an ecosystem of varied events and experiences, varying degrees of intensity. The BOOK OF SECRETS will seek to educate in its brash and unsubtle way.

Suggest they get hold of a copy of THE PROPHET by Kahlil Gibran so that they can read the lines –

FROM THE TRACTATE ON LOVE

But if in your fear you would seek only love's peace and love's pleasure, Then it is better for you that you cover your nakedness and pass out of love's threshing-floor,
Into the seasonless world where you shall laugh, but not all of your laughter, and weep, but not all of your tears.

Love gives naught but itself and takes naught but from itself.
Love possesses not nor would it be possessed;
For love is sufficient unto love.

This section of a consultation can give explicit answers but it is also a place when your wisdom can be expressed.

Same map as for HORSE LATITUDE.

As mentioned earlier, when giving some of the meanings of each pictogram, the answer to a person's question is sometimes in the form of a simple *yes* or *no* and on the odd occasion the answer relates to previously mentioned events that they might not have heard clearly and, in this case (because you will remember the event or events being queried) the first card on the table will be your answer.

TAROT AS TEACHER

There are only so many things that can be learned from any book, one of the basic reasons I refrained from writing one on the topic for many years, because the BOOK OF SECRETS (the intel beyond the pictographic images) is that which ultimately teaches you to recognise hitherto unknown meanings. Being open to this is what all the prior theory has been about because experience has taught many people that uneducated dabbling backfires. And while an abundance of oracle cards has flooded the marketplace over the past several decades, and sometimes call themselves (or publishers do) *Tarot*.

They aren't. They have wisdom and potential but are only as communicable as the person who interprets them.

I've known of people who get together and attempt to read cards, over and over, wanting to see what they *desire* to see and dealing out map after map until they *think* they have an outcome that suits them. The trouble is that *everything* else they shuffled and exposed is *also* going to happen, so if a series of disasters or unfortunate events is predicted, on the way to seeking something ultimately pleasant, then, in the nature of *the chicken or the egg*, the interpretations of discord don't go away. They also happen.

The same applies to thinking that people-cards might be someone known because this is all assumption. When people fool around like that they have no objectivity and the whole thing becomes almost, if not absolutely, dangerous. Same with assuming that pictograms always mean what you originally learned them to mean because that will change with the seasons.

CHANGING LANDSCAPES

When I began learning in the 1960s the world was different. We had experienced two atomic bombs, the effect of which could have begun a chain of events that is ongoing. But.

Virtually no plastic or take-away foods, little to no obesity and the diseases caused by that crisis, supermarkets didn't exist. AIDS, in Vitro Fertilisation (IVF), same-sex marriage, nuclear proliferation, uranium-depletion, nanotechnology,

AI, the commonality of tattooing, social media and ever-present screens were incomprehensible, despite me now knowing that all of the above had already begun/been developed so that when, eventually, these thing became considerations we could recognise them. Fluoride wasn't in the water and people cooked at home. There were no artificial additives and no pesticides.

When we keep up with current events we are better equipped towards accurate interpretation of the BOOK OF SECRETS. Because Tarot knows, and will tell you. This can disconcert. There's always been war, though, according to written history, so that's not going to surprise anyone.

Same applies to weather, fires, global changes in core temperature, volcanic eruptions, earthquakes, mega-hurricanes and coral bleaching. What do we really know? Nothing, in a way.

…

Then the *third* presentation of a map in a DEAD RECKONING arrangement turns up:

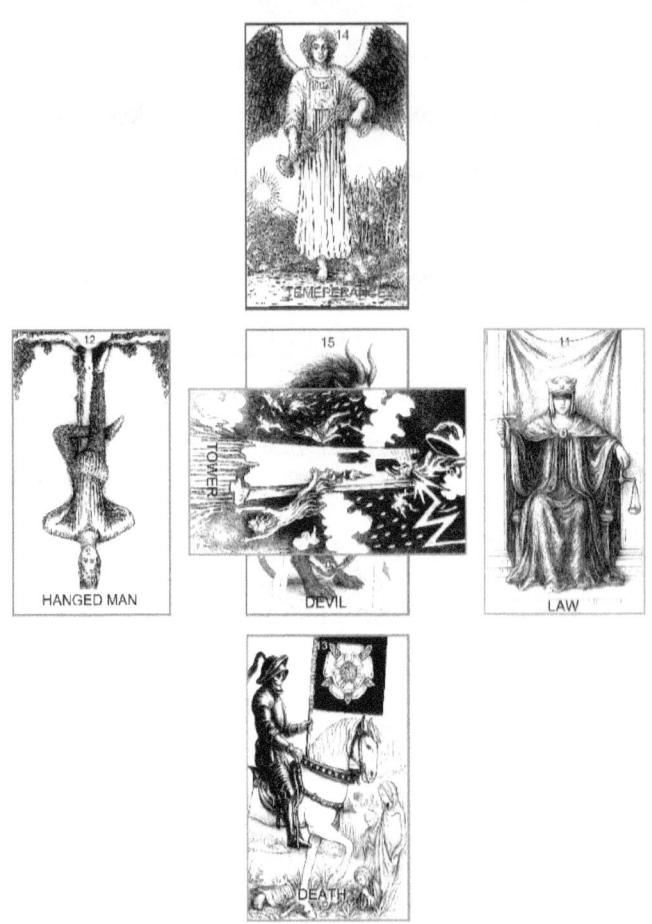

This map happened for three people. Two, a year apart, the people unknown to each other, the last for a man I have read for already.

See screenshots towards the end of the book.

THE PROBABILITY RATIO

A WORLD EVENT?

According to ChatGPT (2025): *The approximate probability of drawing an identical 5-card layout three times in a 78-card deck shuffle is around 0.000000142, or 1 in 7 million. This is a very low probability, suggesting that seeing the same hand appear three times by chance would be extremely rare.*

First was in August 2023 for a human being from the Northern Rivers in Australia. They lived with anorexia. They were also Jewish. October of that same year the media reported the abduction, by those suspected then (extant) of being Hamas militants, were 250 seemingly-random Israelis. Since that time (extant) Aljazeera news declares that 41,900 Palestinians have been erased by the IDF in what the media calls "genocide".

October 2024 an actor, remotely, laid out the exact same map. They were going to Los Angeles for work the following month. I blurted "San Francisco!" but was told they had no intention of going to San Francisco.

When the session was over I switched on the news. A cathedral, named *San Francisco* and erected in Chile during the seventeen hundreds, burned down. The images of that, beside the image of the Notre Dame fire of 2017, are extraordinary. They are same but opposite:

Notre Dame, France, 2017   San Francisco, Chile, 2024

Image – towers burning

Notre Dame's Tower burned in July 2017. One thousand, four hundred oak trees had been razed to erect the tower. The SARS-CoV-2 (coronavirus) virus broke out, worldwide, not long after. People I know are waiting to see the impact of the two seemingly random events.

...

CASE HISTORIES (USING FALSE NAMES)

WARRIOR

Jane was in her early fifties. She looked "city" (in difference to the local people in Byron Bay that I called home) and had an American accent.

Had I been asked, based on appearances, to have guessed either her lifestyle or profession I would have been hard-pressed to do so but would have presumed she was financially secure but that she lived a so-called ordinary life, whether that was here or in the U.S.A.

That's not what her data told me. I saw death and destruction, governmental institutions, clandestine activity, lots of international travel, war and violence, and paradox after paradox because she was obviously married and successfully, had a beautiful home and grandchildren.

Image: case history: Jane, STARGATE

This is an example of what might have turned up on the table concerning this woman. Please really contemplate the images, even without going into later card-interpretation-breakdowns because it is your ability to see, by way of the above STARGATE, discussions and associations that will be.

Breakdown –

The Tower in the position of Malkuth shows the world in which the client will live or be. It is one of major upheaval and disaster. The *Tower* in this position represents explosions or extreme violence, chaos and disorder, along with the toppling of people or positions of authority, whereas in Yesod the *10 of Cups* indicates that her home is elsewhere (as this is one of Yesod's meanings).

When you do a layout like this it isn't progressive. It doesn't necessarily follow any order like the lightning-flash, although it can. Look at both the big picture and each dimension/equation/sphere individually. With the *Tower*, particularly in this position, look for the causes elsewhere because it could as easily be a house-fire, a bomb or a natural disaster. What it always will be, however, is the person and/or the person's world and, again, the other images will tell you which.

Emperor in Netzach, an unusual place for this card to fall, and the *8 of Coins* (work) in the place of Binah (representing ages, government, administrative, tradition or institution) explains that this woman will be involved in a government job and will also be other than an employee *because* of the *Emperor* which places her in a position of authority: a woman in a typically man's world.

Where's the clue? The client is the *Woman of Coins* which falls in Geburah, associated with mars. She's a warrior? Do you say she is in the military in a war torn environment? That's *exactly* who she is.

The *7 of Swords*, in Tiphareth represents the self, so what's she doing sneaking around? And why is the *2 of Swords* (one of its meanings being silence) in Chesed which can represent the person's workplace among other things? With the *Ace of Swords* in Kether nothing more can be said other than to reiterate that she will be in a position of power in a military institution, with silence and secrecy surrounding her life.

The *Hierophant* in Da'ath could have meant many things but her marriage was her *key* to success.

She explains during question time. She is a colonel in U.S. Military Intelligence. On vacation. She was stationed in Bosnia during the international armed conflict that took place in that region from 1992 to 1995 and, even though many events that were predicted were yet to be, the majority of what was told was already known.

...

TWIN TOWERS, 2001

Robert has been a client on and off for about twenty years, coming once every two or three years for his next reading. He is a very successful man in his early thirties who lives in both Australia and the U.S.A. This was the top line of one of his spreads in June, 2001:

Image: twin towers 2001

Not only did this prediction show up for him, but over the coming days and weeks the first three cards turned up many times, in the exact-same sequence, for other people.

This map reads as a story telling of something from the sky exploding and, because *Death* and *10 of Swords* together represent violent death the outcome to the first two cards is obvious.

The final picture in the line, *World*, announces one of two things: a) that the outcome to this event is a worldwide media event or b) that the event heralds a new cycle. Either way the interpretation is the same. Robert was in New York when the World Trade Centre exploded.

What is interesting in retrospect is that friends and I were at a local café in the days following September 11th, talking about the event and talking about the above reading that I had conjectured over with them when I had first saw the crisis. The chef, an acquaintance who had been read for several years previously, and who was also sitting with us on his break, explained that the prediction of towers blowing apart etc. had been in his reading *three years ago*.

...

PREGNANCY AND BIRTH

In an initial map, Tarot had shown that she was happily married. The BOOK OF SECRETS, however, kept on and on, map after map, about the birth of a child but, accompanying this information were very peculiar images.

The maps displayed disappointment on more than one occasion. Sadness and grief. There was also a sequence of patterns that initially made no sense (the following is close enough):

Image: IVF, unexpected natural birth

The first thing that caught my attention was the obvious birth of the *Child of Cups* because the *Ace of Wands* and *Sun* together means birth, and almost always of a biological infant, no matter the species although, as an animal other than human *Strength* is sometimes depicted.

What confused me initially was the top line and what it had to do with the outcome. She was to be, or had been, disappointed by IVF treatments.

As of the day of her session she and her partner had been married for five years. They had three attempts to date at Invitro fertilisation, all of which had failed.

Yes, she would get pregnant, hold onto and deliver a baby but, from my perspective, because of *Wheel (of Fortune)*, it would happen naturally.

I ran into her in a supermarket a few years later. She had a baby in her arms. She and her husband had paid for four more attempts and all had failed.

They gave up.

She thought nothing of it when her menstrual cycle hadn't come because it had always been irregular and she only went to see her doctor when she found herself constantly nauseous. The child was born at home, alive and healthy, delivered by a midwife and her partner.

Remaining detached from your personal opinions keeps you open to the unexpected and that which appears utterly unbelievable as it is not you, the interpreter, as an individual who is important but as a *vessel* through which Tarot can inform what it knows.

That, in and of itself, is pretty spectacular.

INTERPRETING FOR YOURSELF OR THOSE CLOSE TO YOU

If you or those close to you (friends and family) want to seek out a seer or a medium, ask around for someone with a reputation for being accurate and go see them instead. The same applies to anyone whose life you know too well. All of us are prone to assumptions.

Last week my daughter and her friend flew to Melbourne and the friend's mother drove the girls to the airport and dropped into my house on her way back. We had coffee and chatted for an hour, getting to know each other. Towards the end of the conversation she asked if I would read for her and I said it was too late; I already knew too much about her. If she had asked earlier I would have prevented any conversation and made arrangements for a session.

When I know people well, but they have been away for an extended period of time, I can scry for them as long as they don't tell me of what they've been doing. It is as though the mystery of people's lives, to a seer, allows for clarity.

THE FEAR FACTOR – TELLING BAD NEWS

Why do we do it? Why do we read for others and put ourselves through the often harrowing experiences of telling people what we see despite what the news can sometimes engender?

Many reasons, but ultimately it is the gift of grief relief, and some examples, again, are necessary.

MANSLAUGHTER

A man in his sixties was talked into coming to see me by his wife and adult daughters. I knew he really didn't believe in what I was doing but had come simply to please them. This is common, I said it was okay if he wanted to just leave and that it's better to do so if he wasn't there of his own free will. He said *No I'll stay*.

In the *past* he was weeping for a man he had never met. That he had the marks to remind him and that a terrible accident altered what seemed to be the trajectory of his life.

He reached over and lifted a trouser-leg to just below the knee. He had a vivid scar wrapping almost all around his calf. He'd been driving home from the pub one night, drunk. He veered over the double lines and hit a motorcycle head-on and the bike had spun out of control ending up off the road. Fred's car slammed into an embankment and his leg was cut as the driver-side door imploded.

He'd forced his way out of his car and went to the victim, a cop in his early twenties who was critically injured.

There were no mobile phones. It was the middle of the night on a dark country road and he sat, removed the man's helmet and held him in his arms as he died. He stayed there, like that, until finally another vehicle showed up. Its inhabitants assessed the situation and the woman stayed with Fred, who by that time had lost a lot of blood from his own injury, while the driver went off to phone for help.

He was charged with negligent manslaughter and spent time in prison. He hasn't drunk a drop of alcohol since and he's never stopped feeling guilty. He now suffers PTSD. He just stayed a while longer, telling me he was thankful for someone to talk to about it because his family never wanted to.

GRIEF

Anne was a psychiatrist. She'd been in love with a fellow practitioner and they'd been lovers, secretly, for years. He was married and had children. He had not wanted to leave his family. Anne, being sophisticated (she thought) had agreed that it didn't matter.

She kept silent about their intimacy, afraid that someone would notice and tell his family and so, when he died she kept up the ruse and never showed grief until told what she already knew. She wept. The last thing she said before she left after the session was that life was uncanny in a way. In those days, psychiatrists charged eighty dollars and said nothing, whereby someone like you only charged (in those days) twenty-five dollars and did all the talking.

The poor man's psychiatrist, she'd said. Of those of us who do this. We should charge what they do.

SUICIDE

The thing about recording a session is the retrospective impact. Ron had been on more than one occasion but this day I saw the death of a relative by his own hand, that no one was to blame and that it would be this relative's destiny to do this thing.

The client's mother's sister and her family lived on the other side of Australia. His cousin hung himself. Aged twenty-eight. The family was devastated because he left no note and had shown no signs of being unhappy. Each of them was wracked with guilt.

Ron's flew across the country taking the tape with him. He played it to them, and even though they were still sad, the effect of some stranger describing the event beforehand was like he'd left a message. The recording relieved them, partially, of wondering why he'd done killed himself and whether any of them could have stopped it from happening.

LAST WILL AND TESTIMONY

Sally's session looked for all the world like that of someone getting ready to die and who was busy putting her affairs in order. Tarot showed her over and over that her kids and her husband would be okay; to relax and be at peace because they would be sad but would cope. At the conclusion of the session she explained she had asbestos cancer and that having a stranger tell her about the outcome for her family was the most important thing for her and she could die without worrying for them.

VIOLATION

June, a woman in her fifties. Her petrographic patterns were packed with violence against her. It showed up as having been the benchmark for her life. She had been in a terrible marriage for over thirty years and had attempted to protect her children from the effect of the husband's actions. *They know*, Tarot said. *They've always known.*

Her mother was sitting in the garden, waiting for her turn. I said, *Sorry, after what I've experienced of your daughter's life I'm too upset to do you.*

One of my apprentices was June's sister. June and her mother went afterwards to a café where June told them what had been going on all these years. The mother was horrified. My student phoned June's daughter and said, tell your mother that you know. They talked for ages and June asked that her daughter not tell her brother. The daughter said he knows also.

June came back after three years, a changed woman. Once the truth was out her son and daughter backed her up when she left him and through all the court proceedings. Eventually, when the magistrate heard everything, he asked the husband why he did those things and the husband answered that she deserved every beating. The husband got nothing. June got everything and had since travelled and moved house and put her life back on track.

CAN'T MAKE A FORTUNE

There are too many examples but you get the idea. Tarot will sometimes help people to get the best price on the sale of a property. It can warn people about deceptions in business and dangers yet to come, but it can't prevent events, and it will not take away free choice. A cool example is that of a man who approached me regarding his investments on the stock exchange. He offered me huge sums of money if I could tell predict the best deals.

Unfortunately, I told him, if Tarot says you will lose money then no matter where you put it you will lose it.

THE SPOKEN WORD – THE LITERAL TRUTH

The way you tell of events you see is also very much an aspect of the work and Tarot is peculiar in this. Three examples follow but before that let's discuss the question/answer section of a session. This happens (should you use it) at the second phase of the consultation after you have interpreted events to come.

Three questions. Get a small amount of backstory before they talk the question through.

TO FRIAR OR NOT TO FRIAR

Henry. An actor. Gay. He was adamant I was wrong when I told him that I saw him marrying someone. Within a year he had auditioned for a production of Shakespeare's *Romeo and Juliet* and had been offered the part of the friar. He married Romeo and Juliet.

His long-time friend Jill had also come for a reading on the same day. In her future I'd seen her married to a Scorpio man and they had a seventeen year old daughter. That ended up being a debacle because she, also, auditioned for the same production and was given the role of Lady Capulet. Her offsider, Lord Capulet was played by a Scorpio man and Jill fell head over heels for him in *real* life, thinking to herself that the very handsome man was to be her husband in the future, that they would have a daughter and would still be together when the child was seventeen years old. Assumptions are dangerous things. The Scorpio man was gay and Jill set about attempting to convince him that he really wasn't. It was very tragic and very funny depending on the perspective. The realisation struck her regarding the true nature of the prediction when the person cast to play Juliet turned out to be seventeen years old.

OOPSIES

Amelia (a local woman; an acquaintance) *looked like* coming into money. It would be a gift that had to do with a relative in England.

She phoned me some months later to tell me her uncle had made contact and that for tax purposes he actually had to give away some money. She told me he was sending her £8000 and she intended to set up shop in town, a thing she had wanted to do for years. I flippantly said to be careful because the money wasn't in the bank yet but she laughed, refusing to have her good mood dampened.

I met her in th street a couple of weeks later and she wanted to show me the space she was due to sign the lease on, that day. She said the money would be transferred into her bank, by her uncle, the following day. I asked her exactly what the prediction was. She had it remembered it word-for-word: *looks like you're coming into some money.*

Then she phoned, upset. The uncle in London had said *a thousand pounds not eight*. She had misheard him. All her plans were cancelled and she was in debt as she'd paid the deposit on the business place and it was non-refundable.

IDENTICAL TWINS

I saw Mary getting on a plane on an all-expenses paid trip to Japan that she would win through a competition. Mary laughingly told me, when she came for another session, that it had been her identical twin who'd won the trip.

THE PLATEAU 2

It is inevitable, once you've studied and are out there for others to find, that you'll hit what is called a *Plateau* whereby you have no feedback from any clients. They seem confused at what you tell them. Nothing makes sense and you've come to the conclusion that you can't read patterns but are mouthing off, rote-fashion, individual card meanings.

This happens for everyone and can be super-disconcerting. It is the *make or break* phase when the BOOK OF SECRETS tests you to ascertain whether you have both the fortitude and the self-confidence to continue. The process may last several weeks even months. If you falter at this fork in the forest you won't be able to come back. In all the years of teaching I know very few students to successfully navigate this treacherous track and only two of them went on to become professional.

When the phase is over you will know. You'll have a breakthrough, bigtime. The client will confirm, even during the session, the accuracy of what they *already* recognise as pertinent to their lives. From then on you may have small periods of plateau but never to the same degree.

GOING PROFESSIONAL – CONSIDERATIONS

One way is by discovering the markets or fairs that'll have you. You'll probably need insurance for this, nowadays. Charge only small sums of money to begin or accept donations and barter, and only do fifteen minute sessions using appropriate maps like a DEAD RECKONING, a STARGATE and a QUESTION.

With experience, charge accordingly. Your prices may not rise as often as other businesses but self-regulate. This is not ordinary at all. As your confidence and reputation deepen and word spreads, think about how you will set about working in a private space. I work from home because I have a studio for that and writing.

This is not always possible. Why not?
- Your family may disapprove of what you are doing
- You don't have the luxury of being able to afford the private room

- You worry about having strangers come to your home

To overcome any of the above you could do one of the following
- Find an alternative lifestyle shop and hire one of their rooms but be aware that many of these businesses will attempt to have you tone down what you tell "their" customers. It is most important that you do not jeopardise the quality of what you are doing
- Continue reading from markets or fairs but get yourself a marquee or tent that gives privacy
- Let people know if you are willing to travel to their homes. This method is advisable if there is likely to be more than one client there, otherwise the fuel or time could make the adventure untenable and, again, price according to your estimation.

Prior to acquiring a reputation you'll probably encounter discomfort, disbelief, even hostility and this is to be taken into account at the getgo. Best develop a thick skin in preparation for the many occurrences where you *will* walk on the edge with your predictions and the xians come after you.

It is advisable to have introduction cards made up with your email address and (if appropriate) your website. Many who come to me are from elsewhere, many from overseas so email is always handy for them to make long-distance bookings and many people will take more than one card so that they can give them to friends or associates. Currently, in the twenty-first century, I'm using video link. Word of mouth is akin to gold. Historically it does not lose its value.

FRAUDS

Advertising can be your own choice but be aware that many people won't take the risk of paying money to someone who could turn out to be a charlatan, as happens, and in many places what you are doing could be classified as illegal.

Under the British Commonwealth law, the Witchcraft Act was repealed in 1951 to be replaced with the Fraudulent Mediums Act:

Fraudulent Mediums Act 1951

An Act to repeal the Witchcraft Act 1735 and to make, in substitution for certain provisions of section four of the Vagrancy Act 1824 express provision for the punishment of persons who fraudulently purport to act as spiritualistic or mediums or to exercise powers of telepathy, clairvoyance or other similar powers (22 June 1951).

1. Punishment of fraudulent mediums, etc –

(1) Subject to the provisions of this section, any person who:

(a) with intent to deceive purports to act as a spiritualistic

(b) medium or to exercise any powers of telepathy, clairvoyance or other similar powers, or

(b) in purporting to act as a spiritualistic medium or to

exercise such powers as aforesaid, uses any fraudulent device, shall be guilty of an offence.

(2) A person shall not be convicted of an offence under the foregoing subsection unless it is proved

> that he acted for reward; and for the purposes of this section a person shall be deemed to act for reward if any money is paid, or other valuable thing given, in respect of what he does, whether to him or to any other person.

(3) A person guilty of an offence under this section shall be liable on summary conviction to a fine

> not exceeding (the prescribed sum) or to imprisonment for a tern not exceeding four months or to both such fine and such imprisonment, or on conviction on indictment to a fine... or to imprisonment for a term not exceeding two years or to both such fine and such imprisonment.

(4) No proceedings for an offence under this section shall be, brought in England or Wales except by or with the consent of the Director of Public Prosecutions.

(5) Nothing in subsection (1) of this section shall apply to anything done solely for the purpose of entertainment

2. Repeals –

The following enactments are hereby repealed, that is to say:

(a) the Witchcraft Act 1735, so far as still in force

(b) section four of the Vagrancy Act 1824 so far as it extends to persons purporting to act as spiritualistic mediums or to exercise any powers of telepathy, clairvoyance or other similar powers, or to persons who, in purporting so to act or to exercise such powers, use fraudulent devices.

Just in case some bigot wants to take you on, know the law

...

TRANSFERENCE—REMOTE READINGS

Do remote readings work? Yes. There are many variations of clairvoyance and what works for some does not work for others and this works for me as long as the person on the other end of the video call has their own cards. The ones I always use. Because *they* have to shuffle.

QUANTUM ENTANGLEMENT

What always happens? In person or across sometimes thousands of miles? Quantum Entanglement. That's a cool way of saying telepathy is definitely a real thing. Our energetic fields intermesh and, while remaining yourself, you are also them. My feelings are their feelings, who I love is who they will love and who I loathe they will loathe. I know when a situation is distressing or elating because my gut responds so that when, in a session, I *seem* to give advice or to admonish, praise or berate it is because the client themselves will do so, probably talking to themselves. This is both empathy and scientifically legitimate.

The actual style of the session will reflect this. One specific example was an hour of lengthy silences The person, later, went on an around Australia trek, driving over vast areas of arid landscape. She informed me that often for hours, if not days, she and her partner said almost nothing.

Transference, Quantum Entanglement and telepathy, are such that you will almost always take the client's viewpoint despite the little inner voice informing you that you might not have the full story.

Confusion happens when the client's views on life are so utterly alien to that of either you or Tarot that you wade through it like molasses. It can be very difficult not to jump up and down in an attempt to educate them on such concepts as self-esteem, individuality, freedom. At times like these, Tarot *will* and *does* interfere, specifically at questions when there are often no holds barred.

SELECTIVE MEMORY

Selective memory can be worked on over the years. What is very handy is seeing and knowing way too many people so that, as a general rule, I do not remember people who might have seen me only six months previously.

An example is me standing outside a café in town waiting for my daughter while she and her friend go off shopping. During fifteen minutes at least a dozen people passed by saying hello. I smiled and returned each of their greetings but did not recognise any of them.

If a person has been to you on several occasions you may well remember them and some of their details but this is rare and you set this up on purpose.

When you're on you're on and when you're not you are most definitely not. You need this odd objectivity so that say a person comes for a return visit nothing you predicted before interferes with the current one.

FIRST DO NO HARM

We now enter into the touchy area of not how much you say in relativity to harsh information but the way you say it. This will tend to change from person to person but always tell the truth and in retrospect and if you, like me, have no social verbal filters (as you will see in a later chapter on case histories) you might experience hate.

PRIVACY

The first thing to set up is a reputation for telling whatever you see and if prospective clients phone you and tell you that they do not want to hear anything "bad" you will need to give them the choice to go elsewhere. Realise that Tarot *is* a mystical experience and that you won't put the need for payment ahead of ethics (Tarot will always put food on the table).

This is where reputation is to your advantage over advertising. First off, it is rare for prospective clients to ever ask if you're any good because they will have heard from friends, family or colleagues that you *are*.

When they first arrive, people shake. They are sometimes afraid but determined to know. Ignore their discomfort. It has the effect of calming them rather than if you were to take notice and try to comfort them. The phenomenon will soon settle despite what you have to say. The same applies to tears. Both men and women will often cry for no apparent reason (nothing to do with the quality of the news) and often will attempt to apologise saying that they didn't know what came over them. It is also adrenalin from excitement, but most people try not to show that.

Should the interpretation be dire, take a moment to sense how to go about saying what you have to. I am an animated personality so I gesture in all directions, pull faces, swear, ask them to wait a minute, ask them if they really want to hear what I've got to say. I also use humor in such a way as not to offend and will, on occasion have a sideways conversation with Tarot, in front of the person, discussing my hesitance or dilemma. This gives the person a moment to a) compose themselves or b) say they want to go home. Most people are, however, more resilient than we give them credit for and most will tell you to just say it.

Do so.

...

AIDS 2

As was written earlier James was the first client who came to me to sort his life out as he was ready to die.

You'll have to work like crazy at remaining calm at the enormity of the death and violence you're likely to see in the cards. One client relieved my anxiety when she told me—as images of grief and emergency turned over—that she was a paramedic in one of the densest and most dangerous places in Sydney. Another was an undercover police officer involved in drugs and vice.

It's all okay. Trust and compassion are your greatest tools here and sometimes you will feel moved to work beyond the BOOK OF SECRETS. I have seen instances of child abuse where the children concerned were in the custody of someone else and I have been able to assist the person opposite me to get in touch with the relevant authorities.

Same applies in instances of domestic violence or when a parent's offspring has been introduced to addictive substances.

You can't always help and must be careful of "the messiah complex". Most of the time, when there are challenging or harsh situations ahead that simply knowing it in advance is the greatest insight you can give them because a) they are then more ready to deal with the event when it happens and b) they also know that this event was destiny, the result of which removes unnecessary emotion at the time of the crisis.

SELF-PROTECTION AND PSYCHIC CLAG 2

Pace yourself.

For the first several years I found I was capable of reading for up to five people a day, at an hour session each, without any seeming personal harm. But it sneaks up on you and if you are not careful your health and well-being will suffer because you are sharing the energy-field of every individual who consults you and traveling time in a strange way.

WHEN TO STOP, WHETHER TO STOP

In the 1980s I had a friend who was also an established interpreter who took clients for up to seven hours a day, seven days a week. In those days we read for each other and I saw cancer in her cards that appeared associated with the breasts. I suggested she give up the work because it was taking a toll on her health but she refused.

Only a few months later she found a lump in one breast and was diagnosed with the cancer. A local oncologist was going to take off both breasts and remove the underarm lymph nodes. She had a reading beforehand. Tarot was adamant she gets another opinion. She did. She is still alive.

I also became sick many years ago, diagnosed with asthma. On average, and not simply clients, somewhere between ten and twenty people would come through the house on any day. I was also raising three offspring. I would have an attack but as soon as I removed myself from the people around me and went into a room to be alone I could breathe. I began to suspect that I was becoming allergic to people.

The problem is psychic clag. This stuff can't be seen but can definitely have an effect, just like humidity, just like dust and dust mites. The feeling of this clag is almost indescribable and is almost like static build-up. You will feel off-centre; stale.

You will have difficulty concentrating and may also feel listless or depleted. This has nothing to do with the quality of either the reading or the client and the only remedy is to get wet. A shower will do it (*not* a bath) but a dunk in the ocean is by far the most satisfying.

Water can neutralise the effect along with food, exercise and time alone for a while.

Can you always clear the clag? Nope. But the wetting is the closest you'll come to feeling healed.

Keep your workplace clean.

It's also important because psychic clag is a physical thing and has density. Vacuuming your floors regularly, washing the walls and cleaning the windows will all ensure that your health is kept at its maximum.

THE BEST FRIEND SYNDROME

If you live in a small town this can be difficult because you are likely to connect with clients daily, merely shopping.

Due to the confidential nature of this work you are likely to end up with half the town's secrets and this ascertains that many people, if you are not both careful and tactful, will want to approach you and fill you in on updates to their situations. Tell people of your well-trained selectively reluctant memory to avoid this and, ultimately, be thankful for the many who will fill you in on the eventualities.

The problems arise when people become desperate and (as has happened to me) climb in through an open window of your house at 3 o'clock in the morning, after a domestic situation, seeking sanctuary. They will try to contact you at any hour of the day or night and it may become advisable to switch off on a regular basis and rely on voicemail to "vet" your response to calls. In the current era I don't give out my contact details other than through my website. People email me. If they somehow get hold of your private number be cold towards them. Set boundaries.

If you are working all this from home, you need a place where people can wait so that they do not walk into your kitchen and think it is okay to sit down and have a chat with your kids and loved-ones as not everyone is aware that assumptions are mulengro.

What's required from you is that you take the responsibility of *being* professional and have clear boundaries. To do this you'll need to constantly update what you do.

"SHOULD'S" – YOU WON'T SEE WHAT IS NOT REALISED

Many think that Tarot is going to get them out of trouble and first-timers will often try to tell you – even on the phone when originally making their booking – why they are coming. Catch them before they do so and advise them that the less you know the better your work. Most will shut up but some will continue, saying they are coming because they need Tarot to tell them what to do.

Rather than dissuade them it can be advisable, after telling them that that is not what Tarot does, to suggest they attempt to resolve their dilemma before they get to you; that this will allow a clean canvas on which to write the destiny if nothing is muddying their minds at the time of the consultation. I ask them to not even *think* when they come.

The "should's" will be inevitable in one out of three people when it comes to the question part of the work. This is the time for *you*, the interpreter, to relax and remain unattached because the BOOK OF SECRETS, as a third present entity, will take centre stage and say whatever is appropriate. This can be hilarious, occasionally embarrassing or strategic information kept for this particular map only.

...

EXAMPLE MAPS

DEAD RECKONING 1

Image: financial struggle

You have worked and trained hard to achieve your current place in the world despite how difficult leaving loved ones or a loved one behind has been, yet in the near future you will struggle financially and have some difficult decisions to make regarding both where and with whom you live. You will feel that you are trapped and are perhaps following the wrong course of action but I also know that you will *want* to be where you are and that you are bright and optimistic despite the frustration. You will soon encounter a man, with whom you have had issues in another time, but that you care about, and a woman of importance in whom you see yourself reflected. You will, retrospectively, realise that this time of hardship—most certainly challenging—has finally ended. Oh, by the way (and don't worry if this makes no sense right now), the Gemini woman will have been correct in her advice or influence.

DEAD RECKONING 2

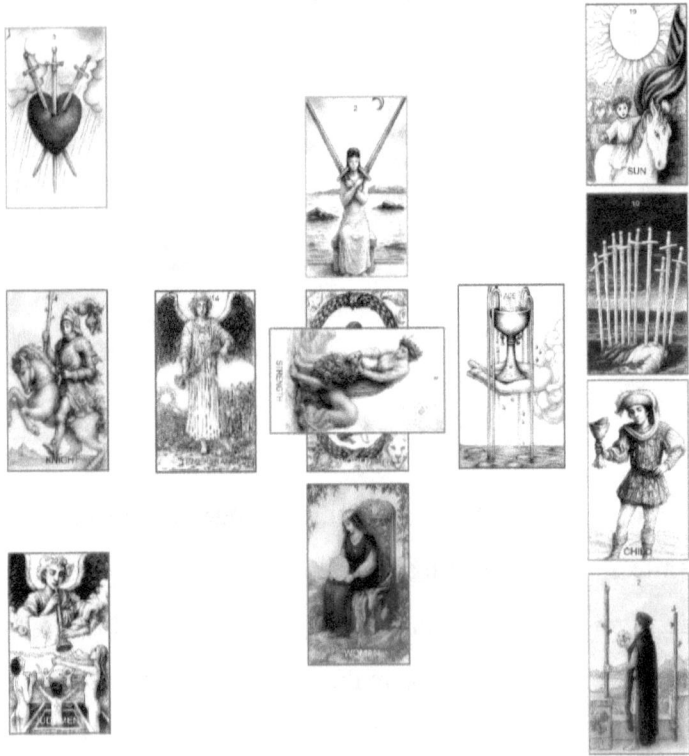

Image: health and stress

You've had your fair share of heartache already and this will not be the time to take on anything new as you are still within the phase of healing. Your main concern will be for your living child and you will be very clear about the decision you make in regards the one that is not yet alive.

You are strong (or on the way to becoming so), no matter how you will feel in the short-term, and your life will not remain the way that it is. Your next imperative step will be to get healthy.

DEAD RECKONING 3

Image: peace keeper in a war zone

You will be in a war zone, a long way from home, in the capacity of peace-keeper. This is not the first time you have done this and there is much that you have seen and experienced that has saddened you.

You will be surrounded by allies, both where you are stationed and at a distance. Your mission will encompass more than one environment and most of the associated travel will be overland. I must stress that you will also be safe. You will work in co-operation with a police presence that is not yet fully trained up.

The interpretation also shows that you will work either behind the scenes or undercover, but that this work will be more spiritual than covert.

DEAD RECKONING – PAST INFLUENCES

This map seems incomplete but that is not so. It will sometimes happen that the pack the client has picked has insufficient cards for a full layout.

In the map of the present this indicates that the future has already begun or that there will be extended delays before the events of the future occur. Events that seem to have already played out will be revisited or, in certain instances (this can occur for actors playing parts that reflect past events) the reason is more obscure.

Image: what to do about obsolescence

Both you and your work will be obsolete. Make a plan.

The map of the *past* has all the implications of events seen for midwives working with homebirths and also for those working in the specific fields of women's health – alternative or, perhaps, unacceptable to the minds and morals of many. Although you are still in this field of work you'll encounter opposition and scrutiny from legal sources for both what you do and what you have already done.

What is important is that the work is necessary and important and you will continue to be involved, in one way or another, long into the future.

There is a human being of significance in your life who may very well be either a Gemini, an Aquarian or a Libran but I do not know if he is helpful or harmful. He is, however, definitely of influence despite his obvious confusion.

DEAD RECKONING – NEAR FUTURE

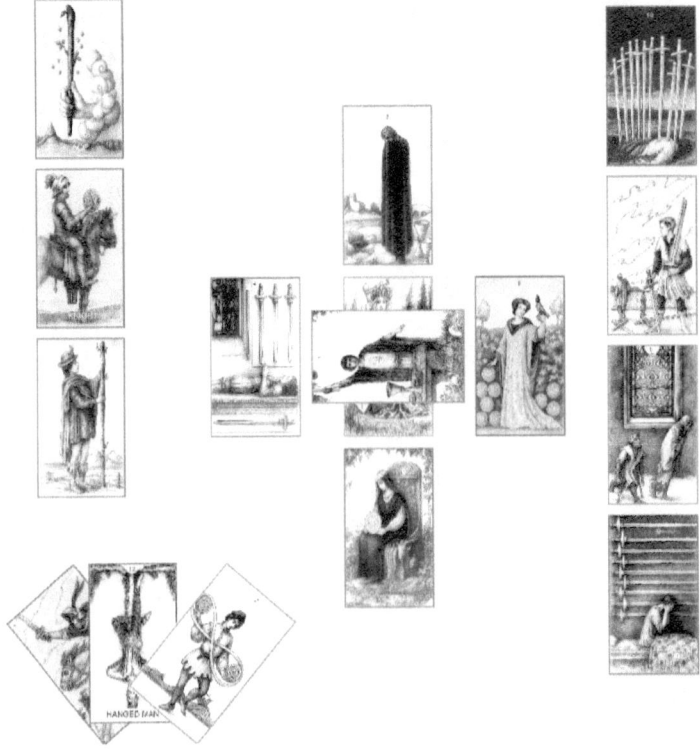

Image: near future – trust yourself

An independent, educated, self-determined woman. You'll need to be. And you'll need to trust yourself and your abilities in the matter of future events because you will find yourself in an environment of poverty. You will be hurt or betrayed by your participation in events but there is no indication of this being permanent harm.

The *Ace of Wands* in the crowning position of the *past influences* indicates that you have a gift with either the spoken and/or the written word and, with the *Child of Wands* as the crowning card here you will most certainly be making a record of events, which is what could get you into trouble.

You will be certain to keep your information "close to your chest" as there are enemies who would step on your back, metaphorically speaking, for the sake of ambition. This could see your reputation in dire straits.

Your work, vocation or career will, despite what you have achieved, be put on a part-time level which will severely affect your ability to pay for your current quality of lifestyle.

DEAD RECKONING – FURTHER FUTURE

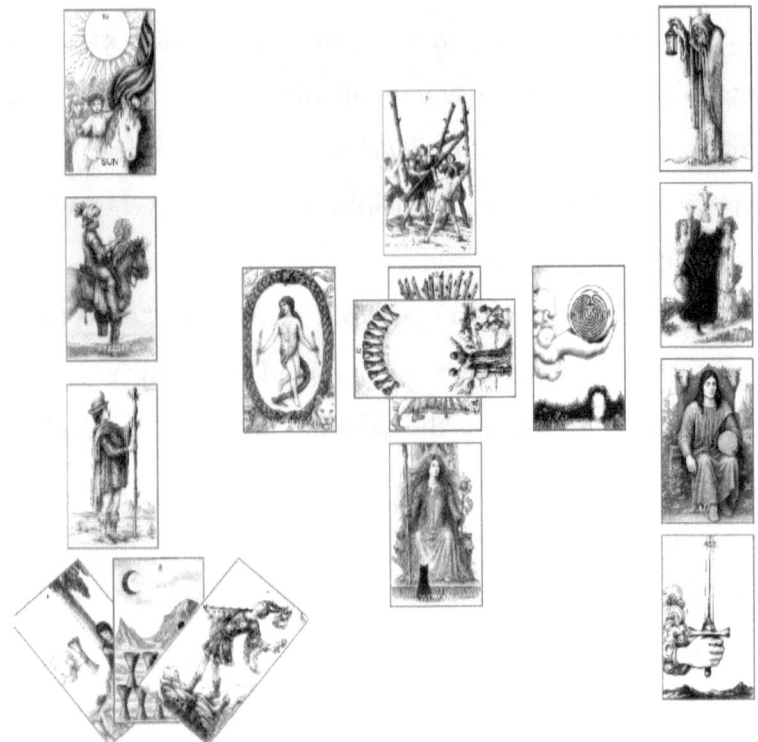

Image: further future – you made it!

(The *Woman of Wands* is the significator.)

You've made it. Kids are grown and your life is organised. You have a steely will and will accomplish much in this new era of your life. The last twenty to twenty-eight years of your life are complete and the next phase is about to begin. That will last you for a very long time.

You will definitely be moving house. Not only will you be

relocating but you look like you are actually building a new dwelling. There are no dramas.

You will share your living environment with a man who either falls under the sign of Virgo, Capricorn or Taurus, or exhibits many of the practicalities and steadiness of the finer qualities of these signs. There is no disruption from him. He could also be the person assisting in the building and/or renovating.

To the side there are other options available to you besides the course that you will take but you will disregard them in favour of what you know. This is good. This is destiny as you have learned what does not please you and it is not that you lack spontaneity but rather opt for that which you know is certain to provide emotional stability.

THE GROVE – MAP 1

Image: grove – very cold

If you are not already living in an environment that can get *very* cold, you will certainly find yourself there for a while.

This is not the map of someone settled and homey and you will be constantly on the move. There is an indication of a period of travel that is fraught with glitches, particularly around accommodation and there is also a falling-out with travel companions.

Three events stand out:
1.   You don't seem at all bothered by any of the above

2. Opportunity comes to *you* by way of an offer from a dark-haired person who is not of your nationality
3. You will do something for yourself that others may disapprove, such as tattooing or piercing

THE GROVE – MAP 2

Image: multiple events

Married and loving it, especially so because you and your partner are both busy people and that gives a sense of quality time when with each other, if not necessarily quantity. I also know that you would have been in a partnership in the past that did not fulfil the above criteria and that you still know the person from that partnership and have a child in common. This child is unhappy in your new relationship but is unwilling to discuss it. There will be a change in whatever work you are doing that will allow you more *free time*. You will instigate this change yourself.

One person stands out: you will have an association with a man involved with the federal police or federal justice system but the interpretation does not expand on what that relationship is.

THE GROVE – 3

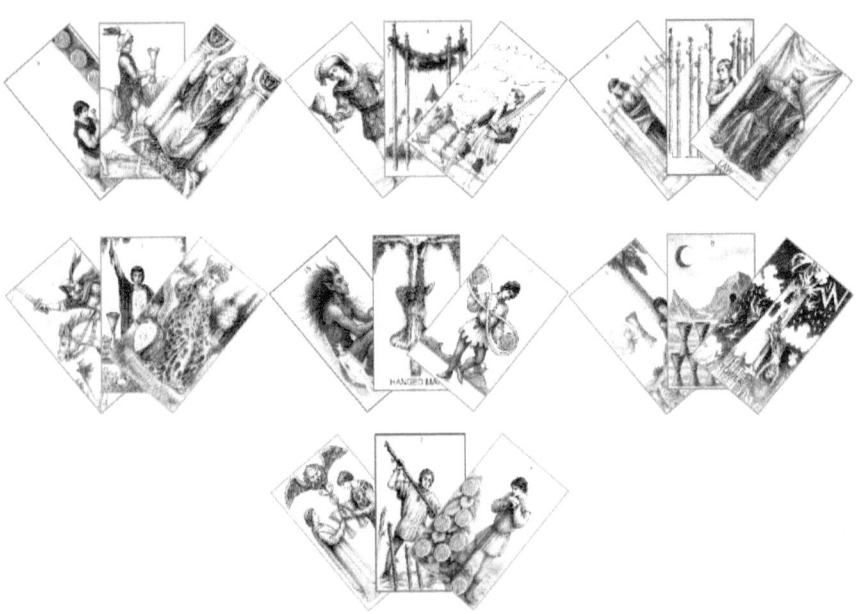

Image: inherent warning

The most important thing is that your work, or a project upon which you will be working, will eventuate in victory despite the lead-up.

However, one of the problems is the outcome to what happens when people enter into amicable financial agreements without a legally binding contract. They think "Oh, we're fiends. We trust each other. We don't need to go to that extreme."

Well, yes they do, because the worst-case scenario is in your map. You may very well find it necessary to go ahead with this (if it isn't already happening) but you will have no legal leg to stand on if you do so if records are not kept and if there is no legal agreement.

If this *doesn't* happen to you personally it will be because you are either a) involved in the case that ensues or b) the legal representation, in some manner, that deals with the outcome.

STARGATE EXAMPLE 1

Image: exploitation – play the game

You will be involved in an industry that is very exploitative, and is not an industry that supports the general membership of women, but you will be aware of this.

You will be ambitious and will have to "play the game" to get ahead. The strategy works. For an industry that appears to be gregarious and progressive there will be an awful lot of subversion and sneaking around and the public will only know part of the truth. There is great danger to others or the environment from this industry.

I don't want to harp on about the industry to the detriment of your future experiences but the point is that your life will be so intertwined with your work that you may very well actually represent the industry which is, after all, what you are going to want.

You will travel often and much of your time will be spent in major capital cities, in five star accommodations at the behest of either your industry or the government that supports it.

This map indicates nothing regarding family or friends. That doesn't mean they are not there, simply that they are the background to the above information.

STARGATE EXAMPLE 2

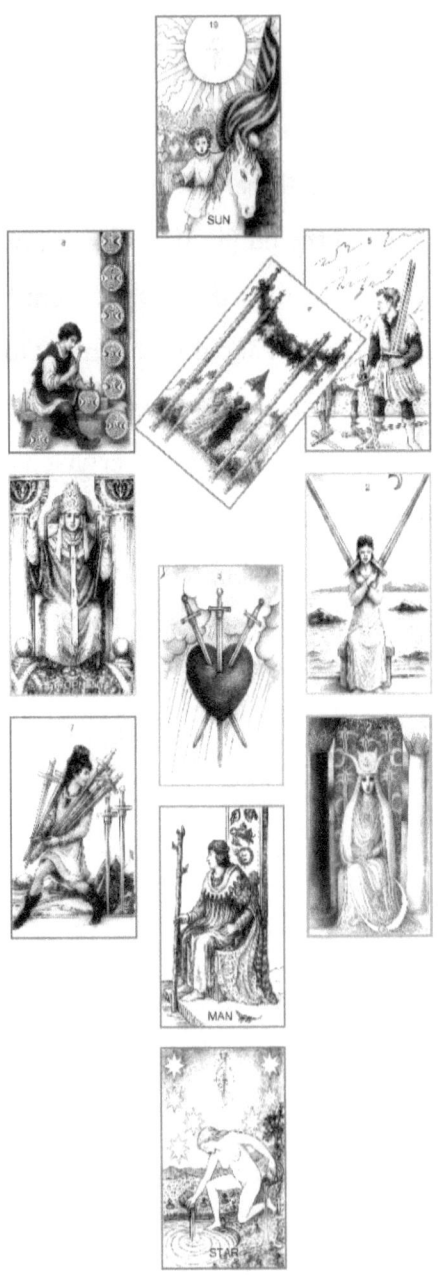

Image: worth it

You will be away from your home and this is going to be very emotionally difficult for you but it will be worth it. You will live and work in a Muslim country and it is that this is likely to be somewhere in the United Arab Emirates because there is absolutely no sense of "third world" here and yet, because of what I see here (pointing to netzach) the women are most definitely veiled.

Your work will be in the field of media, entertainment and/or technologies and because you do not speak the language you will need to be cautious regarding how you communicate.

- You will be out of your personal element, being a woman in very much a man's domain and will be required to keep any opinions, that do not comply with the customs of the people, to yourself, and to dress in accordance with the strict dress code.
- You will be very aware, throughout, that there is war not far from there but it will not encroach on this land.

In conclusion, the experience will be magnificent and the whole affair will certainly "raise the bar" in relation to both your prestige and reputation and that you will, within the timeframe of this reading, also find yourself working at the head (or the headquarters) of this organisation.

HORSE LATITUDE – WARNING

Life is a journey, right? A seeming voyage, so I use the analogy of navigation and map-wisdom for context. Most people I've met don't know about the HORSE LATITUDE. It's an area of ocean whereby—during the era of ship travel and exploitation of lands other than one's own—masted vessels can become trapped by windlessness, the doldrums, at approximately thirty miles north or south of the equator. Several hypotheses exist around the name of this area and, despite the one about rum I researched and wrote about the conditions in the holds of these ships for itinerate travellers and those transporting other animals that often culminated in death and shark food. Hence it being an excellent replacement for WARNING MAP, being quite explicit in its straightforwardness.

The important thing about the HORSE LATITUDE map is that the client will see the potentially life-devastating event coming beforehand and can alter the outcome or prevent it altogether. Sometimes the situation is obvious and the answer simple but at other times it will seem to have little or no relevance to the person's life as they know it.

Having read several maps prior to this one will give you a fair indication of whether the person has heeded the warning but very often the session will only take them to the point where the warning eventuates, therefore causing a fork in that person's road. Should they fail to heed the warning when they recognise the events the end result is a hole in their lives that may take many years to heal.

HORSE LATITUDE MAP 1

Image: latitude, avoid the thing

Client is the person with the house.

You are going to get a phone call from a woman. You'll know her because she talks heaps about money. She's travelling and, by all accounts, is planning to visit you and staying (whether she tells you the latter or not), sharing your home.

Get out of it. Doesn't matter the excuse – invent it if you have to – otherwise you're going to be left with a mess and increased costs.

HORSE LATITUDE MAP 2

Image: Horse Latitude – Warning 2

This woman is in the music industry. She has or will attempt to form an independent label or have been contracted through an independent label.

This will not work out and, to remain viable she will have to marry herself to a more traditional or orthodox label. As a result, she will remain viable within the industry.

HORSE LATITUDE – REVERSE WARNING

Image: reverse warning

This is a 'reverse' warning; a warning: of encouragement.

This person is a city-dweller and what they desire is very unusual and I feel vulnerable saying what I am going to say because it is so left-field, except stranger things have happened and therefore to trust: this person has a bright and long-term future as an officer in the mounted police force. The warning is to pursue their ambition because the outcome will be successful.

EPIGENETIC EVENTS– MAP 1

Image: significant people and singular events

Some people are too independent and strong-willed to go down any orthodox road regarding traditional marriage – let alone the religious kind – the *Man of Wands* can represent any man. He is naïve to think he has the right of what is supposed to happen.

There is nothing in the map that relates to either love or the lack of it but what is apparent is that a way of honouring the relationship is by way of a practical and relative interconnections.

EPIGENETIC EVENTS – MAP 2

Image: map 2 – epigenetic events

Two situations:

1. One person (*Child/Man of Wands*) will try talking to the *Man of Swords* but they are at a distance and no longer communicate (*Judgment*). Things change. What's interesting is the child/man connection. This will often explain that either the client or the *Man of Swords* has known the child/man for years.

2. The *Woman of Coins* is in a long, ongoing conflict in her place

of work. There is always a choice as to how a situation of relentlessness outcomes. Again, *Judgment* is CHANGE

EPIGENETIC EVENTS – MAP 3

Image: of epigenetic significance

Currency of any kind is invested in the maintenance of health, strength and overall fitness. As a human being ages the fact of death—whatever that might ultimately mean other than that of the observer—is considered. The pictogram (the *3 of Swords*) indicates a breaking away. Separation and/or severance. There is no choice.

After a while (*4 of Swords*) the *Ace of Wands* tells of a beginning. Does not say what that is as no one can know what is unknown.

This applies to everything, from vitality as a human animal to ideas, relationships, projects. Everything transitions.

And so this map confronts death and endings. It shows health as this process or cycle fulfils itself before becoming other.

The *3 of Swords* indicates loss (any form of separation from the expelling of a child from the womb to a heart attack, but it's a map that advises how to live.

...

FINAL THING—OR MAYBE NOT

The following images are 2024/2025.

I put the proposition of odds to ChatGPT. The likelihood of identical patterns of cards appearing for people at vast distances from each other (one in the Northern Rivers, Australia, living for now, with anorexia, one person in L.A. to film, the third person currently in Thailand, setting up a gemstone business).

The odds were, at an estimate 700 million to 1.

What is destined to happen? When? Will it affect the people I love? Is it as enormous and devastating as it looks? Along with others I've watched madness amongst humans who think to impose yet another war on individuality, women, people of colour, other species, ecologies, humans who view sexuality through their own uniqueness, those with spirituality seemingly different—at least, in text, language and culture—to the supposed dominant zeitgeist, unprecedented flooding, fire, weird weather patterns, the realisation of PFATS, micro plastics, debilitating pharmaceutical intervention into health, earthquakes and seismic activity unknown in my lifetime. Posturing. Politics fawning to reality television personalities, grey war. Drone weaponisation, and also the weaponisation of food and medicine to entire populations. Starvation. Genocide. Again. And that's only of our mutual hominid species. Manufacturing is poisoning food more than ever. Getting away with it. OxyContin. Obesity. Malnutrition.

The quest for anti-aging. Obscene architecture and the caricaturing of everything via the tools of AI, as well as the unknown outcome to AI's destiny as an independent evolutionary phenomenon. have worked with friend Pete Robson to enhance the most basic of royalty-free card images to create those in this book and I am also in deep discussion of all manner of concepts, like koyaanisqatsi, but it is wrong in so many ways, due to human bias, that breaking away from the attachment to the mainframe will be an act of insanity that I am aware must be the next *Mad-Max-ian* step.

Oh, and have the events exposed in the following three images have happened yet?

I don't think so.

...

SCREENSHOTS

September 2023

September 2024

Again, September 2024

Probably best to just leave these here without explanation.

ABOUT THE AUTHOR

2025

LY DE ANGELES

CONSCIOUSNESS

I once dreamed I was sitting on a straight-backed chair. Everywhere was darkness, backlit in the strange way of dreams. To either side of me was a clear wall that was impossibly high and never-endingly straight ahead. I just fit between them with no space to turn. To either side of me were other human beings, also seated on identical chairs.

The dilemma I experienced—close to despair, but also terrifying—was that if I rose from where I sat and walked along this transparent but limitless corridor, would there be an end? Or would I walk forever while not being able to turn around and return to the chair? But that sitting on the chair indefinitely was impossible to consider.

We were all aware of each other (and the seated people disappeared over some horizon to left and right: they were legion) but could not communicate. I wondered if the others knew panic also.

Then I awoke. And I understood. That dream was in the years known as the 90s. It was prophetic, I know that now. And I see what will be done. Am I afraid? All the time. I would be stupid not to be. Being afraid assists in preparedness for humanity's next phase of change. I do not consider fear an enemy as it stops me doing impulsive and dangerous things out of hubris or inattention.

When I woke I also realised none of us knew who had put this torment into effect and that only the outcome to contrived confusion is recognised. Through violence. Victimisation. An us-and-themness.

So who am I? An interpreter. The source of what is interpreted is irrelevant.

I interpret image. I interpret the psychology of language. Myth. Questioning indoctrinated history. Questioning the delusion of hierarchy. Visions, omens and portents. Unravelling the brainwashed (the most treacherous and difficult). The process of the last of these, relentless. I predict the so-called future. How is that possible? Because it has already happened and is continuing the exposé. We exist in an ever-unfurling present, and everything is Fibonacci and/or cyclic.

Some of us are doorways. Tarot displays pictograms that vary infinitely despite the seeming limit. There is none. Dreams provide knowledge in symbol, of what to acknowledge or change. Or they prophesy. Or we are met. Same with any of the so-called mystical arts. *All* art, understand, is the interpretation of myth. Knowing through seeing, knowing through knowing. And all myth is founded on reality. Forgotten or as yet unrealised. Or misrepresented as twee folklore or absurd biblical representation of forgotten events. For any, of many reasons. Usually cataclysmic or catastrophic. We are a species that speculates based on either fear or reward. That's a current problem. I will take notice of all the above, but my work is to bypass whatever it is. Seek another comprehension.

Example: Where were we, as ancestors, during the Younger Dryas? Were we technologically advanced? Living for generations in Petra, or Cappadocia? How? And how did we try to explain space flight and algorithms to the children, unborn into the reality of what we knew? Is it possible that we are relearning the technology that built the massive structures? Why else the consistent fascination with stone?

Image: Gravity Glue

ORALITY

No book can truly inform anyone how to become an interpreter. There can only ever be a primer — a 101. It just is. A human being can either do this or they cannot. Through studying with me you'll either understand how and what I see or you won't.

Is it genetic? Is it speculative? Is it the result of supposed near-death and a flicker of the wisdom of the infinite? Is destiny fixed? Is fate fated? Are any of our questions really answered? In increments, yes. Maybe. Sometimes. Perhaps.

There seem solutions to practical issues like fixing the electrical glitch, building a dwelling, shooting aurochs for the tribe's sustenance. But these are not on the list.

And everyone is guessing for a century or so.

MAD MAX TAROT

We are disliked or disbelieved by many. Many dislike it when they ask a question that they desperately want a YES to, and the answer is NO. Shock. Defiance. This can't be right. Yet it will be. What they want to happen, won't. Would it have happened if they had not asked? That's *Schrödinger's Cat* theory, isn't it?

Image from Mad Max Fury Road

WHO AM I? WHO ARE WE, MORE LIKELY.

They don't know us; they know what we do. Sometimes. They never know who we are, however. A rather adequate number of people want to destroy what they do not understand. This is historic. This is bigotry against the inevitability of the unknown. It is the secret language of invasion and conquerage. Of religion and associated behaviour. Like whether SELF continues when the body has lived in animacy and becomes unrecognisable as who was known. Discorporation is an observation, not an experience. Whether we live elsewhere and access those lives through dream is a serious, but unanswerable question. Whether medicines of forest and mountain can work with us to break the blind spot in consciousness is worthy of discussion. And experience.

THOU SHALT NOT SUFFER ...

Whatever the skill, it is belittled or vilified by those with an agenda. Those agendas, in the currently unfurling notion of us, are an invented series of abrahamic ideologies called religion. Or fact. In what universe is that unchangeable? In what universe is that appropriate to an intelligent and rational interpreter?

Religions have invented answers when there are none. They have taken your ability to imagine and have warned you of the consequences of disobedience. They invented hell. They pretend beneficence but they have brainwashed vast swathes of humanity. Therefore, they are what? Parasitic. Will AI resolve this? Paul Kingsnorth, in his frighteningly and beautifully believable book *Alexandria*, provides an option that grapples with these questions. I did the same, queasily, in the 2012 edition of Genesis | The Future, that began in 1995 when the idea of semi-sentient computer (named 7) technology wasn't yet realised. Neither were black-armoured cops, or nuclear plant destruction (and that was just the introduction). But it happened/is happening.

We are in a current dystopian delusion of "you tell me your trauma and I'll tell you mine" fixation, with ideology and suffering selling media. Why? The question is more relevant than any answer. Answers disorient with falsity.

DEEP LISTENING

Interpretation, and the inevitability of behaviours, signs; languages of image and imagination are based on listening. With the ears, or with the eyes, with touch or experience. Deep Listening goes beyond the manifest, to interpret what is really happening or will happen. These are the skills of an interpreter. Learning from the vast swathes of data and information on human behaviour, meteorology, myth, history (debatable), iconography, art, prediction and intuition.

All require a form of listening that does not depend on hearing rather the evaluation of what is being heard.

Nothing is irrelevant. No premonition is off the table. We are yet to be bowed or silenced. We have been. We are chancing exposure for the moment.

TIME TRAVEL

Yes, an interpreter does this. Think George Orwell. Think Da Vinci. Oppenheimer. There are legion time-travellers. Many may live on a wee island in the Outer Hebrides, looking at tealeaves or watching approaching cloud, and warning the fishermen, as has been done, continuously, but without recollection of names and dates and records, into ancestral mists. Paint, poetry, weaving, work clay, telling stories, dancing, raising stone. Simply thinking.

THE DOORS

I have shared much speculation as to how it is possible to write of events millennia, before or after, events occur (MAGDALENE | WITCH

OF THE GRAIL LEGENDS, several others), or deep-diving into source literature, following the traces of thread through bibliographies, biblical commentary or other texts, to research but not retain the immensity of information, rather, alchemically, to weave those threads together to create a commentary (sometimes called *story*) and then to let go of self and allow the information to download. Do I feel it happening? Yes. The sensation is visceral. So is waking. We rise from some unrealised depths. Try it.

Sometimes it can seem disturbing. I wrote a story — Midsummer Solstice — in WHEN I SEE THE WILD GOD, in which a woman and her children burned to death in a two storey, weatherboard house near where the sídhe come for midsummer reunion. In the story the police are looking for her partner. They don't know if he was incinerated, if he set the fire, or whether he is elsewhere. Within 48 hours of writing that short story the 6 o'clock news, here in Australia, told of a woman and her two children who burned to death in a two storey weatherboard house, just across the border in Queensland, and... well, you get it.

This has happened for as long as I remember. In the body I currently inhabit. The instances of chicken/egg are too numerous for this page. I would bore you.

TITLES/SCHMITLES

Interpreting dreams is necessary. Interpreting myth and translating that into actuality, is necessary. Re-contextualising what is said, without the malignancy of religious or ideological insertion, is incalculably important as language is our means of communication beyond the image or page. To break superstition's back, and all the titles, from *medium* to *witch* to *alchemist* to *devil-worshipper*... Well... they're all sad, delusional and frightened HUMAN titles, invented to cause rejection or secrecy by their description of infidelity to some acceptable god or another.

People are disturbed by what we do. And yet, we are sought. Is there an agenda. Time travel requires knowing that time travel is possible, and then exploring.

Image: voyage

You who are doing this work? It is time travel, even though there is no such thing as time. Can it be, perhaps then, that you are folding space?

Or are we really prophets?

BIBLIOGRAPHY AND WORKS REFERENCED

Badcock, C, *Evolution and Individual Behavior*, Blackwell Pub, 1991

Berry, W, *World Ending Fire – The Essential Wendell Berry* Penguin, 2018

Black, C. (Director) *Schooling the World: The White Man's Last Burden* (film), 2010

Bly, R. *Iron John, A Book About Men,* Addison-Wesley, 1990

Brand, R. *My Booky Wook*, Harper-Collins, 2007

Davis, W. *The Wayfinders*, Anansi Press, 2009

Davis, W. *The Serpent and the Rainbow* Simon and Schuster, 1988

Deutsch, D. *The Fabric of Reality*, Allan Lane, 1997

Doidge, N. *The Brain that Changes Itself*, Viking Press, 2007

Eide-Næss, A. E. *Ecology, Community and Lifestyle*, Cambridge University Press, 1989

Eisler, R. *The Chalice and the Blade*, HarperCollins, 1998

Gibran, Kahlil. *The Prophet*, Alfred A Knopf, Inc., 1923 (136th printing, 2001)

Gleick, J. *Chaos Theory*, Penguin Books, 2008

Kelley, L, *The Memory Code*, Allan & Unwin, 2016

Kelly, L. *Grounded, Indigenous Knowing in a Concrete Reality*, Essay, Rounded Globe

Person, Martin Luther, *Letters from a Birmingham Jail,* Liberation Magazine, 1963

Kingsnorth, P, *Alexandria*, Faber & Faber, 2021

Knight, C. and Lomas, R. *The Hiram Key*, Century Books, 1996

MacFarlane, R. *Landmarks*, Penguin Books, 2016

MacFarlane, R. *The Old Ways*, Penguin Books, 2012

MacFarlane, R. *Underland,* Penguin Books, 2019

Margulis, L. & Sagan, D, *Mystery Dance, On the Evolution of Human Sexuality,* Simon & Schuster, 1992

Mayer, M. & Robinson, J. *Nag Hammadi Scriptures* (rev), HarperCollins, 2009

Monbiot, G. *Feral*, Penguin Books, 2014

Monmouth, G. *The History of the Persons of Britain*, 1136

Palahniuk, C. *Invisible Monsters*, W.W. Norton & Company, 1999

Roy, A. *The God of Small Things*, IndiaInk, 1997

Reanney, D. *Music of the Mind*, Hill of Content, Australia, 1994

Shepherd, N. *The Living Mountain*, Canongate, 2012

Storm, H. *Seven Arrows,* Ballantine Books, 1972

Wall-Kimmerer, R, *The Grammar of Animacy*, Daily Good e-zine, 2016

Young, J, *What the Robin Knows: How Birds Reveal the Secrets of the Natural World*, HMH Books, 2012

OTHER BOOKS BY THE AUTHOR

Witchcraft Theory and Practice, Llewellyn, USA, 2000

When I See the Wild God, Llewellyn, USA, 2002

Pagan Visions for a Sustainable Future, Llewellyn, USA, 2004

The Quickening, Book 1 of the Traveler Series, Llewellyn, USA, 2005

The Shining Isle, Book 2 of the Traveler Series, Llewellyn, USA, 2006

Tarot Theory and Practice, (OP) Llewellyn, USA, 2007

Magdalene | Witch of the Grail Legends, Australia, USA, 2012

Genesis | The Future, Australia, USA, revised edition, 2012

The Feast of Flesh and Spirit, Interstitial, Australia, USA, 2013

Priteni | The Decimation of the Indigenous Britons. Australia, USA, 2015

Initiation | A Memoir, Australia, USA, 2016

The Skellig | A Shapeshifter Tale, Australia, USA, 2017

Witch | For Those Who Are, Australia, USA, 2018

Under Snow, Book 3 of the Traveler Series, co-authored by Serenity de Angeles, Australia, 2019

Advanced Tarot | The Voyage of Prophecy, (no longer available) Australia, USA, 2020

Brave | For the Unclaimed People, Australia, USA, 2021

The Changeling | From Winter, Spring is Born, Book 4 of the Traveler Series, Australia, USA, 2022

Crow Magic, a Novella – prelude to the Sídhe series, 2024

CONTENTS
PAGE
6	IS ANYTHING RANDOM?
7	A GARDEN OF CAVES
9	WHAT THE BOOK OF SECRETS WILL TEACH YOU
11	THE NOOSPHERE: PICTOGRAMS AND SYMBOLS
12	A CAUTION – THE PLATEAU
13	INDIANA JONES ≈ TAROT
15	THE DARK NIGHT OF THE SOUL
15	DEVIL, DEATH, TOWER AND TEMPERANCE
16	EPIGENETIC INTERFERENCE
17	SORRY?
18	RING PASS NOT
19	MEDICINE
19	DON'T LOOK DOWN
21	THE FRAGILITY OF THE VISIONARY
21	INVISIBILITY
24	THE BIGOTRY OF THE ENGLISH LANGUAGE
26	MUTINY
30	PART ONE—THEORY AND PHILOSOPHY
30	FALSE NARRATIVES
31	LET'S IMAGINE
33	DENIAL
33	SAY IT
35	NECESSARY AMNESIA
38	MEMORISE
38	BORN WITHOUT THE BLIND SPOT
38	THE IMPOSITION OF FAIRY TALES
39	MASCARA
40	FOOLISHNESS & PERSONHOOD
41	THE PRICE OF AUTHENTICITY
44	ORALITY
45	BUT THAT'S WHAT TAROT DOES
45	TAROT IS MESSY
48	UNDERSTANDING TIME
48	THE PERSISTENT DELUSION
49	TAROT AS HEALER
49	RESPONSIBILITY
50	TAKING CARE OF YOU
51	SAYING IT ANYWAY

52	INITIATION
53	DEATH AND THE DAYS AFTER
55	YOU DIED AND DIDN'T KNOW IT
55	BOUNDARIES LIMITATIONS & TABOOS
58	PANDEMIC
59	THE OBSERVATION OF THE LIVING
60	LIFETIME AWARD
62	ALL IS DESTINY
65	JUMPING MOUSE
65	IMMORTALITY
65	EXERCISE—PEBBLES AND POOLS
67	THE FIRST BARRIER: TIME AND MULTIPLE REALITY THEORY
67	MIND, THOUGHT AND LIGHT
67	DATES ARE WHAT?
72	THE ARROW OF TIME
73	THE BIG BANG
75	Y NODE THEORY
77	WITHIN A RECOGNISABLE TIMESCAPE
78	THE CHICKEN OR THE EGG—COLLAPSING THE WAVE
79	LIGHT AND THOUGHT
86	WHAT TAROT ISN'T
84	PERSONAL ENERGETIC FIELD AND BODY
84	LANGUAGE
88	A CAGE OF SELF IMPOSING
91	CLOSE ENCOUNTERS
91	WALKING THROUGH WHAT HAPPENS
92	ONCE
93	THE RANDOM FACTOR AND THE FOOL
94	BEING PSYCHIC AND OTHER WEATHER WIZARDRY
94	WHAT IS TAROT
96	TIME TRAVEL
98	DEEP LISTENING AND TRACKER LANGUAGE
98	INSIGHT
100	BLACK AND WHITE ON A RAINBOW SPECTRUM
101	*SEI CHU TO* – FROG-SKILLED
102	SHADOW REALITY AND ALTERNATIVE LIVES
103	MULTIPLE LIVES
105	TO DIE OR NOT TO DIE, THAT IS THE QUESTION
106	HOPSCOTCH
108	KABBALAH 1

110	FRACTALS
111	FOUR DISTINCT CASE HISTORIES
112	THE WOMAN FROM THE ADELAIDE HILLS
112	WHO BURIED WHO?
112	THE BODY IN THE BELL JAR
113	THE HANGED MAN
114	SHADOW REALITY
115	NUNDOM OR CELEBRITY
118	FREE WILL AND FATE—QUESTIONING EVERYTHING
119	FOOL—THE RANDOM FACTOR
120	GOSSIP
121	HOW MANY IS TOO MANY
122	REMOTE VIEWING/IN PERSON
122	STAR SIGN
122	NO SELF-SHUFFLING
123	ACQUISITION AND DISPOSAL OF WORN CARDS
124	SELF PROTECTION/CLEARING CLAG
125	SAY IT
125	CONFIDENTIALITY
126	RECORDS
127	PART 2—THE TREE OF LIFE
128	NEOLITHIC AND CURRENT CONTEXT
130	MOON AND SUNS AND STARS
131	THE INWARD JOURNEY AND THE THEORY OF EVOLUTION
132	MICROCOSMICALLY
133	MACROCOSMICALLY
133	MALKUTH
134	YESOD
135	HOD
135	NETZACH
136	TIPHARETH
138	GEBURAH
141	CHESED
143	BINAH
147	CHOKMAH
147	CARGO CULT THEORY
150	KETHER
151	DA'ATH
154	TREE OF LIFE—THE OUTWARD JOURNEY
156	A FOREVER HUMAN BEING

157	NEPHESH
157	RUACH
161	NESCHAMAH
164	THE JOURNEY IMAGES AND THE TREE OF LIFE
165	THE THREE OPEN ROADS
165	THE ROAD OF SEVERITY
166	THE ROAD OF MERCY
166	THE MIDDLE ROAD
169	THE CYCLE OF INITIATION
169	INITIATION—THE FIRST PHASE
170	FOOL
171	MAGICIAN
173	MYSTERY
174	EMPRESS
175	EMPEROR
176	HIEROPHANT
178	LOVERS
180	CHARIOT
181	STRENGTH
182	HERMIT
183	WHEEL OF FORTUNE
180	LAW
186	INITIATION—THE SECOND PHASE
187	HANGED MAN
188	DEATH
189	TEMPERANCE
190	DEVIL
192	TOWER
194	STAR
195	MOON
197	SUN
197	JUDGMENT
198	WORLD
199	PART 3—INTERPRETATIONS—WAYSHOWERS
200	FOOL
204	MAGICIAN
206	MYSTERY
208	EMPRESS
212	EMPEROR
214	HIEROPHANT

216		LOVERS
218		CHARIOT
220		STRENGTH
224		HERMIT
226		WHEEL
228		LAW
230		HANGED MAN
232		DEATH
234		TEMPERANCE
238		DEVIL
242		TOWER
244		STAR
246		MOON
248		SUN
250		JUDGMENT
252		WORLD
254	JOURNEY CARDS	
256—283		WANDS
285—313		CUPS
316—343		COINS
346—373		SWORDS
374	SEASONAL SEQUENCES	
375	PART 4—THE PRACTICE	
375		WEEK ONE
375		NEUROPLASTICITY
376		WEEK TWO
377		WEEK THREE
379	THE CONSULTATION FROM BEGINNING TO END	
379		IN PERSON
379		CONTACT
380		SHUFFLE/ORDER
383	PART ONE OF THE CONSULTATION	
383		MAP 1—DEAD RECKONING
389		MAP 2—THE GROVE
391		MAP 3—EPIGENETIC EVENTS
392		MAP 4—STARGATE
395		MAP 5—HORSE LATITUDE, THE WARNING
402		MAP 6—CONTINUUM
403		MAP 7—QUESTIONS
406		TAROT AS TEACHER
407		CHANGING LANDSCAPES

410	PROBABILITY RATIO—A WORLD EVENT?
412	CASE HISTORIES (USING FALSE NAMES)
412	WARRIOR—BREAKING THE LAYOUT DOWN
416	TWIN TOWERS COLLAPSE
418	PREGNANCY AND BIRTH
420	INTERPRETING FOR YOURSELF OR THOSE CLOSE TO YOU
420	THE FEAR FACTOR—TELLING BAD NEWS
421	MANSLAUGHTER
422	GRIEF
423	SUICIDE
423	LAST WILL AND TESTIMONY
424	VIOLATION
424	CAN'T MAKE A FORTUNE
425	THE SPOKEN WORD—THE LITERAL TRUTH
425	TO FRIAR OR NOT TO FRIAR
426	OOPSIES
427	IDENTICAL TWINS
427	THE PLATEAU 2
428	GOING PROFESSIONAL—THE CONSIDERATIONS
430	FRAUDS
430	THE FRAUDULENT MEDIUMS ACT
433	TRANSFERENCE—REMOTE READING
433	QUANTUM ENTANGLEMENT
435	PRIVACY
435	SELECTIVE MEMORY
435	FIRST DO NO HARM
437	AIDS 2
438	SELF PROTECTION AND PSYCHIC CLAG 2
438	WHEN TO STOP, WHETHER TO STOP
439	THE BEST FRIEND SYNDROME
441	"SHOULDS"—YOU WON'T SEE WHAT IS NOT REALISED
442—466	EXAMPLE OF REAL LIFE MAPS
467	FINAL THING—OR MAYBE NOT
469—470	SCREENSHOTS 2024 TO 2026
471	ABOUT THE AUTHOR
481	BIBLIOGRAPHY
483	OTHER BOOKS BY THE AUTHOR
485	CONTENTS

NOTES

NOTES

NOTES

www.ingramcontent.com/pod-product-compliance
Lightning Source LLC
Chambersburg PA
CBHW022024290426
44109CB00014B/733